Disability, Public Space Performance and Spectatorship

Disability, Public Space Performance and Spectatorship

Unconscious Performers

Bree Hadley

First published 2014 by
PALGRAVE MACMILLAN

Palgrave Macmillan in the UK is an imprint of Macmillan Publishers Limited,
registered in England, company number 785998, of Houndmills, Basingstoke,
Hampshire RG21 6XS.

Palgrave Macmillan in the US is a division of St Martin's Press LLC,
175 Fifth Avenue, New York, NY 10010.

Palgrave Macmillan is the global academic imprint of the above companies
and has companies and representatives throughout the world.

Palgrave® and Macmillan® are registered trademarks in the United States,
the United Kingdom, Europe and other countries.

ISBN 978-1-349-48449-2   ISBN 978-1-137-39608-2 (eBook)
DOI 10.1057/9781137396082

A catalogue record for this book is available from the British Library.

A catalog record for this book is available from the Library of Congress.

Typeset by MPS Limited, Chennai, India.

Transferred to Digital Printing in 2014

Contents

List of Illustrations

Acknowledgements

This project has taken some five years to come to fruition. Whilst the shape and scope of the ideas explored between these covers is characteristic of some very personal interests, these ideas could not have become what they are without a long gestation period, and the generosity of a great many friends and colleagues who have been willing to engage in discussions, conversations and devil's advocate-style debates about the content.

There are, as a result, a great many people I would like to thank.

The first, of course, are the artists who have produced the wonderfully provocative work that launched me into this book in the first place. I am particularly grateful to those who have been kind enough to be interviewed about their work, including Liz Crow, Mat Fraser, Ju Gosling, Katherine Araniello, Aaron Williamson, James Cunningham, Suzon Fuks, Noemi Lakmaier, Alison Jones and Bruce Gladwin.

I would also like to thank the colleagues in drama, theatre and performance studies who have given me the chance to present or publish parts of the book during their development, providing opportunities to test the material and push it into new territories. Earlier versions of parts of this book have been presented at the Australasian Association for Drama, Theatre and Performance Studies (ADSA) and Performance Studies international (Psi) conferences over a number of years, two friendly yet fiercely rigorous forums for debate in which I feel I have found my scholarly home. An earlier version of the part of Chapter 3 on Liz Crow's work appeared in the annual issue of *Performance Research* on the Performance Studies international conference ('(Dia)logics of Difference: Disability, Performance and Spectatorship in Liz Crow's *Resistance on the Plinth*, *Performance Research* 16.2, 2011, 124–31). An earlier version of the part of Chapter 4 on modern remobilizations of freakshow motifs in Mat Fraser's work appeared in *M/C Journal* ('Mobilizing the Monster: Modern Disabled Performers' Manipulation of the Freakshow', *MC Journal* 11.3, 2008). I would like to acknowledge the colleagues who have provided feedback, advice and friendship in these contexts, as well as those who have provided all sorts of other support over coffees, dinners or late-night conversations over the last few years. Petra Kuppers, Kirsty Johnson, Rebecca Caines, Jelena Rajak, Andrew Filmer, Bernadette Cochrane, Peta Tait, Helena Grehan, Caroline Heim, Vivienne Muller, Alan McKee and Rebecca Laycock have all helped at one stage or another, in one way or another, and together given me the confidence that others will value this book's insights into work I myself find so valuable. The Creative Industries Faculty at Queensland University of Technology in Brisbane, Australia, also supported the completion of this work through an Early Career Researcher Grant in 2010, which enabled me to travel and take advantage of the local, national and international scholarly and artistic networks that have been so critical to the book's development.

Though this book aims to analyse the performance practices of other artists, exploring the ideas emerging from this analysis in my own practice has been a parallel part of my engagement with these sorts of works. A small group of students, graduate students and graduates of the Drama programme at Queensland University of Technology – amongst them Genevieve Trace, Sarah Winter, Caspian Cunningham, Nikki Ann Tuarau, Susie Pembroke Wilson, Matt Kirby, Hannah Rodda, Eloise Garratt, Kirsty Volz and Matt Gaffney – have acted as improvisers, performers and collaborators in these practical experiments. My thanks go to them, too, and I am hopeful they will enjoy reading about the other side of the coin of our sometimes strange labours here.

Finally, thanks too go to those who have been part of my life beyond the world of art, artists and performances – Robyn, Jane, Gabi, Megan, Suboohi, Bernadette, Jo, Gillian and others – who have, during these same few years, helped me become the person who could write this book.

Introduction: Disability, Performance and the Public Sphere

For people with disabilities, daily interactions in social situations, spaces and places can feel like a series of performances in which their idiosyncrasies are, whether they like it or not, on show.

As hearing-impaired artist Aaron Williamson says:

> I have what is termed an 'invisible disability' that under certain conditions becomes visible, thus extracting or displacing me from the quotidian. If I were in a wheelchair people would immediately mark me as a disabled person, and I'd face a whole range of different responses. But as someone who doesn't have a physical marker of impairment as such (except when I used to wear hearing aids), there's no visual indication of my being disabled unless say, I'm in a newsagents and I don't hear how much something costs or I walk out having forgotten to pick up what I bought. Then I experience this transformation into a slimy monster that crawls down the street with everyone shouting after him! When I was younger it was painfully embarrassing, this 'invisible disability', since I saw it as something that had to be covered up. I developed a very strong desire to fit in and not stand out so it's ironic really that I now do all these things that wilfully displace and set me apart.
>
> (2008: 8)

Although sociological perspectives suggest we all perform our selves, for people with disabilities that are in some way visible – in themselves, or in the bodily techniques, tools and prostheses used to manage them – the sense of being a social performer, playing a social role, and in the process perpetuating beliefs about human bodies, is more acute. This, Phillip Auslander and Carrie Sandahl suggest, is because '[d]espite the fact that disability is a ubiquitous, even mundane, human experience, people with visible impairments almost always seem to "cause a commotion" in public spaces' (2004: 2). As soon as the disabled body enters the public sphere – on the street, in social institutions, in medical institutions or in popular theatre, television, film or literature – it becomes a spectacle. It becomes the focus of more or less furtive stares as passers-by attempt to make sense of its startling, unruly or strange corporeality. These reactions, and the social relationships, scripts and rules that inform these reactions, cast the disabled body as a source of curiosity, discomfort, stigma or pity. Meetings between social performers, spectators and scripts in day-to-day life thus constitute performative conversations in which people try to create common understandings about the state, status and meaning of bodies. These scripts, images, moments and meetings are, as a result, central to the operations of what Jürgen Habermas calls the public sphere, as the public space or stage where people negotiate the accepted beliefs, attitudes and systems that are subsequently adopted as representative by the State (cf. Habermas, 1989: 30–1). For people with disabilities these moments create pressure, eloquently conveyed in artist Aaron Williamson's account of his own occasional transformation into a 'monster', to conceal, control or manage their differences. Or, if concealment is not possible, at least perform these differences in a way that will be most recognizable, comfortable and controllable for fellow social performers and spectators. In this sense, the idea that identity is constructed through a series of social performances – through social acts of looking, seeing and being seen that have all the hallmarks of theatrical performance – is, for people with disabilities, a reality of day-to-day life. The daily social drama of disability is just that, a daily drama in which people with disabilities are unwittingly or unwillingly compelled to play certain roles to shore up the mechanics of a public sphere from which they themselves are often ostracized or excluded.

In conversations with artists with disabilities in the United States, United Kingdom, Europe and Australia over the past five years, I have become conscious of just how strong this painful, embarrassing and sometimes strangely empowering sense of self as a social performer can be for people with differences that are not easily or entirely concealable.

Indeed, I have become conscious of how strong this is for me as someone who, like Williamson, has been known to confuse colleagues, casual acquaintances, neighbours and the odd newsagent with an occasional need to call on a cane to walk. I have begun thinking about it when somebody stops me in the street or in a shop to ask what happened, if they can help, or if they can pray for my health – or, indeed, simply starts doing supposedly too-tricky-for-me tasks like pushing a trolley without so much as a word passing between us. Most critically, I have become conscious of just how much this sense of self as social performer informs the practices – not just the content, but the structure, staging and performer-spectator interface – of many of those who choose to touch on their disability in their performance-making. Musing on this phenomenon has led me to a growing body of work by artists with disabilities who make use of these moments where people pull them into the daily social drama of disability in their performance practice.

Though they have different disabilities, and work in different cultural contexts, the artists I consider in this book – Aaron Williamson, James Cunningham, Noemi Lakmaier, Alison Jones, Bill Shannon, Katherine Araniello and others – have all made works designed to highlight the difficulties this usually unconscious drama poses for people with disabilities. They have presented this work not in conventional theatres, but in galleries, installation spaces, streets, shopping malls and other social spaces and places, in some cases putting their own safety and sense of self on the line in service of a shared desire to change public perceptions of their disability. Williamson (2008), for example, has done everything from putting himself in a glass case in a gallery, to setting tape, barricades and other obstacles up in public streets to give passers-by a sense of what it feels like when power to move freely is lost, to a mock protest pushing passers-by to sign a petition to give supposedly incurable people access to assisted suicide. In each case, the performance has been presented in the very institution, street or social space where encounters that define idiosyncratic bodies as disabled commonly play out.

It is the practices of social-cum-dramatic performers like Williamson, and what they have to teach us about the public sphere, public space, performance, spectatorship, politics and ethics that have been the main motivator for bringing a range of, to date rarely analysed, work by artists with disabilities together in this book.

Seeing, imaging and imagining the other

Slimy monsters. Medical specimens. Cripples. Charity cases. Inspirations.
Though they differ across times, cultures and contexts, there can be no doubting that such personae – and the historical, social and symbolic meanings such personae are invested with – have a strong impact on a disabled person's status, identity and sense of self. What interests the artists I study in this book is the way acts of spectatorship – acts of seeing, imaging and imagining the disabled body on stage, on the street, in social and medical institutions, and in the media – attach such personae to their supposedly all-too-suitable bodies.

The fact that these personae are produced by spectators not by biology is, for disability scholars, activists and artists, demonstrated by the plethora of imagery spectators and societies have attached to their bodies over time.

In the United States, United Kingdom, Europe and their colonies, imaginings of the disabled body have historically been dominated by a teratological impulse, which reached the height of its power in the fairs, sideshows, freakshows, cabinets of curiosity and museums in circulation in the seventeenth, eighteenth and nineteenth centuries. The importance of these practices has been recognized in the publication of at least a half-dozen books that consider the part freakshows play in defining, categorizing and controlling the disabled body in the past three decades. These include Robert Bogdan's *Freakshow* (1988), Rosemarie Garland Thomson's *Extraordinary Bodies* (1997) and her edited collection *Freakery* (1996), Rachel Adams's *Sideshow USA* (2001), and Michael Chemers's *Staging Stigma* (2008), together with chapters and articles by Elizabeth Grosz (1996), Petra Kuppers (2004), Elizabeth Stephens (2006), Collette Conroy (2008) and others. In fairs, sideshows and freakshows, these authors argue, the biological fact of being shorter, fatter, hairier or in some other sense differently configured was subjected to specific teratological scopic mechanisms that turned bodies with these idiosyncrasies into freaks. Spectators were titillated, excited and educated by the sight of what they were not, and would not want to be, in the fleshy form of the fat lady, freak, geek, dwarf or monster. With the advent of new technologies, media and touring circuits in the late nineteenth century, the freakshow's motley cast of characters made their way into mainstream theatre, literature and cinema, offering an ever-expanding audience a warning of what can happen when the human body goes awry.

In the twentieth century, the exploitative imagery of the freakshow started to slip from the centre, if not the wings, of the cultural stage. In the welfare states emerging in supposed civilized, cultured nations at this time, spectators and society were taught to be tolerant of the less fortunate, including people with disabilities, the uneducated, the unemployed, women, children and other not-quite-citizens. The emergence of the welfare state brought with it a medical model of disability. In this model, as Michel Foucault says in *The Birth of the Clinic* (1976), bodily differences and idiosyncrasies become surveillable, controllable and sometimes even curable in an objective, scientific schema of biology. From Jean Martin Charcot's spectacles to the contemporary reality TV of shows like *The Doctors*, *Embarrassing Bodies* and *My Amazing Story,* as Petra Kuppers puts it, '[t]he medical theater is a place of public performance: a body performs its materiality and meaning to a doctor who is empowered to read hidden histories and signs (Foucault 1994)' (2004: 39). Doctors, and the public who come to understand things through their definitions, see the disabled body in terms of mutations, accidents, compliance or non-compliance with medical advice, and 'amazing' tales of overcoming or cure. The disabled body is no longer an extraordinary, powerful or provocative example of the limits of the human body, it is simply an example of human misfortune to be examined, categorized and cared for by medical experts. Disability, disease and illness are seen as embarrassing personal problems, conditions to be cured, tolerated or accommodated, examples of what happens when people fail to follow medical advice, or, in extreme cases, examples of the plight of poor unfortunates who probably need to be put out of their misery.

On the surface, the role of the patient may seem rather more liveable than that of the monster, mutant or freak. It is, though, still part of what David T. Mitchell and Sharon Snyder (2000) characterize as a culturally constructed 'script' that limits the roles, personae and identity positions available to people with disabilities. It is simply that the freak has been replaced with new, and in some ways more problematic, roles – from the corrupt individual whose physical flaws are a sign of personality flaws, to the charity case, the stoic sufferer, and the 'supercrip' who overcomes their challenges and can even display superior insight into the world around them. This script, replayed again and again in dramatic, literary and cinematic cannons as well as in daily life, influences the way sufferers and spectators alike respond to disability in daily life. A medical model TV show like *Embarrassing Bodies* may tell us, 'there's no shame we're all the same', but this is, in fact, an injunction to survey, compare and take steps to control anything about one's own body that is not the same as other people's bodies.

Disability may be a common experience, one that many if not most people will face as they move through illness, injury or aging, but it is still a challenge to comforting narratives about the unity, universality and above all, usefulness of the conventional human form that needs to be dealt with. Disability still needs to be cured, concealed, closeted or otherwise controlled. Failure to do this is treated with derision by doctors, social spectators and society. This is particularly so in Western welfare systems such as those that operate in some parts of Europe, in the United Kingdom, and in Canada, Australia, New Zealand and other commonwealth countries, where taxpayers support the medical and disability care systems. In these societies, people are supposed to want to be normal, productive, contributing citizens who do not unnecessarily bother or burden others with their problems. Accordingly, there is no room for any suggestion that disability might be a natural, normal or even positive aspect of human experience that people might want to live with, or, indeed, valorize as a characteristic a certain community of people share. To be happy with one's disabled self, happy to have a body that is deficient, difficult, idiosyncratic and thus less useful than an able body, can, as Tobin Siebers says, be seen as a sign of a psychological problem, or, at the least, of being a malingerer (2010: 11).

When it comes to dominant ways of imagining the disabled body, the one thing almost all scholars, activists and artists emphasize in their analyses of these and other images, motifs and metaphors is the part they play in defining not just the disabled body, but the non-disabled body. Although the teratological, diagnostic and therapeutic imaginings of disability that dominate in Western culture present disability as a mistake, or a warning of what happens when bodies go wrong, disability is, in fact, central to the continuing cultural labour of defining the productive, useful, unified citizen's body. The disabled body is the extreme edge or margin that allows the non-disabled body to define itself in relation to what it is not (Hadley, 2008).

Herein lies the 'paradox' (Kuppers, 2004) at the heart of those modes of seeing, imaging and imagining disability that encourage us to see it as a source of fear, shame, stigma or pity. On the one hand, these discourses position the disabled body as a very visible part of the host of spectacles, stories and philosophies about what it means to be human that permeate all aspects of the public sphere. On the other hand, though, these discourses see the disabled body only in terms of the personae projected onto it, not on its own terms, and thus position it as very invisible. By using disability as the axial image or metaphor for all that is Other, these discourses prevent us understanding the material realities of human beings who have disabilities, and take some potentially potent symbolism away from the very people who might want to make use of it to shift public perceptions of themselves (Davidson, 2008; Davis, 1995; Hadley, 2008; Kuppers, 2004; Siebers, 2008; Warren, 1988).

For those with a real, material stake in the matter, this paradoxical positioning of the disabled body is a personal, political and ethical issue not just for themselves, but for their spectators and for society at large. According to ethical philosopher Emmanuel Lévinas (1996a: 7), the encounter with the other always automatically compels us to recognize, respond to and take responsibility for the other at a pre-ontological level. However, in an effort to understand, we impose our own culturally determined codes, categories and labels on the other – an imposition that occurs in the ontological realm, and is influenced by the social, institutional and symbolic practices that prevail in a particular culture at a particular time. This is what teratological, medical and therapeutic models of disability do. They equip spectators with ready-made readings and responses that save them from having to truly encounter the other, or take responsibility for their relation to the other, in the street or on the stage. They subject the other to what Lévinas (1996a: 9) calls the violence of recognition, categorization and comprehension. The daily/dramatic spectator's process 'does not invoke these beings but only names them', Lévinas says,

> thus accomplishing a violence and a negation. A partial negation which is violence. This *partiality* is indicated by the fact that, without disappearing, those beings are within my power. Partial negation, which is violence, denies the independence of a being; it belongs to me.
>
> (1996a: 9, original emphasis)

The circumstances of the daily/dramatic encounter transport bodies with disabilities into what Lévinas calls 'the horizon of knowledge' (1996b: 12). Their radical, unreadable alterity is reduced, and they are transformed into something that serves the dominant cultural logic. The responsibility for the other that characterized the original pre-ontological encounter is lost, together with any possibility of an ethical face-to-face encounter between one and other (Hadley, 2008; cf. Grehan, 2009).

Whether wielded by sideshow spectators, medical specialists or modern day Good Samaritans doing their bit to help the less fortunate, the teratological or diagnostic gaze thus does violence to people with disabilities. It does more than attach a label. It defines their identity, and influences the treatment they receive in all facets of life as a result of that identity. It thus has real effects not just on their agency and ability to access status, social institutions and services, but on their most basic understanding of who they are and how they fit in or fail to fit in to the world. This gaze that turns them into monsters, cripples, sufferers or charity cases is, for most of these unwitting social performers, in many ways more disabling than any pain, impairment or physical difficulties that might be associated with their medical, mobility or sensory conditions.

Disability, performance and performative interventions in public space

Attempts to address the paradoxical position in which spectators and society put people with disabilities have, since the 1980s, led to a rise in countermoves and counter-imaginings from scholars, activists and artists who identify as disabled. These scholarly, activist and artistic practices have, according to Kirsty Johnston, become mutually informative elements in a disability movement active in the United States, United Kingdom, Australia and elsewhere (2012: 6, 9–10). What unites those involved in or influenced by this movement is a tendency to see disability as a minority experience that is marginalized by the images, discourses, institutions and architecture of the mainstream. A tendency, that is, to work with a social model of disability which sees society not biology as the most 'disabling' problem for people with corporeal or cognitive differences. Almost all take account of awkward moments in which people ask them to perform a role that aligns with the dominant perception of what it means to be disabled as the point of departure for their work. In some cases, the call to perform is a mere annoyance. In other cases, it is a threat not just to the person's agency but to their very survival, as he or she is confronted with the fact that many people think a life with a significant disability is not worth living, leading them to consciously or unconsciously support euthanasia, eugenics and other practices with the potential to rid the world of people with disabilities. Those working in disability studies, disability law, disability rights activism and disability arts look for ways to agitate for a more inclusive public sphere, in which, though pain and impairment may remain a reality, this typically unconscious performance of prejudice against a person whose life society sees as not worth living is no longer a prevailing reality. This can be through storytelling to alert people to the problems people with disabilities encounter in their everyday lives, analyses of specific situations and struggles, texts, performances or protests that try to tackle these problems head on, or, in some cases, texts that imagine alternative public spheres in which such problems no longer exist.

Although the politically charged practices of performers marked by gender, race or ethnicity have been the subject of much debate, it is only with this recent upsurge in the disability rights movement that scholars have seriously begun to consider the practices – and, as a result, the distinctive aesthetic and political agendas – of performers with disabilities. To date, texts about these practices number in the tens rather than in the hundreds or the thousands. The task performers with disabilities set themselves is to find a way to speak back to the modes of seeing, imaging and imagining disability that do violence to them, with a spirit, if not strategies, similar to other political artists. The work of these performers, and of those who analyse these performers, displays the same diversity of approach, aesthetic, style and interest seen in the disability movement as a whole, and, of course, in most political movements. It is a fascinating and at times fraught field that is growing both in scope and in scope of influence.

Even the most cursory survey of this field indicates that when people with disabilities turn to performance as a political practice, they tend to avoid natural, autobiographical narratives about diagnosis, crisis, overcoming and cure. Though popular on the main stage, these are, it seems, the stories others would tell about disabled people, not the preferred mode when they work as instigators of their own performances rather than interpreters of other people's well-made plays about them. This caution about conventional theatre has roots that are not at all difficult to identify. In Western culture, as Carrie Sandahl says, the dominant discourse insists on configuring disability as an individual problem detached from the sphere of identity politics (2004: 598–9). It casts illness, disease and disability as a private catastrophe a person needs to deal with. This, regrettably, makes it all too easy for spectators to see an account of disability on the realist stage as a portrait of the way a person learns to deal with their problems that is not connected to broader political concerns in the same way that a portrait of gender, race, ethnicity or class might be. The story, though tragic, fails to register as part of the political negotiations that characterize and change the configurations of the public sphere. This, as Kuppers (2009) notes, may be why it is not uncommon to find attention wandering when we hear a straightforward, logical, linear account of pain, suffering, coping or cure. For many spectators, such a story, though sad, is simply a metaphor or moral lesson about how people might cope with any one of a number of different problems or traumas they might encounter over the course of their life.

Instead of working with well-made plays, performers with disabilities tend to be much more interested in working with contemporary comic, theatrical, performance or choreographic practices. Examples, for instance, might include the stand-up comedy of performers such as Steady Eddy (Australia), Liz Carr (United Kingdom) or Zach Anner (United States), the inclusive dance of companies such as Rawcus Theatre (Australia), Graeae Theatre (United Kingdom), or Axis Dance Company (United States), the remobilization of freakshow motifs by modern-day performers such as Mat Fraser (United Kingdom) or Jennifer Miller (United States), or the conceptual, confrontational and at times almost guerrilla performance practices of A Different Light (New Zealand), Ju Gosling (United Kingdom) or Bill Shannon (United States).

Accompanying this diverse body of practices is a body of scholarly texts that has begun to identify, document and describe their most salient and interesting aspects. There are books that look at work that takes place in theatres, turning the victim, villain or hero roles people with disabilities are assigned in traditional theatre on their heads through a diverse range of multi-character plays written, performed and produced by people with disabilities, representing their own perspectives rather than those of the doctor, social worker or do-gooder. This, for example, is the focus of Kirsty Johnston's *Stage Turns: Canadian Disability Theatre* (2012) and Victoria Lewis's collection *Beyond Victims and Villains: Contemporary Plays by Disabled Playwrights* (2006). There are also books that look beyond plays and theatre pieces to contemporary performance, cross-cultural and community performance, and, of course, politicized performance practices in theatre or in day-to-day life – work that has, as even Lewis and Johnston acknowledge, been the area in which disabled performers have been most prolific in recent years.

There are books that consider work within a specific community of affinity. In *Hearing Difference: The Third Ear in Experimental, Deaf and Multicultural Theater* (2006), for example, Kanta Kochhar Lindgren considers the way deaf, community and multi-cultural theatres experiment with new staging practices to show and shift the cultural construction of deafness.

There are also texts that consider the work of many artists and communities in different countries, contexts and forms. This diversity is a characteristic of Petra Kuppers's texts, including *Disability and Performance: Bodies on Edge* (2004) and *Disability Culture and Community Performance* (2011), which capture the way people with disabilities create stories, connections with spectators, and more inclusive forms of community. This diversity is also characteristic of Carrie Sandahl and Phillip Auslander's *Bodies in Commotion* (2004) and Bruce Henderson and Noam Ostrander's *Understanding Disability Studies and Performance Studies* (2010). Although both collections speak primarily from US, UK and European perspectives, they include articles on everything from the daily self-performance of artists, academics, mendicants or other types of people, to dramatic performances in dance, theatre, film or television, to contemporary, community and politicized performance practices.

Still other books look more broadly again at forms that do not necessarily fit the definition of theatre. In *Unimaginable Bodies: Intellectual Disability, Performance and Becomings*, (2009), Anna Hickey Moody analyses the way dancers with intellectual disabilities deterritorialize diagnostic, medical and social discourses of disability to make new meanings and social imaginings possible. In *Concerto for the Left Hand: Disability and the Defamiliar Body* (2008), Michael

Davidson considers prose, poetry, and photography as well as performance art in a study of how deaf and disabled artists harness the aesthetics of pain, impairment and oppression to challenge the position they are assigned in society, and, again, make new meanings possible.

There are also books on disability in visual arts, such as Ann Millett Gallant's *The Disabled Body in Contemporary Art* (2010) and Richard Sandell, Jocelyn Dodd and Rosemarie Garland Thomson's *Re-Presenting Disability: Activism and Agency in the Museum* (2010). Some literary and cultural theorists also touch, however briefly, on performative practices in their analyses of how people are working to create a culture of, or more inclusive of, disability. Mitchell and Snyder (2000, 2001, 2006), Garland Thomson (1996, 1997, 2009) and Siebers (2008, 2010) all analyse the way disabled people are represented in theatre, film, literature and the visual arts, unpacking the ways in which the disabled body has been used as a 'prosthetic' in Mitchell and Snyder's terms, to prop up dominant ideas about body, identity and Otherness in Western cultures. In the course of these studies, each has also written about self-representations by performance artists like Mary Duffy and Cheryl Wade. Recently, Garland Thomson (2009) has also written about the way disabled people become master manipulators of the stare, shifting the starer–staree relations that have defined and could potentially redefine disabled people in daily practices in public spaces. In this sense, though cultural theorists do not necessarily foreground theatre per se in their studies, they are interested in film, freakshows, autobiographical performances, and the work of artists at the far end of the 'theatrical' spectrum in performance art, even if their interest is in the symbolism instead of the specifically theatrical strategies the performers use to interrupt the stereotyping they are subject to.

The performance artists I bring together in this book all sit at this far end of the 'theatrical' spectrum. They are interested not just in illustrating, but in literally intervening in the discrimination they are subject to in daily life, and this takes them beyond theatre in any traditional sense of the word into a disability inflected form of live art, performance art, or social intervention as art. These artists take the moments in day-to-day life in which they most commonly feel compelled to act out a limited and limiting cultural script – the moments in which the doctor, do-gooder or bystander's stare turns them into a monster, medical specimen, cripple or charity case that consciously or unconsciously connects them with cultural assumptions about disabled bodies – as the starting point for their practice. These moments include being diagnosed, being put in a special school, hospital, home or seating area in public spaces, being overlooked, chastised or barred access to a shop, a street or a service, being told their life is not worth living, being told how brave they are, or simply being the one that has to accommodate the awkwardness and embarrassment of others in social situations. The choice depends on the cultural context the artist works in, and, of course, the access to status, services and public spaces the artist is commonly allowed in this context. In the United States and United Kingdom, for example, continuing debate and court cases about euthanasia make this the compelling choice it would not be, say, in Australia, where access to medical care, education and career are (as we at last move to a National Disability Insurance Scheme that catches us up with some of the legislative and medico-legal progress made in the United States and United Kingdom over the past three decades) much more prominent in public discussions of disability. Whatever the moment, the artists restage it, and the stares, readings and responses they draw in it. Aaron Williamson and his collaborator Katherine Araniello, as I have said, started a petition in a public square in London to prompt passers-by to consider their assumption that the most caring response to Araniello's supposedly unliveable life in a wheelchair with care workers responsible for the routines of her day-to-day life might be to ask the government to allow her to fly to Switzerland to take advantage of their assisted suicide laws. Liz Crow places herself atop the fourth plinth in London's Trafalgar Square, in a Nazi uniform, in her wheelchair, to prompt passers-by to consider eugenics, euthanasia, the supposedly unliveable life of people with disabilities, and just how far some states will go to solve this problem for sufferers and society at large. James Cunningham re-enacts the effect of the mirror-box medical specialists employed to create the illusion of movement in his paralysed arm, asking spectators to put themselves in a similar position, and, in the process, consider their attachment to a whole, able body.

Though not part of a named practice or movement per se, these works all deploy a number of common strategies when they remobilize the images, moments and meetings the artists experience in the public sphere, and in public space, to try to intervene in how the public sphere operates. Though the moments in focus differ as a result of the different ideologies that drive the looks and comments the artists receive in public spaces in their cultural context, the artists all re-engage, re-enact and attempt to re-envisage the tragic, terror-inducing roles people with disabilities are forced to perform in public spaces and places. They replay these stereotypes across their own bodies, with different degrees of amplification, exaggeration, counter-position or critical commentary, in the very public spaces and places where this stereotyping typically plays out, or, at least, outside conventional theatrical spaces. This stress on installation, intervention or interruption of the smooth flow of life on the street, or in medical, social or aesthetic institutions, or in the media, is what links these practices with what scholars in the United Kingdom typically call live art and what scholars in the United States typically call performance art (cf. Hadley, Winter and Trace, 2010; cf. Keidan, 2007; cf. LADA, 2008). Like most exponents of live art, these artists deconstruct or do away with the stories, characters and staging elements traditional realist theatre employs to prevent the potentially disruptive intrusion of real life into the closed fictional world unfolding before spectators (Lehmann, 2006: 30–1). They work not in a theatre, where darkness, stillness, silence and separate seating protect spectators from direct contact with the action unfolding before them, but, instead, in productively live spaces such as galleries, pubs, shops, streets or cyberspace. In doing so, these practices blur the boundaries between stage and social process. They position spectators – whether they are there to see a performance (as in Cunningham's installations) or simply passing by (as in Williamson, Araniello, or Crow's interventions) – as active witnesses, participants or co-performers in a conscious repetition of the usually unconscious social drama of disability, and, therefore, responsible for the encounter, and the effects of the encounter (Hadley, Trace and Winter, 2010; Schaefer, 2003: 5–6).

In effect, each of these artists takes the more-than-theoretical link between disability, performance, spectatorship and the meanings spectators make as the point of departure in their activist politics and performance. They firmly believe it is not just usually unconscious acts of performance, but usually unconscious acts of spectatorship that bring the sometimes unfortunate realities of disability into being. Both, therefore, need to be differentially repeated, disrupted and transformed if there is to be any chance of creating a change in how disability and disabled people are figured in the public sphere. These artists hijack popular display platforms, places and spaces, and highlight the sort of responses disabled people draw in these spaces, by having spectators replay their own habitual responses to disabled people in that space. The hope, of course, is to draw spectators' attention to how their habitual ways of seeing, imaging and imagining disability are complicit in the Western cultural compulsion to define the disabled body as an object of curiosity, discomfort, fear, pity, stigma, shame or embarrassment, by and large excluded from the public sphere. Will spectators see the disabled body as monster, mutant or freak? Will spectators feel discomforted by disruptions to their own sense of being a whole, able person? Will spectators feel the desire to help the supposedly less whole, able person that is so pivotal to the current culture of disability in welfare state countries? What will the spectator do if this causes awkwardness, embarrassment or any other slip in the standard dramaturgy of the social encounter? What if helping, in fact, means helping a disabled person to terminate their supposedly too-difficult-to-live life? What would he or she do if the position were – as it so readily can be via accident, disease or aging – reversed? The emphasis on spectators' reactions, spectators' performances of spectatorship, played out in front of performers, fellow spectators and society at large, raises the stakes of these practices above those of either standard social performances or standard theatrical performances. There is, as a result, a chance – though not a certainty – that spectators will start to reflect, reconsider the scripts that underpin their social interactions, and, potentially, come to a change of perception they can then carry through into future dealings with disabled people.

What these practices try to create, above all, is a method of intervening in the cultural construction of disability. This work, like most live art, engages what Hans Thies Lehmann (2006: 134) calls 'an experience of the real' – real lives and real traumas, in real spaces, places and social situations. It does not, however, attempt to show spectators a real, essential identity, and it does not attempt to spell out a specific counter-position to the current cultural logic of disability identity. Instead, it tries to unravel the mechanisms of oppression from within, whilst, at the same time, acknowledging the real impact of pain, impairment and oppression in disabled people's lives. The politics, then, is aligned not just with a social model of disability, but with a 'realist' model of disability that acknowledges that culturally constructed identities come to have real effects, and thus, for theorists like Tobin Siebers, Tom Shakespeare and others, has much more potential to create a concrete transformation in our relation to corporeal differences and idiosyncrasies (Siebers, 2008: 82; Siebers, 2001). These artists use installation, public space intervention and performance to encourage spectators to consider the real implications and consequences of current discourses about disability. They create the conditions of possibility for a political encounter, an ethical encounter, and a change of perception amongst spectators, even if – as the artists themselves acknowledge – it will be the spectator and society that determine if, and if so how, this change flows through into concrete outcomes in the public sphere.

In the last few years, director of the Live Art Development Agency (LADA) Lois Keidan, LADA itself, and other auspicers such as the National Review of Live Arts in the United Kingdom have done a lot to assist the increasing number of artists with disabilities who find this approach apposite to their political agendas. The affinity between disability and live art has been the subject of a recent seminar series at LADA (2011); a recent festival called *Access All Areas* hosted by LADA in London (2011), at which artists like Mat Fraser, Bobby Baker, Noemi Lakmaier, Katherine Araniello, Aaron Williamson and others performed; and a book called *Access All Areas: Live Art and Disability* (2012) which documents the *Access All Areas* events, and conversations that emerged during it, in still and moving images. Reviews of disability inflected live art at Access Arts and Disability and Deaf Arts festivals in the United States, United Kingdom and Australia have acknowledged the fact that artists with disabilities 'who work with Live Art have engaged with, represented and problematized issues of disability in innovative and radical ways' (Paterson, 2011; cf. LADA, 2012: 55). With this sort of interest, moving beyond showcasing of this sort of practice into a full-scale scholarly analysis of why artists see it as appealing, what strategies they use, what success they have, and what personal, political and ethical issues they encounter, is clearly worthwhile. Critical attention to these practices answers the call of scholars such as Davidson (2008: 2) to consider not just the thematic or therapeutic agendas of disability performance, but also, its aesthetic strategies, structure and style, and the link between its aesthetic strategies and its activist agendas. It also has the potential to tell us a lot about the efficacy of a remobilization of once offensive motifs of Otherness in activist performance practice, about spectatorship, and about the politics and ethics of spectatorship, topics currently of interest not just in disability performance, but in performance practice more broadly at the present moment.

Protesters, pranksters or pity seekers? – the motivations and conundrums of interventionalist performance

If the spectrum of disability performance is so diverse, what is it about an interventionalist, at times almost 'pranksterish' style of performance in public space – a style that, in fact, puts responsibility for meaning-making and for any potential change of mind beyond the hands of the performers themselves – such an appealing choice for the artists I study in this book? Why would they want to replay the problematic roles Western culture assigns them not in a theatre where they have some level of control over what happens, but rather in a public institution, shopping mall, street or in social spaces where the work's reception will be so much more uncertain than almost any other style of practice in circulation in the field of disability performance today?

Although the motivations are complex, and vary from artist to artist, there are at least three motivators above and beyond the aesthetic and philosophical underpinnings of this style of practice that make it appealing to the artists I study here. These are motivators that in many cases apply regardless of whether the artists choose to create this sort of work instead of, or in combination with, one or more of the many other types of in-theatre practices people with disabilities contribute to the contemporary performance scene. Some, such as Aaron Williamson and Liz Crow, are, after all, also highly proficient in other forms of practice and have moved towards live art after work in other forms.

These three motivators relate to the practicalities – and, of course, the philosophies – of theatre production, development and funding today. It is all very well to say that restaging a stereotype lifted from everyday life can be an effective way of using the theatrical stage as a space to speak back to systemic discrimination again specific sorts of people. It is, after all, a strategy that has been used with success in many forms of autobiographical performance for years now, even if these performances are also still more likely to be presented on independent, alternative or cabaret-style stages rather than on mainstream stages (cf. Heddon, 2008). For many disabled performers, however, there is an additional challenge in accessing the theatre stage, subsidy or training required to create these sorts of performances. This, of course, is the fact that they do not have the same physical, social or financial access to a stage on which to speak back to stereotypes that performers marked by gender, race or class do. A long legacy of discrimination makes it difficult for disabled performers to access a legitimate theatre stage, subsidy or training school – or, at least, a legitimate theatre stage, subsidy or training school that is not already overwritten with so many unwanted discourses about disability as to make the whole process difficult and disheartening. Architecturally, theatres can be inaccessible, and it is only in the last decade or so that arts agencies have begun to fund the sort of refits required to address this problem for disabled spectators if not for disabled actors, directors, designers and producers.

This literal issue of access is, though, in some ways the least of the problems. To this day, dominant discourses about disability place unwanted interpretative limits on people with disabilities when they try to access stage, subsidy or training.

The first set of difficulties arises when disabled performers try to access the stage. Though we do see characters with disabilities on stage, they are rarely played, let alone written, directed or produced, by people with those same disabilities. Accordingly, if and when people with disabilities do take to the stage, their practice is already overwritten with problematic discourses. In some cases, this is still the traditional theatrical discourse that makes disability a metaphor for personality flaws or problems people have to get past in life that I discussed above in identifying the dominant aesthetic agendas of disability arts. In other cases, though, this is the therapeutic discourse of 'arts for people with disabilities', 'integrated arts' or 'amateur arts'. Though therapeutic arts does undoubtedly benefit some people, it also leads to the much-lamented tendency to draw professional theatrical practices by people with disabilities into its 'helping and healing' paradigm. This sort of practice is not expected to be innovative, interesting or even watchable, let alone politically provocative, because it is an instrumentalist practice designed to occupy and develop people with disabilities, not to express their opinions to spectators beyond family, friends and caseworkers. It is something many professional performers with disabilities struggle to dissociate themselves from.

The second, related set of difficulties arises when disabled performers try to access theatre subsidy systems. The majority of the artists I analyse in this study do work in contexts where the performing arts is primarily produced through public subsidy systems, as is the case in the United Kingdom and Australia, although not so much in the United States. It is another hallmark of the modern welfare state, and the methods it uses to develop, manage and maintain good citizens. Here again, though, many artists lament the way disability artists tend to be funded as part of a health, therapy and diversion agenda that, again, draws professional practice by disabled people into a helping and healing paradigm that overlooks the possibility that their work might in fact be about experimentation, innovation and the pursuit of excellence, or, of course, the pursuit of an activist politics, in the same way as seen amongst other artists. The artists I study here are more than willing to take advantage of any funding opportunities for professional disability artist practice in place in their cultural context – in the United Kingdom, this includes new opportunities that have come with the live arts community's embracing of disability arts, which have brought pools of money for Lakmaier, Williamson, Araniello and some of the other artists discussed here, though in Australia access to arts rather than access-oriented funding remains available only after a long track record of work of the sort Back to Back Theatre can boast. Indeed, those opportunities, which were not available in the United Kingdom a decade ago, are only now slowly starting to emerge in a country like Australia, and are rare in the United States, may be why the majority of the artists in this book, unlike in many books on disability in performance today, are not from the United States. (Although, of course, personal interest in an access to artists and their work has also been a factor in determining the practices discussed in this book – this text, like all texts on disability and performances, represents not only a specific set of artists, but a reading based on an author's own specific geographical, social, cultural and identity positions, and the places where artists and author's positions overlap.) Still, at the same time, these artists are more than willing to create small-scale solo works, where this sort of funding is not available, if it means they can retain their emphasis on work that is aesthetic and political rather than therapeutic in its impacts. Frequently, these artists are supporting themselves through teaching or other ancillary arts practices while they work. Many hold higher degrees in drama, theatre, performance or visual arts, which, in addition to influencing their complex perspective on their position as unconscious performers, opens up the academy as a potentially less hostile space in which to pursue their practice, particularly for the UK live artists like Williamson.

The third set of difficulties arises when disabled performers try to access theatre training schools. In many contexts, professional theatre training opportunities, like professional theatre production, development and funding opportunities, are inaccessible for performing artists with disabilities. This can be because theatre training schools – as distinct from performance and visual studies programmes which deal with contemporary live art practices and the like – cannot see themselves taking on a student for whom the future professional opportunities seem so limited, or, of course, because they cannot or will not cater for corporeal differences in their largely naturalistic training approaches (cf. Sandahl, 2004). This is why contemporary, cross-disciplinary inclusive practices – from storytelling, satire and comic scenes of encounter with social and medical institutions, to plural modes of imaging, moving and corporeally connecting bodies, to public space intervention – still tend to be most serviceable for artists with disabilities who have not had access to conventional theatre training.

Together, these three factors create an 'inhospitable and sometimes hostile' (Johnston, 2012: xiv) context for many professional disabled performers that can be a motivator to turn away from the theatre and towards alternative forms of practice. For the artists I study in this book, turning specifically to installation, live art, performance art or public space intervention provides a cheap, convenient, mobile and, at least in some ways, less frustrating form of practice. This form of practice takes the day-to-day reality of disability, performance and spectatorship as the point of departure for real-life interventions in public institutions, shopping malls, streets or cyberspace. In doing so, it bypasses a lot of the problems associated with larger scale, more labour intensive production practices in traditional theatre spaces that tend to require a lot of time, technique or financial backing. It allows the artists the authority, and autonomy, they need to be able to pursue their own individual agenda in small, most often solo, performances in a range of spaces and places.

There is also one last motivator for many of the artists I study in this book to move into interventionalist performance practices, and it is to do with the audiences for traditional in-theatre practices today. This is a motivator that would, I think, exist even if the issues with representational politics, platforms and funding policies that prevail today were resolved – perhaps via the activism of agencies like LADA and others that do acknowledge the professionalism, politics and activist agendas of all people – and there was no longer any risk that practices in theatres would be drawn into what some of those I discuss here describe as the 'disability arts ghetto'. It is the fact that interventionalist performance can be done anywhere, anytime, in front of anyone who happens to be using the institution, space or place the performer co-opts for presenting their piece. Interventionalist performance is as mobile as a demonstration or a protest or a flash mob. It can move anywhere, anytime, to connect with any audience, in any gallery, street, shop or website. Accordingly, its audiences are not necessarily limited to traditional theatregoers, or traditional disability theatregoers, as a practice that is more firmly anchored to a traditional theatrical presentation might be. At a time when theatre audiences are not what they once were, and not necessarily representative of the whole of society, this is an important factor in choosing an interventionalist practice with the potential to move beyond the theatre into other institutions, spaces and places.

The combined effect of these motivators makes performative intervention in public spaces a practice that is apposite to the personal, professional and political agendas of artists who are looking to create work that connects – albeit in different ways – with non-disabled audiences, disabled audiences within the artistic community, and, of course, disabled audiences within the wider community. Just as disabled artists find performative intervention in public institutions, spaces and places more real, relevant and accessible than traditional plays, many disabled audience members find such interventions relevant, accessible and of interest to them in one way or another.

Clearly, it is no more possible to generalize about disabled audiences than it is about any other audiences. The disability community, and disability culture, is a broad church that represents many different views, which may be more or less critical of medical, social or other models of disability, more or less critical of the many institutions disabled people encounter in everyday life, and, of course, more or less critical of the beliefs, behaviours and attitudes of the other members of the public they encounter in these institutions. In this sense, although a focus on mundane, daily difficulties and moments of discrimination does make this work readily identifiable and relatable to audiences with disabilities – whether these are the same corporeal, sensory or cognitive disabilities the artist experiences or not – it does not guarantee non-critical acceptance.

The works discussed in this book have often been well received by disabled audiences, if not in the initial interventions (often targeted to non-disabled spectators, participants or co-performers), then, at least, in documentation, performative lectures and performances that recount the results of the intervention in a critical, confrontational or comic way (often targeted to non-disabled and disabled spectators simultaneously). There are, though, instances in which disabled audiences – in particular disabled audience members who are part of the wider community instead of the 'disability arts crowd' community – have expressed concern at the extremes of provocative, prankish public space actions the artists will go to. These audience members have aligned themselves with caregivers, experts and doctors, who express more concern about the work and the person who would make such work, than with the artist who expresses interest in its provocations. Views about the need for a change in culture, and the pathways to change in culture, differ depending on the disabled audience member's history, their experience of the positive and negative aspects of living with this particular identity label, and their different approaches to claiming agency in, or in spite of, this label. As the chapters in this book will show, however, even in cases where work causes controversy even amongst disabled audiences, there is usually at least an appreciation that the artist has created time, space and interest in negotiating cultural attitudes towards disability in a way that is not always common in the public sphere. It is the choice of live, interactive actions that blur the boundaries between drama and daily life – and, of course, the choice to document and further discuss these action in shows that do offer accessibility aids such as audio description, signing and so forth – that enable the work to do this, and to make it possible for a wider than usual range of audiences to participate in viewing documentation, discussion and debate in a way that amateur, therapeutic or in-theatre work sometimes cannot.

Ironically, the very things that make this form of practice most appealing – the fact that it can, like a demonstration or a flash mob, confront almost any spectator in any institution, space or place – are also the very things that make it amongst the most challenging of contemporary forms of practice to create, present, or indeed to analyse. This interventionalist approach is, as I have said, based on the assumption that asking a spectator to perform and reperform their part in the daily social drama of disability can prompt them to consider their own ideas about disability. It is about making the usually unconscious call to perform conscious, so that performers, spectators and societies can, together, consider its consequences. But, as I have argued elsewhere, if we accept the poststructuralist suggestion that the meaning of a performance is always partial, provisional and unfinished until the point where a spectator constructs his or her own meanings and conclusions about that performance (Hadley, Trace and Winter, 2010), then, as Lehmann (2006: 85) says, we need to acknowledge the part the spectator's own position in a complex social field plays in determining the outcome of interventionalist performance practice. It is the spectator, as much as the performer, or, in fact, more so than the performer, who determines how the intervention will be perceived, interpreted and have, or fail to have, a future impact in the public sphere. This means the history, habits and *habitus* of the spectator – the mechanisms by which, as sociologist Pierre Bourdieu (1977) argues, the world structures spectators and spectators structure the world – are critical to the outcomes of these interventions. Depending on their experience of the world to date, each spectator will have a distinctive *habitus*, which they will, inevitably, bring to the encounter. It will be influenced by their prior experience with disabled people, with theatre, with disabled people in theatre, if any, and innumerable other factors. Each will have what Bourdieu (1977) calls a *doxa*, or suite of ideologies, discourses and assumptions taken for granted to be true. Each will have what Bourdieu (1998) describes as an *illusio*, a socially constructed (via *doxas*) sense of what is right, why, and the way social 'games' or interactions should play out. This attitude, approach or sense of how one should interact with others (and the Other) will not be uninterested or neutral or anywhere near as uniform amongst spectators as it might be in a traditional theatre. The attitudes of an individual, or a class of individuals are, after all, what allow for action, agency and authority in social spaces. Given how difficult it would be to function without automatic answers to the questions day-to-day life poses, it is understandable why they become too stable, naturalized and invisible to individuals and societies to give up. These habits of being impact on the way spectators act, react to and read any attempt by an artist to engage them in a consciousness-raising encounter, and only become more and more impactful as an artist moves further out of a theatrical frame into public spaces and places.

The only certainty here, then, is that the call to recite one's common response to disability will be different for each and every spectator, depending on his or her position in the social field. What might, for one spectator, seem like an extreme, exaggerated, comic or offensive image of disability might, for another spectator, seem like little more than the reality that literature, film and television has taught them to expect. What might, for one spectator, seem like a condescending call to 'help' a 'poor', 'suffering' disabled person might, for another spectator, seem like a call to tolerance, inclusion and community-mindedness they cannot ignore if they are to retain their position in the social field. And so on. The range of possible interpretations of a subversive restaging of the Other in public space runs from protester, to prankster, to pity seeker, to psychologically unstable person, to simply what a spectator expects of a disabled person. The possible interpretations are much more varied than what would be expected of a restaging of the Other in a standard theatre space. They can even, in a worst case scenario, lead to a performer being berated, assaulted or brought up on charges as the result of an intervention gone wrong. This is because the spectator's ability to read the blend of fact, fiction and fantasy in play in this sort of encounter will differ, if for no other reason than because the performance takes place in installation spaces, shopping malls or streets where a prior history with interpreting disability as disability, or interpreting theatrical acts as theatre, cannot be taken for granted. Indeed, it is precisely these differences in play in social actions and interactions that make nego- tiating the ideas, ideologies and discourses that come to dominate in the public sphere so difficult. Negotiations that have only become more messy, self-interested and piecemeal, or in Habermas's (1989) terms 'decayed' in today's society with the advent of ever-more identity categories, communities and channels by which individuals can communicate, confirm and contest these ideas.

On the one hand, the complexity of spectatorial practices and interpretations is a positive. Negotiation, contestation and uncertainty amongst spectators are only likely to increase the chance that a work can provoke personal, ethical or political questions. On the other hand, it is also a challenge, because this very uncertainty makes it difficult to determine if, and if so how, interventionalist performance practices prompt personal, ethical or political responses.

Studying the performativity of spectatorship

Though the idea that theatre's power comes from its capacity to prompt spectators to think about social life has, as Freshwater says, become an orthodoxy of contemporary theatre practice (2006: 56), there are no ready answers about how to understand, analyse or create in relation to this critical part that spectators play in politicized performance practices. It is still far easier to emphasis what artists do, and what audiences are assumed to make of it, than to acknowledge the range of possible responses or the way these responses prompt individual spectators to reflect on their own social, ethical or political position. There has, therefore, been a historical tendency toward theories of spectatorship that think in terms of blocks of spectators – a singular, somewhat passive 'audience' (Freshwater, 2009: 5; Grehan, 2009: 4; Lehmann, 2006: 106) – instead of in terms of a collective of individuals who encounter the work from a variety of perspectives. Authors of articles on specific plays, performances and performance paradigms have often identified the parts of the practice that prompt author, critic or specific spectators to 'think', and assumed that all other spectators can or will be prompted to 'think' about their beliefs, attitudes and behaviours too. To do this, though, is to ignore the differences of opinion, conflict and confusion that come out in interpretations of performances, and to universalize spectators and spectatorship (Grehan, 2009: 14; Ridout, 2009: 54, 60–6). It is not useful – not in contemporary performances in which clearly interpretable characters, storylines, crises and resolutions are not central features, and certainly not in the interventionalist practices I consider here.

In order to offer a more complex, nuanced account of spectators and spectatorship, analysis of interventionalist performance practice in this book will be more aligned with newer approaches to spectatorship – from reader response theories (Bennett, 1997; Thom, 1993), through into phenomenology (Garner, 1994; Rayner, 1994; States, 1985), cognition (McConachie 2008) and more recently, relational, political and ethical approaches (Bishop, 2006; Freshwater, 2009; Grehan, 2009; D. Kennedy, 2009; Oddey and White, 2009; Ridout, 2009). I will draw on reviews, critiques, commentaries and observations of spectator responses, together with performance theory, disability theory and the ethical theory of Lévinas, Lehmann and Dwight Conquergood to develop a framework for understanding the way spectators are positioned in the performance practices of disabled artists, the sometimes unpredictable ways spectators bring their 'self' to the exchange, and the pleasures, risks and perils of using public sphere exchanges to try to prompt spectators to think differently about disability. In the initial chapters, I will concentrate on identifying the strategies artists use to create their work. In later chapters, I will increasingly use artists' documentation, critics' descriptions and social media commentary to delve further into individual and shared responses to the work. I will raise questions about the risks involved in a practice where impact, and therefore any eventual political efficacy, lies beyond the work itself in the hands of spectators and bystanders, especially when the full parameters of the work may, in fact, be much clearer to secondary spectators seeing documentation of it than to primary spectators participating as co-performers in the initial public space action or interaction. I will raise questions about whether the presence of the disabled body is, or is not, critical in creating the conditions of possibility for an ethical encounter in this type of practice. I will also raise questions about what happens when the images, metaphors and motifs of disability at the heart of this type of practice are appropriated by non-disabled performers. In this sense, my analysis will connect with continuing debates about whether the live encounter with the body in performance is a privileged site for the emergence of an ethical face-to-face encounter with the Other, and how performance practices create – or fail to create – the conditions of possibility for (if never the certainty of) this ethical encounter. I will not offer any certain answers about the way this sort of work affects each and every spectator, because that simply is not possible. I will, though, offer insight into how interventionalist performances work to create an ethical encounter – one that can, as Nicholas Ridout puts it, become 'the basis for thought, feeling or action within the sphere of politics' (2009: 65–6) – and into a range of distinctive and at times surprising responses to the work of artists with disabilities.

Book structure

In *Disability, Public Space Performance and Spectatorship*, I consider the ways in which interventionalist performance practices allow artists with disabilities, and their spectators, to negotiate new ways of relating with self, others and society. What the artists I examine here share, above all else, is a desire to re-engage, re-enact and re-envision the daily and dramatic performances in medical institutions, aesthetic institutions, social institutions, hospitals, schools, homes, streets and the media that have historically defined the disabled body as Other. They use this recitation of recognizable cultural tropes, together with exaggeration, confrontation, anecdote and, most critically, spatial arrangements in which performers and spectators are aware of each other's presence, participation and complicity in how the encounter unfolds, to try to challenge cultural anxieties about corporeal and cognitive differences. Subjected to critical attention here – not to legislate in favour of this specific form of practice but to find out why artists with disabilities find it so appealing and how it works – these practices have a lot to teach us about public space performance, spectatorship, ethics and politics in disability performance and, as a result, in performance more broadly.

In Chapter 1, 'Weebles, Mirages and Living Mirrors: The Ethics of Embarrassed Laughter', I begin by analysing works by James Cunningham, Noemi Lakmaier and Alison Jones which, though not yet literal interventions in public space, do take place in installation spaces in the public institution of the gallery where the boundaries between performance and social process start to blur. Though they work in different countries, contexts and media, Cunningham, Lakmaier and Jones all mobilize the modern medical or diagnostic gaze that has come to define the disabled body, as the discourse of freaks, mutants and monsters has given way to more politically correct ideas about disability in the twentieth century. These artists all select mundane moments from the daily social drama of disability – from medical imagery, to struggling to wheel a chair through public spaces, to snide comments from passers-by in those same public spaces – and lift them from their usual social milieu. They recite these moments in more or less metaphorized ways in installation-style performances, with commentary and critical perspective coming from shifting images, shifting styles of engagement, and shifts in the point of view from which participants or passers-by respond to what they see.

In these works there is a sense of uncertainty about how spectators are supposed to respond to work in which facts, fictions and fantasies about human bodies, particularly human bodies in the process of becoming Other, collide. Indeed, Cunningham, Lakmaier and Jones raise the stakes for spectators struggling to respond. In the installation space, the spectator becomes a performer, on the spot and in the spotlight as they act, interact and play out a relationship with a body becoming Other in full view of fellow spectators. They must literally move, speak, or summarize their response, in a situation where the right response is not clear. For some spectators, entering the relation to the Other that Lévinas (1991a; 1991b) calls 'substitution' – the relation in which they identify, identify with, yet ultimately fail to fully grasp an Other – is awkward, alienating or embarrassing. In these works, I suggest, embarrassment may in fact be a signal of an ethical process taking place. This process is, however, still unpredictable. In the absence of critiques, reviews or comment books, it is impossible to be sure if a spectator is performing a ready-made response to an Other, improvising to cover the absence of a suitable ready-made response, or providing a glimpse of a moment in which they truly start to connect with an Other in a new way. In some ways, I suggest, the politics of the work may be clearer to secondary spectators, who see documentation of the primary spectators' struggle to respond. This raises questions about the practice, politics and ethics of inviting spectators into this sort of encounter, particularly if spectatorial responses start to seem like displays that serve mainly to spark thoughts in other secondary spectators after the encounter. Questions that, I observe at the close of Chapter 1, only continue as other disabled artists take this sort of work from galleries into public spaces and places.

In Chapter 2, 'Drug Deals, Samaritans and Suicides: Bodies on the Brink of the Visible', I turn to the work of artists who do literally take their practices into public streets, spaces and places. In Back to Back Theatre's *Small Metal Objects*, Aaron Williamson and Katherine Araniello's *Assisted Passage* and Bill Shannon's *Regarding the Fall*, artists with disabilities commandeer public spaces, replaying the relations they are subject to in these spaces – in particular a desire to 'help' poor suffering disabled people – as a sort of guerrilla theatre. They challenge passers-by to reperform their own socially prescribed role in the daily social drama of disability via spontaneous responses, spontaneous reperformances of their own attitudes, beliefs and behaviours. Whilst this work relies on strategies similar to those identified in the works studied in Chapter 1, there is a greater degree of subtlety or subterfuge in the framing of some of these works. Indeed, passers-by pulled into these works may not realize they have become part of – a performer in – a deliberately deconstructive recitation of dominant ideas about disability. Again, the impact of the work may be felt more strongly by secondary spectators who see it in deferred form in the artists' documentation, and reflect both on the passers-by's attitudes towards disability and their own simultaneously. Again, this raises questions about whether artists may be dealing with spectators-become-performers identities in a reductive way. In these works, the spectator's response enacts – or, at least, is presumed to enact – established ways of seeing the disabled body as tragic, hopeless or helpless. It could, therefore, be criticized for setting spectators up to perform a specific, standard response to the disabled body instead of accepting the sometimes surprising idiosyncrasies individual spectators bring to the situation. Analysing this sort of practice in Chapter 2, it becomes clear that artists are aware of and accept the risk that they could be accused of 'playing pranks' on passers-by. They do so, primarily, because their style of intervention in the public sphere is, in fact, a call to engagement with an Other that cannot be fully comprehended on both the spectators' and the performers' side of the equation. It is not just the spectators, but the performers' too, who are putting themselves in a risky position, where they may be witness or party to a reductive reading of an Other, as a necessary condition for creating an encounter in which new relationships with specific little 'o' others rather than the usual universalized large 'O' Other might be negotiated.

In Chapter 3, '"That you would post such a thing…": Staging Spectatorship Online', I suggest that analysis of spectatorial responses to interventionalist performances on social media can provide a record that has not historically been available as fodder for the analysis of spectatorship. I draw on four diverse examples – Rita Marcalo's offline *Involuntary Dances*, Liz Crow's offline/online *Resistance on the Plinth*, Katherine Araniello's online *Suicide Messages* clips on YouTube, and *Cast Offs*, a TV show about disabled people coping with nature *Survivor*-style also available on Channel 4 and YouTube – to examine how spectators respond via social media. Whilst these works differ in style, tone, structure and what spectators respond to – in some cases it is live work, in others it is webcast work, in others a combination of the two – they do display distinctive common features. In each case, the posters perform a debate about disability politics. In each case, social media becomes a platform not just for recording memories of an original performance, but for new performances, new encounters and new negotiations, which go well beyond re-membering or re-mediating the original. There are several common features of these new performances, which typically move from clarification of the original act's parameters, to claims of disgust, insult or offense, to counter-claims confirming the comic or political efficacy of the act, often linked to disclosure of personal experience of disability.

There is, above all, a lot of anxiety about acts that blur the boundaries between fact, fiction and fantasy. This produces a desire to think and talk about how oneself, others and society should respond to these acts. It draws posters into varying levels of dialogue or debate between different cultural logics. Although it is not characteristic of every post, consistent or coherent, these online performances – these online replays of the daily social drama of disability – do give glimpses of posters thinking through their perspective, and others' perspectives, as they try to come to a clearer view. Whilst the impact of these encounters is still unpredictable, these performances, and the cascading circles of new performances that come from them, still present the same risks and the same potentials seen in the live performances considered in Chapters 1 and 2. There is a risk of reductive, recuperative readings of each party's Other within the encounter. Yet, at the same time, there is a potential for posters to improvise or 'riff' off their existing views and adapt, expand or alter others' views. Accordingly, whilst the process can raise passions, tempers and anxieties for those who participate, it can also offer people who might not otherwise have an opportunity to participate in public sphere debate a voice, or an opportunity to develop a new voice, that some posters considered very worthwhile.

In Chapter 4, 'Same Difference?: Disability, Presence, Performance and Ethics', I extend the framework for examining the ethics of staging spectatorship in public space performances developed in *Disability, Public Space Performance and Spectatorship*. I return to the question of whether an encounter with a disabled body – in a context where fact, fiction and fantasy blur, creating uncertainty and a call to consider one's own beliefs – is, in fact, the privileged site for the emergence of an ethical face-to-face encounter scholars like Peggy Phelan (1993) and Lehmann (2006) suggest it to be. I consider this question by considering the work of a number of non-disabled artists who have appropriated one or more of the images, metaphors or strategies identified as distinctive in the work of the disabled artists discussed in Chapters 1, 2 and 3. As noted earlier, disability has traditionally functioned as a sign, symbol or metaphor for negative character traits in Western popular culture and in Western dramatic, literary and cinematographic cannons. Yet, as Sandahl (2004) notes, the signs, symbols and somatic idiosyncrasies of the disabled body are today transported into cultural narratives in theatre, literature, film and television as potent metaphors or master tropes for expressing everybody's experience of – or desire for – Otherness.

In Chapter 4, I consider the way performance artist Guillermo Gómez Peña, choreographer Marie Chouinard, and television show *Glee* mobilize disability as a positive symbol of difference, self-determination or sovereignty over one's own mode of being. I find that, whilst some of this work can be seen to fall into the ethical traps or pitfalls Conquergood (1985) identifies for performers presenting an Other, and, indeed, for spectators interpreting an Other too; some do have the undecidability, and resultant call to reflect, debate and reconsider their own position, that calls people into an ethical process. In the context of work like Gómez Peña's and Chouinard's, the fact that a non-disabled body is appropriating disability signifiers needs to bleed through into the spectator's perception, just as the fiction needed to bleed through into the facticity of performances such as Back to Back's, Shannon's, or Williamson and Araniello's. This is the factor that pushes, if still not predictably drives, a spectator to engage in a dialogue in which different cultural logics compete for traction. The live, concrete encounter with corporeally specific Others may not be the only way to create the conditions of possibility for this dialogue between different ideas, discourses and ideologies, but, no matter the medium, something of this complexity is required. Where it is not present, non-disabled artists' deployment of disability as a rhetorical device to tell a story about different differences that all start to seem like the same difference can indeed be read reductively, and can, as Sandahl (2004) claims, reduce disability's currency as a category around which a corporeally specific group of people could enact an activist politics.

In the Conclusion, '(Dia)Logics of Difference', I end my examination of disability, public space performance, spectatorship, ethics and politics. I affirm that the emergence of an ethical encounter in performance is premised on a theatrical frame, a blurring of facts, fictions and fantasies, and a resultant deferral of meaning-making which draws spectators into a liminal space where reflection becomes possible. I reiterate the importance of recognizing the ways that spectators bring the modes of being, behaving and seeing that are part of their bodily *habitus* to the construction of this liminal space, making monolithic approaches to the ethics of spectatorship in this mode of practice impossible. I reflect on the way I have staged my own spectatorship of this fascinating set of practices in *Disability, Public Space Performance and Spectatorship*, as an example of the risks, perils and pleasures of engaging in a process in which multiple participants – in this case the artists, the spectators, and myself as scholar – bring their own ideas into productive conversations with the potential to impact on public perceptions of disability.

If there is a dominant theme throughout the Chapters of this study, and the specific twists, turns and returns in it, it is the idea that performance can make a productive, material intervention in the public sphere, one that allows disabled people to speak back to dominant ideologies, discourses and social formations. To repeat, replay and problematize the positioning of the disabled body as Other through performances on the same public stages, spaces and places where it has been positioned as Other in the first place is a logical point of departure for people with disabilities looking to shift their position in the public sphere (cf. Kuppers, 2004: 1, 2, 4). The artists I consider in this book are well aware that disability is a constructed identity that is, at the same time, all too discomfortingly real for those who live it daily. They pick moments – in medical or social institutions, sideshows, streets, homes or the media – that capture these discomforting stereotypes by which others see them and by which they are forced to see themselves. They restage these moments with subversive intent. Their practices are, as I will reiterate again and again throughout each Chapter, risky. There are risks for the artists themselves, the spectators, and for society as a whole. The nature of the work necessitates not just taking these risks but taking others into these risks, whether they consent to this or not. These practices are, though, also rich with the potential that comes with taking these risks. They provide moments in which able and disabled people can turn difficult daily encounters into one, tens, hundreds or thousands of chances to negotiate their way into new relationships. This, for people who live their whole lives as unwilling social performers, is a risk well worth taking.

1

Weebles, Mirages and Living Mirrors: The Ethics of Embarrassed Laughter

'What are you?' 'What is wrong with you?' 'How can you live that way?' These sorts of questions, asked in hospitals, schools or social situations, put the diagnostic gaze that typifies modern ways of seeing, imaging and imagining disabled bodies into practice in day-to-day life. They are designed to draw people with disabilities into negotiations of their corporeal differences, and, in the long run, render their idiosyncratic bodies more readable, relatable and docile for spectators and for society at large (Foucault, 1976). As I indicated in the Introduction, these questions, these moments of questioning, are an ever-present part of everyday life for people with disabilities. In attempting to address a long history of oppression, disability theorists, activists and artists today almost all begin their work with accounts of these awful, awkward moments in which they become the object of stares or scrutiny. The moments, they argue, where they feel most compelled by social spectators to perform the role of the monster, medical specimen, cripple, charity case, malingerer, inspiration or whatever other personae prevail in the given context at the given time.

Artist and author Victoria Lewis (2006), for example, talks about the effect of this experience for people with visible disabilities. Lewis describes a moment in childhood where a group of bullies jumped from behind a hedge and started chanting 'cripple', instantly casting her as an object of pity (should she choose to accept this role) or contempt (should she choose to challenge or rile against this role). Academic Tobin Siebers (2008) talks about the effect of this experience for people with less visible disabilities. Unlike Lewis, Siebers

34

focuses not on an originary traumatic moment in which he first knew himself as Other, but on the many trivial moments where he feels forced to perform his disability in particular ways – including moments where he plays his disability down, as he struggles through a social outing with friends who naturally head for steps that are for him difficult to negotiate, and moments where he plays his disability up, for gatekeepers such as airline attendants who will not accept a request for access to services without a visible sign of disability such as a wheelchair. Supervisor Deanna Fassett and student Dana Morella describe the very painful process by which Dana is again, and again, and again 'outed' as dyslexic, and then asked to define her invisible disability, describe it and defend its status as a legitimate reason for special treatment and services, as she seeks text readers and other resources to accommodate her learning disability while studying. 'More than once', Morella says:

> I've been called an imposter, and told I was dishonest and unethical, that I was making a mountain out of a molehill, since not only am I an adult, but I am in graduate school... Time and again, this includes admonitions like, 'You should be grateful just to be here!' or 'I never got to go to graduate school', or 'You got yourself into graduate school – what did you expect?' and 'Do you know that only a small percentage of people in the world even get to go to college?' It's as if, in asking for what I need in order to succeed, I am greedy or ungrateful. It's as if I am spoiled, pampered, and spared from the 'real' challenges of academic life.
>
> (Fassett and Morella, 2010: 148)

Morella goes on to describe the almost warlike tactics and techniques she uses to work through the challenges she encounters in the, to her, hostile and suspicious environment of her school.

Though the specifics vary, the situations Lewis, Siebers and Morella describe here are clearly all too common. I, as a spectator, feel a strong identification with some of their anecdotes and comments. As Lennard Davis (1995: xvi) notes, the questions, clarifications and accusations those of us who function as reluctant social performers encounter in everyday life are about much more than mere curiosity about their bodies, or confirmation of bystanders' interpretations of their bodies. They are part of the continuing cultural labour of defining and policing bodies. Those with disabilities are confronted with probing and sometimes highly personal questions about the state and status of their body much more often than people who are part of any other marked or marginalized identity category. It could, for instance, be characterized as the equivalent of being asked to define, prove and defend one's race, gender or sexuality not just on the occasions where one seeks to access specially provided services, which might be justifiable, but, say, every time one goes to enter a women's toilet, or a shop, or even a public square or street. In these moments, people with disabilities are asked – by social spectators who probably do see themselves as comic, curious, helpful, or simply charged with maintaining value-neutral rules and regulations everyone in a given culture has agreed on – to perform their disability in specific, socially acceptable and socially serviceable ways. There is, as Lewis (2006) suggests, almost no way around this call to perform for many people with disabilities. Either they take up the role and the associations that come with it, or refuse the role, but, in the process, risk being assigned the more alienating role of the bitter cripple, or the malingerer with its even more problematic set of associations.

The artists I consider in this chapter all base their practices on these awkward, alienatory, but for many people unavoidable moments where their identity is called into question in public spaces and places. James Cunningham, Noemi Lakmaier and Alison Jones all begin their practice with some basis – albeit a very loose basis – in what Deirdre Heddon (2008: 7) calls *bios* or life story. They make pieces about diagnosis, medical devices, the daily process of accommodating architecture, furniture or other features of the landscape, or the daily process of dealing with the confused comments of others, because they themselves have experienced encounters of this sort. They are aware of the way the gaze at the heart of these encounters brings them power (to access medical institutions, treatments or liberties in social spaces), as well as prejudice and pressure to conform to social expectations about the way their bodies should be and should behave. They are even more acutely aware of the awkwardness, unpredictability and opportunities for embarrassment this constant need to negotiate their bodily idiosyncrasies can bring. What is interesting, though, is the way each engages these embarrassing moments in their work. Each of these artists avoids telling their story as an authentic, autobiographical narrative, summarizing the encounter, the embarrassment it causes, and the way it effects their sense of self – the theatrical equivalent of the stories Lewis, Siebers and Morella tell in their theoretical texts. They do not want to present these moments as their own individual problems for fear that this might, as Heddon (2008: 4) acknowledges, become an essentialized account of pain, prejudice or exclusion that fails to move, teach or make audiences think about discrimination against so-called deficient bodily identities. Instead, Cunningham, Lakmaier and Jones play out moments drawn from their day-to-day lives as disabled people – medical imaging, a momentary struggle to get a wheelchair around an obstacle, a comment called out while crossing the street – in a more abstract, amplified or metaphorized way. They confront spectators with images of bodies that are ambiguous, between two states, or in the process of becoming something new. Bodies that are, fundamentally, unfixed. Indeed, they present images that spectators might at some level relate to, if they have ever found themselves under scrutiny, had trouble fitting in, or been taunted in the schoolyard.

Most critically, Cunningham, Lakmaier and Jones present these images in live, interactive installation spaces. In Cunningham's *Mirage*, Lakmaier's *Exercise in Losing Control* and *We Are For You Because We Are Against Them*, and Jones's *Portrait of the Artist by Proxy* series, spectators are very visible participants in the encounter. These artists demand what Helena Grehan (2009) calls activated spectatorship, as the spectator quite literally becomes an active participant or co-performer in their pieces. Spectators are asked to move around an installation space, interact with the space, interact with the performer and with fellow spectators, and, in Jones's work, quite literally speak their thoughts on what they see. In this sense, spectators are asked to respond, and take responsibility for their responses, in a context where a whole host of people can see them doing this, either in the space itself, through windows that allow passers-by to see into the space, or through recordings to be shown to any number of people after the fact. The spectator is not drawn into a story on a stage, from which they can depend on a safe level of distance, but, instead, into something that is at once a performance and a very public re-enactment of a social process. They find themselves in a highly charged space in which their attitudes towards the fundamental unfixity of the human body are on show, and they are, at least potentially, embarrassed by, or forced to evaluate, the effects of their attitudes. This, in the end, is how these installations hope to interrupt, disrupt and intervene in the diagnostic gaze that is such a difficult part of the day-to-day lives of people with disabilities.

Bodies in becoming – Igneous's *Mirage*

Illness, injury or accident has the potential to put any body in the position of being defined as disabled. Pain, paralysis and amputation can, as Elizabeth Grosz says in *Volatile Bodies* (1994: 71,72, 76), present a challenge to a person's perception of themselves as an integrated, individuated, well-shaped, and thus useful bodily whole of the sort Western culture valorizes. Indeed, pain, paralysis or amputation as a result of an accident might be seen as more challenging than congenital disability as a person accommodates – perhaps all too suddenly – to a new image of themselves in the mirror, in their own eyes, and in the eyes of others.

In *Mirage* (2006), a performance installation by Australian company Igneous, dancer James Cunningham and multimedia artist Suzon Fuks investigate precisely this sort of shift in a person's perception of self. *Mirage* – like past Igneous works *The Body in Question* (1999) and *Liquid Skin* (2005) – is based on Cunningham's experience after a motorcycle accident in 1992 left him paralysed in his left arm, and on his subsequent study of pain, paralysis and the phenomenon of the phantom limb that is common to these conditions. The specific motif is the mirage-like perception of movement in a painful, paralysed or amputated limb that Cunningham experienced in a device called a mirror box after his accident. A mirror box is a therapeutic device designed, according to Cunningham's programme notes, by neurologist Vilayanur Ramachandran to provide the synaesthetic illusion of movement in a still or missing limb. The mirror box had a 'profound' effect on Cunningham when he encountered it in his research about pain, recovery, and the recovery of bodily movement in the wake of an accident.

> Observing the movement of his intact arm reflected in a mirror, it was as if James could suddenly feel his paralysed arm moving again, along with perceived weight, joint articulation and position

in space. A bizarre experience when one knew that in fact the immobile arm was lying flat on the table.

(Cunningham and Fuks, 2006a)

In effect, the mirror box mobilizes the same visual mechanisms that, according to medical science, allowed an individual to achieve bodily wholeness in the first place, to promote a continued perception of wholeness. According to Grosz (1994: 40), an individual's body image is, like the broader set of body images that populate the Western cultural imaginary, based on both individual and collective fantasy. As an infant, an individual starts life as a set of undifferentiated stimuli. It becomes a subject, with a social identity, and agency, only when it is able to see itself as an integrated, individuated whole (Grosz, 1994: 273). This, according to psychologists, happens by means of a series of visual identifications with images of its own body, and other bodies, in what Jacques Lacan calls the mirror stage (Grosz, 1994: 32). These identifications are based on what Lacan calls a moment of (mis)recognition in which the infant mistakenly recognizes, relates to and aspires to realize an idealized images of wholeness, at odds with its currently much more muddied, disseminated mode of being. This (mis)recognition – like the social spectators' (mis)recognition of the disabled bodies displayed in fairs, sideshows, freakshows, museums, medical institutions or the media – is productive, performative and world-making. It allows an infant to acquire a sense of what their body is, should, and should not aspire to be.

Obviously, theorists like Grosz argue, the infant's acquisition of a body image happens in a specific social, cultural and historical field – which, in Western culture, tends to figure the able body as the norm, and the disabled body as mutant, monstrous, or to use more psychoanalytic terms, hybrid and *unheimlich*. The sight-based identifications that structure the mirror stage mimic and are mimicked by the sight-based identifications that structure Western cultural forms like the fairs, sideshows, freakshows, museums, medical theatres and other modes of performance. Both are characterized by performative acts of identification, interpretation and categorization that inscribe bodies and bodily characteristics with meaning, and bring them into what Emmanuel Lévinas (1996a) characterizes as sphere of the known and knowable. In this cultural field the infant aspires, usually, to the integrated, individuated wholeness of the able body. Its body image is, therefore, always already structured by the sexist, racist and ablest framework that articulates, and affirms, the binaries between one and other, male and female, able and disabled, that subtend Western cultural logics. It is this aspiration to wholeness – and the disabled person's inability to achieve this wholeness they are taught to aspire to – that makes it difficult, both privately and publicly, for disabled people to accommodate the images by which Western culture defines bodies. 'The disabled body causes', as Davis says, 'a kind of hallucination of the mirror phase gone wrong' (1995: 139). The medical profession seeks to cure this maladaptation through surgeries, prostheses and exercises that help individuals adapt to their limitations, overcome their limitations, and even artificially create the illusion of bodily wholeness for themselves or for others. The mirror box, which uses a mirror image of a patient's functioning limb to create the illusion of movement in the other non-functioning limb, does exactly this, to help the patient accommodate to their dysfunction. It is, however, a process that is ambiguous, alienating and empowering for the patient.

Mirage is a two part performance installation, designed to share Cunningham's experience in the mirror box with spectators so they can 'gain a first-hand experience of the illusory nature of perception, the "mirage" of the mind' (Cunningham and Fuks, 2006a). The performance installation re-imagines Cunningham's experience in the mirror box to interpellate spectators into it, and show them how their (socially structured) minds trick them into cohering multiple, fragmented states into a meaningful whole (Figure 1). It works with what Jennifer Parker Starbuck might call a 'cyborgean' (2006: 649) aesthetic, integrating dance, data projection, video, installation and other technologies to interpellate spectators into a mutable, plastic perceptual space in which parts of the body can be mirrored, multiplied, transposed and transformed. The images – though not 'monstrous' images of disability, disease or illness – are definitely striking and strange. They are reminiscent at times of a hall of magic mirrors that might be found at a fair, sideshow or freakshow, at times of the medical mirror box, and at times of medical imagery of bodies such as diagnostic diagrams, scans, MRIs and X-rays. Cunningham and Fuks describe the imagery as 'a poetic anatomy inspired by molecular and neurological biology, particle theory, prosthetics, mutation, and dissolution-reformation of matter' (Cunningham and Fuks, 2006a).

Figure 1 James Cunningham in *Mirage*, Australian Choreographic Centre, Canberra, 2006 (Photo: Leighton Hutchinson)

In the first part of the performance, the installation space is white, clear and clean. It is set up to look something like a sideshow hall of mirrors and also something like a surgical ward. Spectators are invited to look at themselves at mirror stations, quite literally placing them in a series of mirror boxes of sorts. The mirrors' strange angles and surfaces swap one body part for another, or morph one's own body into that of another, leaving spectators – at least on the night I attended – giddy, giggly and confused by these tests to their perceptual integrity. The experience, amongst spectators who have paid to be part of it, is ever so slightly awkward or embarrassing, in a light, community-building sort of way.

Although I have described this as the first part of the performance, the fact that spectators can pass through multiple performance cycles over the course of an evening, move about at will, and stay as long as they like, means these experiences in the first space sit as a sort of palimpsest over experiences to come in the second space. They enable spectators to relate both visually and viscerally to the mirroring and fragmentation Cunningham goes on to explore in the second part of the performance. As critic Jody McNeilly says:

> For those willing to interact with reflective mirrors casting images and affecting neurological states of body disjuncture (enabled through instructed positioning of limbs and perspectives of vision), the ante-chamber of white generously prepares the audience member to wade into the black pool of this piece's exquisitely constructed mythology.
>
> (2006)

In the second part of the piece, the space is darker, more abstract and more ambiguous. Spectators are invited to move around a triangular pool of water with cords, cables, scaffolds and a six-foot scrim-covered triangular frame hanging above. These, and Cunningham's body, become the canvas for the mirroring, morphing and transmogrification to come. Turning and moving in the dimly lit space, Cunningham uses one limb to push another, giving it weight and momentum, and with time it becomes less and less clear which is leading and which is following. He plays with a shifting, shrinking, growing doppelgänger of himself reflected on the water, on the scrims, and on the frame he is shifting and tilting around him. His image is doubled, tripled and quadrupled, but always asymmetrical or truncated in some way. In McNeilly's words:

> *A duet lived and layered with choreographed intention and streamed from data projectors high in the theatre's ceiling starts to unfold.*
>
> James, with his life-size, light-weight, triangular scrim-stretched capsule pulled over him, shares his isolation with the projected image of himself, both men alongside the other with reflected synchrony. There is a simple, yet powerful distal initiation of the head. Live James peels away to the left, his silver other responding with some delay to the right. They enter into a play of mixed timing, a slight delay instigated by temporal manipulation, shapes formed into a mesmerizing relief. Images of antiquity come to mind. The sound score is reverent to the composition. Is video James streamed live/delayed, with the image flipped for directional purposes? Or is it a pre-recorded James? These questions fall away as the dance resists its mediatisation to draw

me towards the bodies, one [real and the other] a mere virtual reproduction.

(McNeilly, 2006)

'*Mirage*', as Cunningham and Fuks say, 'plays on perceptual illusion, the construction of hybrid forms, and the real and virtual fusing and separating' (Cunningham and Fuks, 2006a). Through its dance, data projection and constantly shifting images, *Mirage* images, imagines and implodes binary relations with and within the body. Signifier and signified. Fixed and fluid. Live and mediatized. One and other. Able and disabled.

The dance between these various presences suggests struggle, co-operation, at times one is overlaying the other, fusing and then separating. Sometimes one is simply watching the other, mirroring their actions or guiding them like super-conscious forces.

(Cunningham and Fuks, 2006a)

It creates a series of moments in which one image of the body, and another image of the body, merge. Still body, shifting image. Shifting body, still image. Sometimes acting together. Sometimes acting separately. Sometimes Cunningham's image seems to lead. Sometimes Cunningham's body seems to lead. Sometimes parts of Cunningham's body – able parts, disabled parts – seem to lead, providing weight or momentum. Things move in and out of sync, and the body's status as a solid, definable object dissolves. The in-between states blend into new, hybrid, unheimlich sorts of bodies. And, in the choreography, Cunningham and Fuks allow moments of stillness, so the spectator can – even if only briefly – perform the perceptual trick necessary to reconcile multiple images into (or misrecognize multiple images as) a new, hybrid state.

This is not, however, a mutation that stops in a single, new state – it is not a new monster, mutant or freak we might recognize, relate (or unrelate) ourselves to, and categorize, in order to escape the threat of the encounter with the radically Other. In *Mirage*, spectators are not just confronted with images of Cunningham, themselves or their fellow spectators as unwhole. They are not just confronted with their own response to images of unwhole bodies. They are, rather, drawn into a visceral experience of what it is like to have one's body defined, redefined and redefined again. There is never a moment at which the body comes into permanent sync with its image or vice versa. There is never a moment in which signifier comes into permanent sync with signified, shoring up – as Rebecca Schneider (1997) following Walter Benjamin might have it – significatory assumptions about disabled bodies. There is never an overcoming narrative in which shoring up a disabled body's identity starts to seem desirable. Instead, states of the body are always broken, by Cunningham's breath, by the intrusion of Cunningham's small impulses and movements, by confusion as to which of Cunningham's limbs, movements or images is leading, by ripples in the water, or ripples in the movements of fellow spectators as they move freely to and from different vantage points in this open space. There is, throughout *Mirage*, a mesmerizing quality to the images, which – as a result of the reflections in both parts of the performance – has the potential to catch the spectator in a visceral recognition of their own capabilities as well as Cunningham's. In one sequence, for instance, Cunningham played with a pendular swinging of his paralysed arm, reflected in the water and on the screens, and as I said in a review at the time, 'I felt foreshadowings of motion in spite of my own arm's stillness, before realizing my musculature would make this motion impossible, except in the mirror space made possible here' (Hadley, 2007).

It was in this way that *Mirage* increased my own spectatorial awareness of the visual identificatory mechanisms that define the disabled body in established categories such as mutant, hybrid, unheimlich or tragic. Cunningham replays recognizable images, combined with commentary, counter-position and questions – not through words Cunningham himself might offer, but through comments amongst spectators, the 'mirage' images, and the constant proliferation and change of these images. The spectator, whose presence in the space is always clear and acknowledged, is asked to respond through words, motions or movements. Their responses variously replay the visual schemas of freakshow spectators, doctors, specialists, do-gooders, and even the disabled person themselves looking in the mirror. The proliferating, morphing and transforming images in play are 'monstrous' in a sense, not just because they are in-between, hybrid or unheimlich, but because they are constantly becoming more so, challenging the idea that any of the bodies in this space should be whole, or should be the same from moment to moment. In this visual, visceral meditation on the experience of embodiment as something marked by mutation and change, spectators' reactions and responses to this idea play out in full view of Cunningham, his collaborators and fellow spectators. There is a discomfort, but it becomes a strangely pleasurable one, prompting laughter, hypnotized attention, and the occasional bump into one another that is happy in tone. As the performance unfolds, the constant shifts in the relationship between body and body image challenge spectators to recognize, re-recognize and re-recognize again new movements, and new mobilities, in the face of what the dominant cultural logic would consider a catastrophic challenge to corporeal integrity. In this mirage-like space of encounter with images of oneself, others and oneself in the eyes of others, it becomes clear that the way we perceive is not the same as what we see, what we perceive is not the same as what is true, and what we perceive is not necessarily as stable, unified and universal as we might make it out to be in day-to-day encounters where we simply see and dismiss others.

Cunningham and Fuks did capture some of their spectators' responses to *Mirage* in a comments book (2006b), clarifying the tenor and outcomes of this engagement with the idea of the body in becoming. 'It's like an optical illusion', one spectator said. 'When I used the mirror box with my left arm', another spectator said, 'it really did feel like the rigid arm was moving the same.' 'The interaction between body, reflection and multiple projections was fantastic to look at', and made another spectator wonder, '[w]ho's moving first, who's chasing who?' Spectators characterized their experience as '[a] perceptive glimpse of a seeming afterword', and one said, 'I never thought that my eyes would make me see the unseen in such a way.' In lengthier reviews, Zsuzsanna Soboslay and Jody McNeilly both echo and expand on some of these sentiments. They affirm that *Mirage* presents an abstraction that, paradoxically, feels somehow familiar – 'a more abstracted realm that is paradoxically even more immediate for the viewer', as Soboslay puts it (2006). They acknowledge that they feel both an invitation, and a sense of awkwardness, at being asked to join Cunningham in this strange new perceptual space provided by the installation performance. 'To walk freely as audience within a space when the performance as installation offers such freedom', McNeilly says,

> places a new form of demand on our responsibility to witness. Both I and other audience members filter awkwardly, together,

adjusting our positioning with hesitant manoeuvres to finally make a decision about how we wish to view the performance in all its measure.

(McNeilly, 2006)

Both acknowledge that their response is one of immediate positioning within perceptual space, and of reflection on what the act of seeing, imaging and imagining Cunningham's disabled body in this way might mean. 'Despite my own perceptual work that vivifies video James as this corporeal other creating a similitude in such terms', McNeilly says, 'there is something in the experience that reminds me of the manufactured illusion that I participate in' (McNeilly, 2006). 'This restorative process', Soboslay says, thus 'both questions the "reality" of permanent injury, as well as the "reality" of the body' (Soboslay, 2006). Though challenging, watching and participating *in Mirage* is ultimately – for Soboslay at least – a joyful, exhilarating experience.

> At its heart, this is a work that actually cares for and about the body, for and about the performer, but also the spectator/audience, and in a larger sense, the human condition, allowing for the fact that seeing, listening, witnessing, are themselves alchemical processes. I felt an exhilaration in watching this work.
>
> And that rare experience: what it costs to watch, and think and be in watching, is rewarded by a message much larger than the performance.
>
> (Soboslay, 2006)

These spectatorial responses suggest that *Mirage* invokes the relationship to the Other Lévinas calls substitution (1991a: 203; cf. McHenry, 2007). For Lévinas, substitution invites spectators into proximity with the Other, and invites spectators to perceive themselves as Other, although, as in this case, not necessarily to put themselves in the place of Cunningham as Other. Indeed, it is by almost, but not quite, putting spectators in Cunningham's place that *Mirage* establishes a sense of exposedness to the Other in the face-to-face encounter (1991b: 75), which calls the spectator's own mode of existence into question (Shildrick, 2002: 92), precisely because it reminds the spectator that they can never fully, reductively, comprehend Cunningham's experience.

As a spectator, I am indeed in two minds, two frames of reference, simultaneously – I identify with Cunningham, yet, simultaneously, am pushed out into reflection on my inability to identify fully with Cunningham, identity in general, difference in general, what it means, and thus on what my relation to the Other is. *Mirage* expresses the ambiguity and in-betweenness of the disabled body, and invites me as a spectator to experience my own body's ambiguities. But it does so without erasing the specific, somatic intensities of experience of either myself, or my others. I am not part of a unified, utopian community of self-differentiated identities which includes Cunningham, Fuks, myself and my fellow spectators. I do not necessarily intend phenomenologically towards Cunningham's otherness in the same way as my fellow spectators (McNeilly, 2006). The experience stays specific, individuated and differentiated, as spectators work to recognize, re-recognize and re-recognize again their relationship to a body becoming, breaching the bounds of signification, and eschewing any status as stable identifier in the encounter between self and Other. It is, as a result, more difficult for spectators to contain the radical alterity of the other in ready-made responses, dismissing it before a relationship of vulnerability, responsibility or respect might emerge. There is dis-ease, awkwardness, embarrassment, but only briefly before a sense of connection in and through difference seems to emerge.

In this way, *Mirage* challenges spectators to experience – if fleetingly – the uncertainties of the face-to-face encounter with other bodies, in which we acknowledge the specificity of other bodies, without immediately being about to abstract, domesticate or abdicate responsibility for our reaction to other bodies. In *Mirage*, the spectator's encounter with the other is characterized not by the categorization, domestication and containment that serves to change 'o'thers into a universalized 'O'ther, but by respect for the other's radical alterity, by vulnerability, and, in Jacques Derrida's reformation of Lévinasian ethics, by a singular reciprocal and undecidable responsibility towards the other (Derrida, 1995: 60–70). This is what Lévinas would call a truly ethical relationship. In this relationship, the other exists, but as an excess, a class of being that can be recognized but never seized by comprehension (1996a: 7; 1996b: 17), or dismissed as a mere complement or contrast to the one itself (1996b: 13; 1996c: 51). Here, the other is a class of being that presents us with questions we may never be able to answer, and cannot – or, at least, cannot instantly – escape via application of established cultural readings, responses and answers. Whilst each spectator's willingness to further reflect on the way these sorts of encounters may or may not change unique others into a universal Other remains an open and individual question, the relationships explored in *Mirage* do at least create the conditions of possibility for new ways of thinking about other bodies to emerge.

Bodies ambiguous – Noemi Lakmaier's *Exercise in Losing Control*

Images of the body as ambiguous, in-between and in the midst of becoming something more or other than a standard human being are also harnessed, albeit in a very different way, in the work of Noemi Lakmaier. An Austrian born artist who lives and works in the United Kingdom, Lakmaier, like a number of the artists in this book, identifies herself primarily as a visual artist who incorporates performance, installation and what she (following Marina Abromavić) calls 'living installations' in her work. 'I don't feel that the term "performance" in relation to my work is entirely accurate', Lakmaier says. 'I would rather describe it as "living installation" or "live art"' (Lakmaier quoted in Moore, 2010). Working in the United Kingdom, Lakmaier is frequently part of disability and live arts events, such as the *Access All Areas* event held by the Live Art Development Agency in London in 2011. Although diverse, Lakmaier's living installations are all linked by the fact that they deal with the theme of Otherness in distinctive ways, despite differences in the medium or the degree to which performance, installation and interactivity is central in exploring the concepts at the core of the work. 'Through the use of everyday materials and the human body', Lakmaier says, 'I construct temporary living installations – alternative physical realities – exploring notions of the "other" ranging from the physical to the philosophical, the personal to the political' (Lakmaier quoted in Moore, 2010). Indeed, the inclusion of performance, performers and living participants was, for Lakmaier, a natural evolution in her practice as she became interested in the way people – as social performers – react to the themes of control, lack of control, and vulnerability in her work.

Though Lakmaier addresses Otherness from a modern medical, social and personal perspective – addresses it, in other words, as something that comes from the way her body and her use of a wheelchair is seen, imaged and imagined – the images and moments at the core of her work are not as directly representative of what happens in streets, social institutions or popular culture as some of the other work discussed in this book. The images she invokes are not straight replays of real life. They are, rather, like concrete metaphors that work by capturing what it feels like to be out of control of one's own body, an image a whole range of people might relate to. Accordingly, her work is typically characterized by absurd images, metaphors and interactions between people. 'The concept', as Tammy Moore says of Lakmaier's work, is to '[...] [refram[e] the ordinary, taking everyday objects or events and adding an element of the absurd to make them "other"' (Moore, 2010). 'I think', Lakmaier agrees, 'I am really interested in that, and in setting up very average sort of situations that have something profoundly wrong with them, and that absurd element to it' (2010). It is, she says, about investigating Otherness conceptually, rather than in terms of any single instance or example of Otherness, and 'exploring that on different levels, on a personal level and on a political level' (2010). Lakmaier's work tends to thrust spectators into ambiguous, absurd situations that deal with Otherness in an abstract way, ask spectators to watch, think about or participate in the situation, and think about what they do when confronted with the challenges it presents. Lakmaier acknowledges that this can make it difficult for spectators to perceive, interpret and react to her installations – but, at the same time, believes this difficulty in itself 'encourages people to have very different readings' (2010) of the work. She is, therefore, happy to leave it to spectators to enter her installations – as a viewer, voyeur or participant – start playing off the not-quite-normal situation they encounter, and make meaning of it as best they can. Indeed, in recent years, the transfer of roles to make spectators the main performers in the installation has become more prevalent in her work. 'I am quite interested in [myself] being the passive bystander in [the process of] observing my voyeurs or my viewers and their different reactions', she says, and '[...] I find it makes it quite interesting, [observing] the different viewers' attitudes and different behaviours' (2010).

In *Exercise in Losing Control* (2007) and *We Are for You Because We are Against Them* (2009), Lakmaier represents Otherness, and the experience of Otherness as one of feeling vulnerable, uncomfortable and less than fully human, by placing first herself then a group of participants in large circular balls she calls 'weebles'. The weebles are, Moore notes, 'based on the American toy marketed with the phrase "Weebles wobble, but they won't fall down"' (2010), a small round figurine that rocks from side to side in a fun or funny way. According to Lakmaier, though her weebles are sturdy, with about 70 kilos of concrete at the base to keep them upright, when you first get into one 'you have the feeling that you have absolutely no sense of control' (2010). 'The objects are physically restricting to the people inside them as only their heads and arms stick out. They rock and wobble with every movement and therefore create a sense of instability and loss of control' (Lakmaier quoted in Moore, 2010). Even if this sense of uncontrollability later dissipates, it is still very difficult to do things in the weeble, leaving those who enter the weebles vulnerable, dependent, and highly visible as Other in any given situation.

> The yellow ball looks bizarrely small, too small surely to fit Lakmaier's body into it, and elicits conflicting impulses. Viewed as an object Lakmaier-as-ball is cute enough to be a new, big-eyed soft toy from Japan; empathized with as a person and the performance is one of horrifying claustrophobia and inability.
>
> (Moore, 2010)

In her first piece in the weebles series, *Exercise in Losing Control*, Lakmaier herself sat in a small 50-centimetres tall yellow weeble in a gallery, and in a range of public spaces and places around the gallery. Initially, *Exercise in Losing Control* was inspired not so much by notions of physical difficulty, control and constraint that come with disability – though Lakmaier herself does use a wheelchair – as by notions of psychological control and how people feel when they cannot exercise control over every element of their environment; as, for example, in obsessive compulsive disorder. Lakmaier says 'the physical aspects only really occurred to me when other people attached them to the piece' (2010) – which, perhaps, is only more appropriate given it is other people's interpretation of what it means to have a physical limitation, like using a wheelchair, more than the physical limitation itself that determines a body's status as disabled. Although Lakmaier did not directly ask people to engage or interact with her in *Exercise in Losing Control*, she found they did want to do this, and found that there were a variety of different responses. These ranged from people – in particular children – who would run off screaming, to people who would try to talk with her, to people who would try to kick or tip her to test the reality of the weeble. Some thought the size of the weeble meant there must be an optical illusion in play, such as a trap in the floor in which Lakmaier was standing. Some realized the weeble was really real. 'There was', for instance, 'an eight- or nine-year-old that came up to me and was like "sorry, miss, are you a midget?"' (Lakmaier, 2010). That said, Lakmaier thought 'the oddest ones were really the ones who sort of insisted on talking to me like there was nothing wrong. [The people who decided the best solution was to] just ignore the situation, [and say something like] "would you like a glass of wine?"' (2010).

The variety of reactions was, Lakmaier believes, due to the spectators' discomfort dealing with such an unnatural, unusual situation. 'I think there was a clear sense of discomfort, [of attitudes such as] "how can this work?", and "it just looks wrong!", because it does not look like a human body anymore', she says. 'And it was clearly funny, as well. [T]hat border between funny and uncomfortable. [There were] people wanting to laugh at it but not really daring to laugh at it' (2010).

In *We Are For You Because We Are Against Them* the absurd situation was a posh dinner party, with wonderful food cooked by a chef who works for a Michelin-starred restaurant in Dublin, for eight weeble-wearing participants (Figure 2). The event ran for about two hours, in a gallery in Dublin, with spectators and passers-by watching as the participants – in a normal situation, a dinner, made not normal by the fact that the weebles made it difficult to eat, drink and develop relationships with others – had their meal. For Lakmaier, '[c]ommunal dining and therefore the dinner party is one of the oldest types of social interactions humans engage in. This is why I am particularly interested in it' (2010). Adopting this scenario, Lakmaier's staging included

> everything one would expect of a high end dinner: beautiful, delicious, chef-prepared food, great wine and elegant, professional

Figure 2   Noemi Lakmaier's *We Are For You Because We Are Against Them*, The LAB, Dublin, 2009 (Photo: Hugh McElveen)

waiters serving, as well as eight guests and interesting conversation. For the duration of the dinner [though] the guest will be seated in 'weebles'. Taking part in a dinner party while being inside one of these objects requires participants to rethink the normally everyday tasks of eating, drinking and social engagement with other diners.

(Lakmaier quoted in Moore, 2010)

According to Lakmaier, 'the title [also] adds to the absurdity for most people' (2010). 'It is', she says, 'actually taken from, it is slightly changed and translated from a really, really disgusting political advertising poster in Austria from the far right party, which said pretty much that, "we are for you because we are against them"' (2010). The installation, the situation, the various modes of participation, and the title attributed to it, all invoke ideas of Otherness, and how we, whatever our position, deal with what is outside the natural, normal order of things. 'It also makes viewers question who is we and who is us and who is they', Lakmaier says. 'Is it the people who are having dinner who are Other? Or is it the people who are having dinner who are We? And who is the audience in this context?' (2010). Because of the way Lakmaier structured *We Are For You Because We Are Against Them*, there were, in effect, two ways of encountering and engaging with the work – as a participant recruited to wear the larger 80-centimetre weeble at the dinner party (a little larger than the 50-centimetre weeble to make it easier and because most people are larger than the artist), or as a spectator who happened to come to, or even just pass by the window of the gallery. The participants were chosen on the basis of their ability to fit in the weeble, and remain in the weeble for a period of time, without feeling too uncomfortably claustrophobic or anxious to continue, which, according to Lakmaier, is quite challenging (2010). The spectators and passers-by were, of course, self selecting.

> What was quite important about this piece was that it was not like a theatre performance where you buy a ticket, you arrive at a certain time, you stay for two hours, and you leave. It was a lot more like an installation piece where you go to a private view and you may want to watch it for five minutes or you may want to watch it for two hours.
>
> (Lakmaier, 2010)

For the weeble-wearers, and those who watched, this structure is much more like the structure of real life – and, as a result, they were much more involved in making choices, making decisions, and making the interactions unfold over the course of the evening.

As the installation progressed, weeble-wearers started to play, to test what they could do, and get into the atmosphere of an – admittedly odd – dinner party. In a sense, then, this work, like Cunningham's work, offered an image of a mutation that did not stop in a single, new state, but instead saw participants perpetually expanding and exploring their movement possibilities. The participants explored their new movement possibilities with a good humour that surprised Lakmaier, who had wondered if they would get frustrated (2010). Having done a variety of works with the weebles – she has, for instance, recruited two people to try to kiss in the weebles – Lakmaier is interested in the future in taking them to even more public spaces and places, because, she says, whilst a conversation, dinner party or cuddle in a gallery enacts everyday social process, she wants to make this situation even more everyday to make the absurdity more extreme. As the weeble-wearers in this work explored their new range of motion, in a semi-everyday space, passers-by were to lesser or greater degrees arrested by the absurdity of what they were seeing. 'It drew a lot of attention from invited audiences as well as random passers-by', she recalls. 'A very interesting dynamic developed between the participants in the piece and people watching it. The two started sparking off each other, which I believe influenced and changed the event' (Lakmaier quoted in Moore, 2010). As Lakmaier says:

> [M]ost of these people walk past this gallery every single day, because it's on their way home, or their way to work, or to the shops, or whatever, and they will be used to seeing paintings in there, sculptures in there, videos in there, whatever, installations in there, probably the odd performance occasionally. But I think what encouraged such a strong double take was the kind of something so different going on in there from what they, normally they just walk past and don't pay any attention.
>
> (2010)

It was interesting, Lakmaier found, because it was in a rough area of Dublin, and its absurdity was surprisingly engaging for some of the local youth in the area. There was 'a discomfort with the "in-betweenness"' (2010), ambiguity and absurdity of the bodies and the situation, but, at the same time, options to stay behind the glass or on the balcony, or get closer, as spectators and passers-by tried to make sense of what they were seeing.

In her weeble works, Lakmaier blurs the boundaries between the symbolic and the social, and between performer, stage and spectator, to present an image – albeit an ambiguous or absurd image – of Otherness, of what makes people feel Other, and the ways in which people respond to seeing or being an Other. The idea of a fixed bodily state is, again, challenged in the content, aesthetic, form and stage-spectator interface of the work as everyone tries to come to terms with the absurd intrusion of the weebles. Artist, participants, spectators and passers-by are all invited to play a role in a performance which is at once both a performance and a performed reality that seems to require some sort of response. The odd situation, the visibility of the spectators, their actions and their interactions in this odd situation, creates uncertainty and confusion. This, in turn, asks spectators to make choices in their reactions that – as the variety of comments, collaborations, confrontations and struggles to ignore the weeble as an addition to the weeble-wearer's body show – rehearse a whole range of different reactions to a whole range of different corporeal differences encountered in day-to-day life.

Lakmaier's work in pieces like *Exercise in Losing Control* and *We Are For You Because We Are Against Them* invites an active response from spectators that goes beyond just watching, choosing a space to watch from, and even beyond choosing to experience things like the mirror box in Cunningham's *Mirage*. Lakmaier asks spectators to engage in activities that actually affect the structure and progression of the work. Which, according to Gianna Bouchard, is something that can significantly raises the stakes for spectators. 'Approaching the stage [or the performer] during a performance is', Bouchard says, 'fraught with contradictory sensations' (2009: 173), because it forces the spectator to consider their own level of responsibility for what is happening on that stage. Bouchard recalls, for instance, Nicholas Ridout's reflection in *Stage Fright, Animals and Other Theatrical Problems* (2007) on the ill-at-easeness or embarrassment he has felt when directly addressed by a performer, attributing it to 'his inability to place himself, either as a fellow performer with a duty to maintain the fictional narrative, or as a spectator who has become invisible to the circuit of reception that usually operates in the theatre' (2009: 226). Approaching or interacting with actors can become, according to Ridout (2007), a surprising, confusing or embarassing call to act that the spectator simply is not sure how to respond to. An uncertainty about how to act, react or answer the question a work poses that is, for Ridout (2009), a precondition of any possible ethical engagement between performer and spectator. For, he suggests, it is the work that takes spectators by surprise, suddenly confronting them with something inassimilable to their current sense of what should or should not be, and so demanding answers to hereforeto unconsidered questions, such that they have little choice but to open themselves to new thoughts, issues or ideas, that 'provoke[s] a truly ethical encounter, in Lévinas' terms' (2009: 67).

Although it is different to the types of theatre Ridout (2007) analyses in his consideration of the awkward predicaments the audience can find themselves in, confusion about how to act or react certainly characterizes spectators' responses to Lakmaier's weeble works. Describing the work or watching documentation of the work cannot, Lakmaier (2010) says, fully capture the intensity of sensation of the demand to do something that many spectators (as they ignored, questioned, commented or kicked the weeble-wearers) clearly felt here. The awkward moments that marked *Mirage*, and the giddy giggles they drew from spectators, seem in *Exercise in Losing Control* and *We Are For You Because We Are Against Them* to give way to moments of full-scale, stomach-churning embarrassment which could not necessarily be covered with a quick smile, laugh or gesture of supplication.

The sort of embarrassment spectators experienced in these works can be characterized as feeling awkward, unclear or confused – and, indeed, self-consciously so – in a social situation. As the Latin roots of the word attest (Houghton Mifflin, 2000), embarrassment is born of a block, barrier or obstacle to our efforts to move smoothly through a social or communicative encounter. In a disability context, embarrassment is something that can be felt by both disabled people as social performers and non-disabled people as social spectators-become-performers. The former may slip, trip, fall, leak, limp or otherwise transform into the slimy monster Aaron Williamson (2008: 9) spoke of. The latter may not know why this happens, what to make of it, or what the most suitable response to this interruption of social flow might be. In some ways, as Antje Diedrich argues in her discussion of embarrassment in Jewish theatre, excluding people who cause such problems from the public sphere might be seen as a strategy to escape embarrassment by symbolically or socially 'destroying' (Diedrich, 2011: 144) the cause of it. Or, more accurately, a strategy to escape an uncomfortable disruption to meaning-making, an uncomfortable demand, by categorizing, eliminating or controlling the cause of it. In Lakmaier's work, a range of potential blocks to moving smoothly through a social encounter present themselves. A spectator may suddenly realize they are not clear on how to respond to the weeble-wearers. Or, indeed, a spectator may suddenly realize something about what their response to the weeble-wearers is, what it means, and how it fits or fails to fit with the social rules their *doxa*, *illusio* or sense of the game recommends as the right ones. Whatever the cause, encountering the weeble-wearers did seem to embarrass some spectators, disrupting the flow of their self-performance, and demanding something less straightforward than typical social or dinner party performance of them. Their responses – from ignoring the weeble, to querying the weeble, to asking visual, verbal or physical questions about how the weeble works, and so on – were ways of managing the interruption and moving forward. They were strategies for moving from confusion to comprehension, from the unknown to the known.

Understood this way, embarrassment, whether in the mildly awkward moments in *Mirage*, or the more awkward moments in *We Are For You...*, may in fact be a flag of an ethical struggle taking place for the spectator-as-performer in these sorts of works. It may be a flag that seizing wobbly, weeble-wearing diners within existing categories of meaning is not easy. *Exercise in Losing Control* and *We Are For You Because We Are Against Them* make it difficult for spectators to latch rapidly onto a response. Unlike Cunningham's *Mirage*, Lakmaier's works are not just poetic, but personal, political and highly interactive, which may be why responses to them were more 'ambivalent', in Grehan's (2009) terms, than responses to *Mirage* seemed to be. For Grehan, ambivalence is anything but indifference. Rather, it is a dynamic, physical, emotional and intellectual engagement with, and estrangement from, a work which leaves spectators wondering how they should respond, and thus 'keeps the spectator engaged with theatre, with the work, and with responsibility and therefore an ethical process long after they have left the performance space' (Grehan, 2009: 22). An effect that Lakmaier clearly is hoping to engage with her weeble works, as participants, spectators and passers-by wonder about what they have seen or experienced and what it means.

'I can hear you looking at me' – Alison Jones's *Portraits By Proxy*

Alison Jones takes the idea of spotlighting a spectator's role as co-performer – and creating a situation of embarrassment for her co-performers – even further again when she restages herself, and the stares, readings and responses that define her self, in the interactive one-on-one installation performances of the *Portraits by Proxy* series (2008–9). In her *Portraits by Proxy* series Jones presents her disabled body for us to look, see and stare at. Here, what we stare at is not an image from the sideshow, the medical theatre, or even an abstract, exaggerated or absurd moment drawn metaphorically from everyday experience. It is Jones's body, silently doing its daily performance of disability – in this case, losing one's vision – before us, leaving us to fill in almost all the blanks about what we assume this disability to be. Jones's installations offer a compelling example of the way deliberate re-engagement with the dynamics of staring that define the disabled body as different or deficient can draw spectators' attention to the background knowledges, biases and assumptions they bring to daily acts of staring at disabled bodies in public spaces and places. What makes Jones's installations particularly interesting is that they make spectators co-performers even more explicitly than the other performances discussed thus far – we, as spectators, become living, breathing human mirrors who are asked to react, summarize our reaction, then speak it back to Jones and to society at large as part of the one-on-one encounter. The dynamics of the starer-staree encounter, and the spectator's complicity in it, is challenged from within. Jones's *Portraits by Proxy* series highlights how discomforting it can be to have our habitual ways of seeing things thrust into the spotlight, but, at the same time, how productive this can be in prompting us to rethink the way we see things.

Jones is a visual artist who lives and works in the United Kingdom. Jones identifies as disabled as a result of a medical condition that has, over the last decade or so, caused her sight to deteriorate. In the early stages of her career, Jones's work was often based on smell installations with foodstuffs, including installations in which the foodstuffs were animated to give off smells or make sounds. Jones's interest in working in this medium emerged from a desire to explore how her visual arts practice could become more accessible to non-sighted spectators, and a desire to experiment with the way in which senses like smell invoke memories in both sighted and non-sighted spectators. More recently, Jones has moved into what she calls sonic interventions as part of the *Portraits by Proxy* series, which includes three works – *Art, Lies and Audio Tape* (2009), *Voyeurism by Proxy* (2008), and *Portrait of the Artist by Proxy* (2008). According to Jones, her motivation for moving into sonic interventions was twofold. At one level, Jones as an artist was ready to move on from the smell installations that had previously been a mainstay of her work, and was interested in working more with the medium of sound. At another level, Jones was becoming more aware of the way strangers were seeing her – staring at her – in everyday social encounters in public spaces and places. 'What really prompted it was', she says, the fact that 'although I was visually impaired my sight was deteriorating and it got to a stage where I started to use my white cane' (Jones, 2010a). It was, Jones says, 'like a public sort of declaration'. At the moment Jones began using her white cane, her bodily behaviours became strange, because, she says, we only 'expect to see older people who are blind' (Jones, 2010a). This challenge to people's expectations meant they 'suddenly started staring' (Jones, 2010a). It was, Jones says, 'like I was this object of curiosity', or an 'exhibition or display for them to ogle at' (Jones, 2010a). So 'I suddenly began to become aware of being – and I've heard disabled people says this – an unconscious performer' (Jones, 2010a). As an artist, Jones immediately felt a desire to interrogate the conditions of this unconscious performance in which she and her onlookers had become bound. 'It was weird, but I said to my friends, if you see someone staring, tell me, because then as I walk past them I can say something – "I can hear you looking at me", you know' (Jones, 2010a).

What Jones describes here is a lived encounter with the way the meaning of the disabled body emerges, as Rosemarie Garland Thomson suggests, through social relationships, social rules and the responses a body elicits from others during every-day performances (Garland Thomson, 2000: 334). 'Staring', Garland Thomson argues in her recent *Staring: How We Look*, "is an ocular response to what we don't expect to see" (Garland Thomson, 2009: 3). Staring happens when bodies or bodily behaviours – in this case, Jones's use of a white cane – do not accord with what we expect to see. When we stare at the disabled body, we are in fact looking for a way to define, categorize and control it – looking, as Garland Thomson puts it, 'for narratives that impose coherence on what appears to be randomness' (Garland Thomson, 2006: 174). For narratives that allow us to read, recognize and relate to others. In this sense, staring is a productive cultural process in which staree and starer alike are confronted with questions about whether and where their own body, their own identity, fits into the scheme of things (Garland Thomson, 2006: 179). These questions require answers, or stability of self and the flow of day-to-day social life may be disrupted. This, Garland Thomson argues, is why 'staring can roil up common unease on both sides of those ogling eyes' (Garland Thomson, 2009: 6), resulting in a range of more or less productive responses.

Jones's experience of becoming the object of stares as passers-by interpreted her bodily behaviours – interpretations informed by tragic narratives about what it means to be blind – together with her desire to speak back to this objectification, prompted her to 'make a piece where I actually give people permission to stare'. This became the impetus for the *Portraits by Proxy* series, three works in which Jones investigates what happens when people are asked to ana-lyse, interpret and articulate what they see in an image – including an image of Jones herself – to others. In *Art, Lies and Audio Tape* (2009), Jones asked spectators to audio-describe artworks, such as W. F. Yeames's *And When Did you Last See Your Father?*, on display at the Walker Art Gallery in Liverpool, back to her. In *Voyeurism by Proxy* (2008), Jones asked spectators to audio describe erotic drawings by Gustav Klimt, on display at the Tate Liverpool, back to her. In *Portrait of the Artist by Proxy* (2008), Jones – who, due to her deteriorating sight, has not seen her reflection in a mirror in many years – asked spectators to audio-describe her own image back to her. In this work, Jones sat in a gallery, wearing headphones, to prevent her hearing what describers were saying directly. A gallery attendant told people Jones was a vision-impaired artist who was asking people to 'describe what she looks like to herself because she's not seen her image for about five years' (Jones, 2010a). In creating this work, Jones was interested 'to see if people's descriptions were going to be sort of how I remembered myself' (Jones, 2010a), and also to highlight the fact that 'I was only ever getting that actual reality of my visual appea-rance secondhand through their descriptions' (Jones, 2010a).

In each, of these works, Jones interrogates the instabilities inherent in acts of seeing, looking and staring that are always already framed and informed by the history, habit and memories of the person look-ing. Although the three works operate in slightly different ways – not least due to the fact that the last is asking people to describe Jones's own image back to her – analysing the describers' reactions together provides an interesting insight into how Jones's sonic interventions became unsettling, demonstrating the instability of vision, and dem-onstrating the way the identity of both starer and staree are on the line in the face-to-face staring encounter.

In all three works, Jones says, the describers' accounts were inevita-bly effected by conscious or unconscious expressions of discomfort, censorship, self-censorship, error or a tendency to embellish. However, the ways in which describers' spoke, held forth or held back differed. In some cases, Jones says, the descriptions differed as a consequence of 'an individual's language' (Jones 2010a). According to Jones, some describers found the task very difficult, and would run out of things to say rather quickly. Other describers, who had more access to, for example, art historical languages, found the task easier, and had an abundance of things to say – right down to the detail of the individual threads in the clothing the people were wearing in the Yeames painting described in *Art, Lies and Audio Tape*. 'I think it d[id] make people aware of their linguistic ability', Jones says. 'When you got someone who was quite well read, I'm assuming maybe they were well read, you got really interesting use of language, whereas with other people, it was quite basic sort of straightforward description' (Jones, 2010a).

In other cases, descriptions differed as a result of an individual describer's inclination to respond to a specific visual stimulus in a specific way. 'When people are describing', Jones says, 'it's affected by what they deem is important to impart in their descriptions and what they think is important, but what they leave out as well' (Jones, 2010a). In this sense, Jones says, 'they sort of bring their own experiences, and you could say their baggage as well, on how they view certain subjects' (Jones, 2010a). For example, Jones noted variations in describers' accounts of the Yeames painting – variations in the age of a young boy in the painting, or variations in the colour of the dress a young girl in the painting was wearing, that could differ quite widely depending on who was describing it. What became clear, according to Jones, was that 'people's descriptions vary' (Jones, 2010a). 'It's got to do with their own preconceptions of things, and how they see the world, and, you know, they sort of bring their own experience to the work' (Jones, 2010a). In this context, the fact that describers did undoubtedly bring their own histories, memories and habits to their descriptions raised questions about the relationship between description, discourse and power as the describers became a proxy set of eyes for the vision-impaired Jones. 'I'm so reliant on people's audio descriptions that the information I'm getting [about the world around me] is second hand', Jones says, 'and to a degree [this series asked] how accurate is that? How close to the truth is it?' (Jones, 2010a).

Most interestingly, describers' accounts also differed as a consequence of self-consciousness as they started to become aware of what they were describing, how they were describing it, and how reliant on their – potentially embellished, erroneous or otherwise unstable – descriptions Jones was. This happened in all the works. For example, Jones says some women were embarrassed when asked to describe Klimt's erotic drawings in *Voyeur by Proxy*, both because of the erotic content, and because, whilst a gallery is a space where staring is permitted, 'you're not really asked your opinion of things' (Jones, 2010a) in a regular gallery viewing session. This self-consciousness was, though, most apparent in *Portrait of the Artist by Proxy*, in which the object of the stares, and the potentially unstable descriptions, was Jones herself. According to Jones, 'people who knew me couldn't [describe me,] they just couldn't do it' (Jones, 2010a). In *Portrait of the Artist of Proxy*, then, background knowledge of the object described did not have the same effect as it did in *Art, Lies and Audio Tape* and *Voyeur by Proxy*. 'The people who had background knowledge of the paintings, they would give me, like, the art history sort of background on everything', Jones says, offering detailed descriptions based on specific discourses, 'whereas the people who knew me doing the portrait were almost lost for words' (Jones, 2010a). Strangers typically started by talking about Jones's face, hair and other superficial features, but soon started describing Jones's presumed personal traits, demonstrating the way in which physical traits are taken as signs of psychological or moral traits in the cultural scripts or narratives we use to make meaning of bodies. 'We got people saying, "Oh, I don't know, she could be vegetarian, she's very slim, she could be vegetarian"' (Jones, 2010a), Jones says. It was

> a bit spooky, really, because, you know, they're just looking at me and they're saying 'Oh, I imagine this person to be...'. And they were talking about my personality, you know, 'She could be fairminded, straightforward, or open hearted' and all this sort of stuff, and it was interesting, just people's insights really into your personality and just how you look and how people judge.
>
> (Jones, 2010a)

Even with strangers, Jones noted that – though early experiments doing this with a photo rather than herself in person did draw comments like 'I don't know, there's a sadness in her eyes' – in the live encounter 'most of it was all very generous, there was nothing offensive or negative' (Jones, 2010a). The spectators' were clearly still attached to the idea that staring is a socially regulated activity that, at least in public spaces, outside the specific social, theatrical and medical contexts set aside for staring at unusual bodies, we are cautioned against from childhood (Garland Thomson, 2009: 6). In this context, 'some of the describers suddenly got self-conscious'. 'When they start', Jones says, 'some people are very sure of themselves, very self-assured early on, saying "I'll do it, yeah", and then they start and they do, I think, become very aware of their voice and they do get quite self-conscious' (Jones, 2010a). It was, Jones says, a little like 'when you stand up to do a presentation' (Jones, 2010a). 'They were okay, and then they suddenly became aware, and then it would fizzle out', and they'd say, '"Oh, that's all I've got to say"' (Jones, 2010a). One woman, Jones says, 'was laughing all the way through it, and I'm sure that was because she was so aware that she was sort of being, you know, I suppose thrust into the limelight, really, being asked to perform' (Jones, 2010a). Another man, Jones says,

> started to describe and then just walked away. And when I took the headphones off the assistants said he said 'Oh, I'm so sorry, I feel really uncomfortable, I don't think I'll be able to continue with the description', and had to leave. So he was obviously put in a quite difficult position which was maybe out of his comfort zone.
>
> (Jones, 2010a)

Jones attributed these self-conscious reactions – self-censoring, laughing, or leaving – to the describers' sometimes quite sudden awareness of the way in which their stare was projecting stories, narratives or cultural scripts onto her body. By re-engaging the dynamics of the starer-staree encounter in the *Portraits by Proxy* series, and in *Portrait of the Artist by Proxy* in particular, Jones created a situation in which spectators were not just actively re-enacting the way we project narratives onto bodies in public spaces and places, but articulating those narratives. They were in the frame of representation and the frame of reality at once, reacting to Jones, and reflecting on their reaction to Jones, in a way that provided challenging, embarrassing or confronting insights into their own habitual responses to the vision impaired. 'I was inviting visitors to the gallery to describe me', Jones says, and 'it very much was like a collaborative process with the viewer or the audience' (Jones, 2010a). In effect, by re-enacting the staring encounter, and giving spectators permission to stare and to share, Jones made them conscious of the way they, too, were unconscious performers actively involved in the production of meaning not just in this encounter, but in the everyday encounters it replicates, replays and questions.

As Garland Thomson says in her investigation of staring at people with disabilities, the staring encounter, and the way people see disa-bled bodies during the staring encounter, is commonly theorized in terms of the gaze, 'defined as an oppressive act of disciplinary look-ing that subordinates its victim' (Garland Thomson, 2009: 6). Despite their many differences, this is as true for performance theorists of disability like Kuppers, Sandahl, Lewis and Davidson as for literary and cultural theorists of disability like Garland Thomson herself. The gaze is seen as productive, performative, insofar as it produces and perpetuates the identity positions that populate the cultural stories, narratives or scripts that inform our way of seeing, doing and dealing with disability in Western culture. In Garland Thomson's words, the stare, as a domineering, disciplinary way of looking 'draft[s] starees into a story of the starer's making, whatever that story might be, whether they like it or not' (Garland Thomson, 2009: 8)·. It defines the disabled body as terror inducing, useless or tragic, and, in doing so, brings these realities into being. However, Garland Thomson believes that staring – as a live, unpredictable, performative encoun-ter in public spaces and places which brings both staree (the disabled body) and starer (the non-disabled body) into being – also has the potential to problematize, trouble or transform the dominant cul-tural logics it enacts. This, she says, is because staring can result in a variety of more or less ethical responses. These responses can be categorized in terms of the inability to concentrate that she calls a blank stare; the intense, uncontrollable attention she calls a Baroque stare; the aggressive, controlling attention she calls a domineering stare; and the unanticipated extension of initial attention that leads people to think about their own ready-made responses she calls an engaged stare (Garland Thomson, 2009: 22, 40, 50, 117). Because it can result in exoticization, estrangement, empathy or longer term engagement that cannot be resolved via an instant, ready-made response, Garland Thomson says, '[a]n encounter between a starer and a staree sets in motion an interpersonal relationship, however momentarily, that has consequences' – it can tell us 'something about how we look *at* each other and how we look *to* each other' and can, potentially, offer us a chance 'to rethink the status quo' (Garland Thomson, 2009: 3, 4, 6). For Garland Thomson, then, the staring encounter does have the potential to create the dialogue and discussion between different viewpoints that characterizes an ethical encounter – a potentiality that is pivotal to what an artist like Jones is attempting with her work.

In her *Portraits by Proxy* series, and in *Portrait of the Artist by Proxy* in particular, Jones invokes a whole spectrum of staring encounters, including the generative, productive potential of an ethical staring encounter that is, in Garland Thomson's terms, rechoreographed or recontextualized by an accomplished staree (Garland Thomson, 2009: 7, 10). Some spectators blanked, bereft of words to describe what they were seeing, and what they were thinking about what they were seeing. 'Um', 'I don't know what to say', and 'I don't know what you want' became their dominant refrains. Some spectators were unable to concentrate, or control their reaction, responding with embarrassed laughter as they struggled to reconcile the image, the situation and the social regulation against staring, with the request to both stare and share their thoughts about what they were seeing. Some spectators used narratives to control, or make sense, of what they were seeing – though, in *Portrait of the Artist by Proxy*, they were clearly focused on finding positive rather than negative narratives. Some spectators, particularly the well-educated ones, with a lot of language available to them, used dominant cultural discourses to create quite extended accounts. But others fizzled out fairly swiftly. And, for some spectators, they were unable to reconcile the image, the situation and the socially awkward moment of suddenly becoming aware of the way in which they were being asked to perform or play out a response to Jones, prompting thoughts and reflections they were not necessarily comfortable with sharing. Here, again silences, stilted reactions and embarrassment signal the existence of a set of questions spectators-become-performers cannot necessarily answer in simple or straightforward ways and thus, potentially, an ethical encounter.

In offering her own image and other images for interpretation, Jones draws attention to the way sight is privileged as a mode of access to fixed, fundamental truths in Western culture. A mode of access to truth often thought to be untainted by filters of history, memory and habit that skew our perception of an object, but which, in fact, are wholly informed by these filters. 'In a culture where vision is by far the dominant sense', Jones says,

> and as a visual artist with a visual impairment, I am reliant on audio-description both from professionals and friends. Inevitably, there are limitations imposed by language, time and the interpreter's background knowledge of the subject viewed, as well as their personal bias of what is deemed important to impart in their description.
>
> (Disability Arts Info, 2009)

In the *Portraits by Proxy* series, Jones draws attention to these background knowledges, biases and assumptions. She reveals different perceptions, as well as tendencies to censor, edit or exaggerate descriptions. Most critically, she set up a situation in which the describers, as they heard their own opinions, out loud, started to become aware of the complex weave of physical, personal and cultural factors that inform the act of seeing. Jones highlighted the fact that in staring encounters in public spaces and places, we are all – starer and staree alike – performers, and highlighted the fragile foundations on which our spontaneous social performances are based. Jones's works thus enabled her describers to think about these biases, without necessarily knowing how to answer, deal with or address them. The works rendered describers vulnerable to moments of reflection, reconsideration, and change of perception.

What Garland Thomson's account of staring does not anticipate or theorize, of course, is the way that Jones edited the audio-descriptions after these encounters to further demonstrate the instabilities of sight and, in *Portrait of the Artist by Proxy*, to reclaim authorship of her own image in a way that usually is not possible in the staring relationship. 'I turned it around again', she says, 'because I could then reclaim the editing process and put my own interpretation on their verbal descriptions of my visual appearance in relation to how I remembered myself.' In this respect, Jones says, 'the final piece is as much about what I want others to see as what strangers observed about me' (quoted in Disability Arts Info, 2009; Jones, 2010b). The edited track of the *Portrait of the Artist by Proxy* descriptions was presented on the BBC Big Screen at the Liverpool Disability and Deaf Arts (DaDa) Festival in 2009. Whilst Jones was concerned by the organizers' desire to present a blurry photo of her face coming into focus as an accompanying image – believing it was 'important that the audience be put in the same position as me, just listen to the descriptions, and from the description make up the image in their mind's eye' (2010a) – it eventually went up with an animated screenplay panning in and out on written transcriptions of some of the descriptions the spectators were hearing (Figure 3). By remediating the remediated descriptions of her own image in this way, Jones says, she 'put the viewers in the position of how I'm having to see the world, through verbal descriptions which are unreliable' (Jones, 2010a). In doing so, Jones says, 'I'm confronting the audience and saying, "Look, this is what disability is all about", and in an indirect sort of implicit way it will make people think in a different way of how they see the world' (Jones, 2010a).

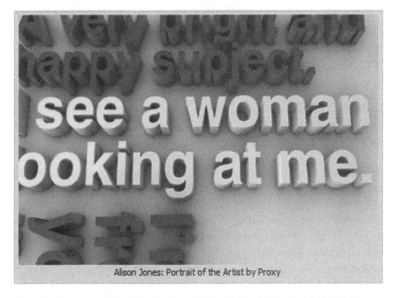

Alison Jones: Portrait of the Artist by Proxy

Figure 3   Portrait of the Artist By Proxy, DaDa Festival, Liverpool, 2009 (Photo: Glenn Maguire, Sparkle)

By re-engaging the roles in the starer-staree encounter again, and turning things around again, Jones's *Portrait of the Artist by Proxy* confirmed the importance of positioning spectators as co-performers to the political agenda of her work. It also confronted a second set of spectators with the way we call on history, memory and habit to interpret what they see, the way what they see can change depending on where they see it from, and provided an opportunity – albeit momentary – to step into the shoes of the other party, the other performer, in day-to-day interactions with disabled people. The *Portraits by Proxy* series, particularly the one-on-one interactions and subsequent remediation of these interactions in *Portrait of the Artist by Proxy*, challenged spectators to play out the disruptive dynamics of the staring encounter in a live, embodied, physically and emotionally engaging interaction. In this interaction both Jones's identity, and their own identity, was momentarily spotlighted, shifted and destabilized. Demonstrating the partial, perspectival nature of the interpretations by which disabled bodies are accorded meaning, the *Portraits by Proxy* series thus provides a compelling example of the way deliberate re-engagement with, rechoreographing and recontextualization of the dynamics of staring can – at least potentially – prompt us to rethink the way we see things.

Stepping into someone else's shoes?

Despite their differences, the dominant feature of Cunningham's, Lakmaier's and Jones's installations is the way they blur the boundaries between stage, spectator and the day-to-day social processes that inspire their works. It is this blurring of boundaries that, according to Lehmann (2006), leaves spectators in such a difficult position in non-traditional theatrical or performance works. In such work, spectators encounter a representation and a reality simultaneously. They encounter a representation of a small, ambiguous or blind body (something framed as a 'fiction') and a real small, ambiguous or blind body (something framed as a 'fact') simultaneously. Fiction blurs into fact. Fact blurs into fiction. The frame of reference for the action becomes fuzzy. The spectator is seemingly subject to two different, competing and potentially conflicting sets of demands. They, like Ridout (2007) when he wondered whether he should respond to the direct address of an actor as a fellow performer in the fiction, or as a spectator floating outside the fiction, or something else, are (at least potentially) left anxious, ambivalent or wondering what to do. What is more, in these works, spectators are subject to these competing demands in a context where – with lights up, little by way of fourth-wall protection, and little distinction between performance and daily life – performers, fellow spectators and society all seem to be watching them to see what they will do. Should they simply watch, as the frame of representation or fiction demands? Should they take some action, as the frame of reality or fact demands?

The dual frame of reference, dual readings, and dual possibilities for response mean spectators can experience what Lehmann calls an uncertainty, or an undecidability, that leads to interpretative anxiety and a sometimes uncomfortable deferral of meaning-making (2006: 102–3). Stuck between distanced reflection and direct response, spectators can find it difficult to fix a reading, apply a ready-made response almost altogether unconsciously, and move forward. They are, instead, confronted with gaps, choices and decisions to be made. This can, at least potentially, cause spectators to reflect on their own beliefs, attitudes and behaviours. As Lehmann explains, to enclose an event in a single frame – be it fiction or fact – allows spectators to reduce it to the status of a symbolic object they can relate to in ready-made, reductive ways (2006: 99). To open an event to dual framing, on the contrary, draws spectators into a liminal space in which attempts to apply habitual, ready-made responses are deferred, delayed or thwarted. Spectators can find their values, views and ways of being brought into question, but find it difficult to know how to respond, and find further debate, dialogue or discussion is required. In this sense, Lehmann says, it is not engagement with representation, or engagement with reality, but self-reflective engagement with a reality, inside a representation, inside a reality – and so on – that creates the uncertainty that in turn creates the conditions of possibility for an ethical encounter in these sorts of works (2006: 102–3). This is what creates the conditions of possibility for the questions that cannot be answered, and the ambivalence that for theorists Grehan (2009) and Ridout (2007, 2009) characterize the ethical, reflexive or self-reflexive encounter.

This, clearly, is exactly the sort of encounter Cunningham, Lakmaier and Jones are looking to create in their installations. Each lifts a mundane, medical or metaphorical image of disability out of its day-to-day milieu. In Cunningham's *Mirage*, it is the image of bodily ambiguity he experienced via medical interventions, now literally, metaphorically and technologically re-enacted in an installation set up. In Lakmaier's *Exercise in Losing Control* and *We Are For You Because We Are Against Them*, it is the image of bodily ambiguity she creates via a ball that makes her body's position in the world altogether awkward, also re-enacted in an installation. In Jones's *Portraits by Proxy*, it is the image of body-becoming-other that she experienced when using a white cane, taken from the streets into the new surrounds of the gallery. These are all images of a body that is, in one sense or another, in the process of becoming Other – becoming asymmetrical, unbalanced or unstuck – and thus becoming the object of scrutiny, observation or stares. These images evoke disability, disabling experience, and more diverse experiences of becoming Other many people might (emotionally if not literally) relate to. In each case, the artist plays this image out across their corporeally 'suitable' body. In each case, the spectator sees a reality, and a representation of something more than its own reality, simultaneously. The theatrical mechanisms that fuzzy the frame are not necessarily verbal commentary, anecdote or critique. They include, rather, a proliferation of perspectives and points of view in the imagery of the performance (in Cunningham's *Mirage*), or a proliferation of perspectives provided by spectators as they interact with the performance (in Lakmaier's *Exercise in Losing Control* and *We Are For You Because We Are Against Them* or Jones's *Portraits by Proxy*).

Whatever the mechanism, the complexity of the frames of reference in play creates uncertainty for spectators. They have a range of potential readings and responses available to them. There is a call to direct response to a body-becoming-Other. There is a call to a more distanced reflection on one's response to a body-becoming-Other. There are uncertainties, demands and choices to make. Most critically, of course, these installations ask spectators to perceive, interpret and perform their response – stepping into the mirror box, manipulating the massive balls, or making a summary of what a blind woman looks like – in full view of the artist and their fellow spectators.

All this means there is quite a lot going on in what might seem, on the surface, to be fairly simply structured performances. At one level, spectators are invited to identify what is unusual about the artists' bodies. At another level, spectators are invited to identify with the experience of a body becoming unstuck, unstable or Other. And, at yet another level, with Cunningham's, Lakmaier's or Jones's body present, there is also a reminder that the artists' corporeal reality and perspective is different to the spectators' own corporeality and perspective. Spectators are, in a sense, invited to stare at an Other, step into the shoes of an Other, only to realize that stepping into the shoes of an Other is impossible, extending the uncertainty that already exists in these works. Uncertainty, confusion and (in Lakmaier's and Jones's works in particular) embarrassment in spectators' responses under such a spotlight signals more or less significant interruptions or blockages in the flow of the meaning-making encounter for some spectators. It thus signals the emergence of liminal moments in which realizations, reflections or new perspectives may or may not start to emerge.

To complicate matters further, the more or less conscious choices spectators make under such a spotlight are showcased not just for the artists and for their fellow spectators, but for society at large via documentation, recording, and in Jones's case re-representation of the encounter. Will a spectator approach or keep a distance? Will a spectator interact with the mirror box, the ball or the blind woman? Will they do it subtly, playfully, aggressively or otherwise? What does the performer expect them to do? What do fellow spectators as performers expect them to do? What does society expect them to do? Asking these questions, these works create the sort of difficulty, undecidability and uncertainty that can lead to an ethical encounter, and, later, to action in the public or political sphere. A proliferation of images, in an open performance space, where the line between the performance and the social process of the doctor's surgery, dinner or street is not clearly drawn, encourages spectators both to react and to reflect on their reaction. This is what gives the work the potential to draw spectators into ethical encounter. This is what gives the work the potential to 'do' something in the public sphere. To query or challenge – if not to change – our ways of being in the world.

Interpreting spectators' self-performances

In each of these works, it is the spectators' self-performance as much as the artists' self-performance that takes centre stage. The spectators' chatter in the hall of mirrors in Cunningham's *Mirage*, the spectators' chatter at and around the dinner table in Lakmaier's *We Are For You Because We Are Against Them,* and the spectators' responses or retreats in Jones's *Portraits by Proxy,* all signal that the spectators are well aware that they are in the spotlight here. They signal, moreover, that spectators are well aware of the social and personal stakes at play here. In effect, these artists share the responsibility for performing a potentially embarrassing social role, response or trait – as disabled people are so often asked to do – with the spectator. Performer and spectator alike are invited to step into an Other's shoes. Each is each other's Other, performing something that may or may not be offensive to the Other or to others.

What makes further interpretation of what spectators do in this situation difficult, of course, is the fact that the precise aspects of the performance that will cause them to start performing the sort of embarrassment that signals an ethical process is taking place cannot be predicted, and can differ from spectator to spectator, depending on their own status within the social field. For some, seeing their face morphed into that of another in a mirror box, bending to talk to a woman in a weeble, or telling a blind woman she has wrinkles on her face, might be an unusual and challenging moment in which they feel pressure to improvise a response, be it evasive, playful, deceitful or otherwise. For others, it might be well within the field of their experience, and they may find ready-made responses without much difficulty at all. In a social context, where blushes, bluster and laughter can be contagious, it will never be easy to tell what is happening for each individual spectator in the situation.

We get a glimpse of this variability of response in reviews of Cunningham's work. Whilst some spectators were most affected in the mirror box, McNeilly (2006) was more affected in the moment when she worked to reconcile live and mediatized images of Cunningham's amorphous and morphing body, while Soboslay (2006) was more affected when she sensed a link between the individual, internal and the social. I myself was most affected in a moment where my own body seemed to try to mimic the swing of Cunningham's arm only to realize it – marked not by paralysis but by the stilted, subluxating, over-articulating movements of the aging hypermobile – would never swing so smoothly (Hadley, 2007). This was a moment where I felt like an Other's Other, aware of my reaction, and my reflection on my reaction. This, of course, is but a sampling (and a sampling translated into language at that) of the way the generally well-received *Mirage* may have worked for spectators.

Information on spectatorial responses to each of these performances is, of course, still based primarily on artists' documentation of these responses. This is partly because – at least in the case of the works considered in this book – the performances have not necessarily been subject to a lot of critical analysis or review. This is, though, also partly because it is always difficult to perceive, interpret and make meaning of spectators' performances. Although documentation, discussion and analysis can capture a nervousness or anxiety that seems to characterize a response, and conjecture that this is caused by a challenge to meaning-making, it cannot fully know what is happening for the individual spectator. Documentation cannot fully determine whether a spectator is performing a ready-made response (in the ontological realm), improvising a performance to cover a difficulty or breakdown in ready-made responses (between the onto-logical and pre-ontological realms), or giving us a glimpse of some-thing more (such as a sensibility in the pre-ontological realm). It cannot capture how much a response is (culturally) prepared, how much it is improvised, and what sort of meaning-making is in motion. In most cases, it cannot capture what this may have led to, unless there are comment books, critiques or other forms of commentary made available – which are clues, but, of course, still remediated representations of more immediate phenomenological responses.

Interestingly, though, this difficulty in interpreting spectators, their performances, and the ontological and epistemological positions influencing these performances may be critical to the efficacy of the encounter. It in fact serves to confirm – or to remind us – that if these performers are the Other, then these spectators are the Other's Other. As such, they are beings a disabled artist might like – but might not necessarily be able – to establish a relationship of respect and reciproc-ity with. This being the case, these performances may be more than an invitation to embarrassment, and to ethical questions, for their spectators. They may be an invitation to reciprocity, and a relationship in which performer and spectator – no longer simply living, breath-ing mirrors that see meaning reflected in each other's supposedly 'suitable' surface – enter a more permeable, plastic relationship in which neither can seize the other within their control.

If these sorts of performances do engender a reciprocitous encounter in which each participant is (at least potentially) surprised by the other, in an effort to see what new meanings, relationships and realities might emerge, then both parties are presented with difficult questions, and with risks. Both walk a knife-edge where gestures give way to responses, which give way to new gestures, and new responses, and each new move raises questions the parties do not necessarily know how to answer. The artists, as much as anyone, face uncertainties about the personal, ethical and political valency of the encounter. The only certainty is, perhaps, that these uncertainties are essential preconditions for the emergence of an ethical encounter.

In this context, it is interesting to think further about the fact that Jones at least makes an effort to make meaning of her Other when she edits the responses she received in *Portrait of the Artist By Proxy*. On the one hand, this could be seen as bringing these people into her power. On the other hand, this could be seen as trying to build a relationship of (perhaps bound to be imperfect) understanding of who her Other – sometimes so different in beliefs, behaviours and attitudes to her self – is. Might she, and the second set of spectators who see or hear her edited recording, be guilty of exploiting the primary spectators for their own purposes? Or might she, and her second set of spectators, momentarily step into the shoes of those first spectators, feeling a fit or lack of fit, and thus at least potentially facing uncertainties of their own about how to make meaning of their attitudes? Who is it that is opening up to vulnerability, responsibility, and some sort of respect for the Other and the way others exist in the world? Here, clearly, all parties find themselves on the cusp of uncertainty that characterizes the ethical encounter as artist attempts to engage spectators as much as spectators attempt to engage artist.

Whatever the answer to these complicated questions, the encounters examined here do still take place in a performance installation space which, for all its challenges and uncertainties, is a space where each participant has (presumably) entered the encounter willingly. There are, however, a great many artists who take the challenges, complexities and potentials of this form of performance further, into public streets, squares and shopping malls, and thus further into actual social processes beyond the gallery or museum setting. In doing so, they raise further questions – about whether participants are using, substituting themselves for, or seeing themselves as vulnerable to, responsible for or respectful of the Other – worthy of consideration in an effort to unpack what is happening in these forms of practice.

2
Drug Deals, Samaritans and Suicides: Bodies on the Brink of the Visible

The *mise-en-scène* of social places and spaces is, as artists like Alison Jones make apparent, critical to the definition of disability, and the disabled self's position, power, or lack of power in the public sphere. Streets, schools, hospitals and homes are set up in normative ways – traditionally, for people with disabilities, difficult to navigate ways. Spectators and society watch to see who can or cannot 'correctly' navigate these spaces, making the look, layout and relationships that prevail in public space a constant source of concern for people with disabilities. In Western culture, exclusion has been the main strategy to control the 'commotion' (Auslander and Sandahl, 2004) people with disabilities can create in public spaces and places. This means public spaces and places can, for people with disabilities, be invested with traumatic histories, memories and associations. This also means there is – at least for Back to Back Theatre, Bill Shannon, Katherine Araniello and Aaron Williamson, the artists I consider in this chapter – a clear inducement to interrupt the daily social drama of disability by commandeering the very spaces and places in which it plays out. In their practice, it is not just interactive installation and performances spaces in galleries, but actual public streets, squares and shopping malls which become sites for subversive practices. In this work, a move into public space further blurs the boundaries between stage, spectator and society, and further pushes spectators into performing (and potentially reflecting on) their habitual response to people with disabilities, and thus their role in casting people with disabilities as Other.

As one of the foremost theorists of space in the twentieth century Michel Foucault (1984) makes clear, the methods by which people with illness, disease or disability have been excluded from public spaces and places have been many, varied, and in many cases very effective. For Foucault, 'space is fundamental in any form of communal life', and, therefore, 'fundamental in any exercise of power' (1984: 252). Space, and the social relationships that prevail in particular spaces at particular times, both serve to produce, clarify and perpetuate dominant discourses about which bodies fit in, where, why and how, and which bodies do not fit in. Spaces – via their architecture, the interactions their architecture facilitates, and the attitudes of the inter-actors – become tools in the exercise of power. Streets, schools, hospitals, prisons and even private homes are set up to facilitate (or prevent) particular attitudes, actions and interactions. Their layout assists the power regimes that prevail in a given society at a given time to assure the public that order, propriety, productivity and safety are being maintained. As Foucault suggests in his discussion of Jeremy Bentham's 'Panopticon' as a model for a perfect prison, surveillance and self-surveillance are critical in compelling people to speak, act and interact 'correctly' in public spaces and places. Power, enacted through our tendency to self-survey our own actions in public space, 'reaches into the very grain of individuals, touches their bodies, and inserts itself into their actions and attitudes' (Foucault 1980: 39). It determines how we move, speak and think, and detects when we deviate. In this way, Foucault says, power, exercised via established socio-spatial norms, transforms bodies into readable, reliable, docile subjects. For Foucault, power, in this sense, is not negative. It is a productive, all-pervasive network that 'runs through the whole social body' (Foucault, 1980: 119), and produces bodies personal and the body politic. According to Foucault, all bodies are isolated, individuated and positioned in the field of power. All bodies are disciplined to act, interact and perform according to dominant socio-spatial logics determined not just by authority figures (the fathers, husbands, doctors, police or politicians that dominant our private and public spaces), but by the habits of bodies themselves, in a self-perpetuating cycle. Gendered, racialized and disabled bodies are, however, positioned at the margins, as outsiders more at home in private than in public spaces, if at all. These bodies thus do not have the same agency in social space as the dominant white male, whose gaze both structures and is structured by the preferred ways of seeing, moving and speaking in a given social milieu.

In Western culture, the 'commotion' people with disabilities can cause in public spaces and places is typically controlled by excluding them – that is, by relegating them to the private realm of the home, hospital or special school. In modern society, Foucault says, boundaries between public and private are critical in categorizing, compartmentalizing and controlling human bodies (Foucault, 1980: 141–9). In the modern house, for instance, people's behaviour is separated into functionally specific rooms to support proper personal roles and relationships (Foucault, 1980: 148–9). Relegating disabled people – and, of course, other marginalized people like women – to the private sphere also supports supposedly proper personal roles and relationships. Positioned in the private rather than the public realm, people with disabilities are less likely to interfere with the order, propriety, productivity or safety of the public at large, as that public – the useful people – go about their business. People with disabilities have, as Rosemarie Garland Thomson says, either been compelled to use medical techniques, tools or prostheses to conceal their disability, or are concealed in 'asylums, segregated schools, hospitals, and nursing homes' (2000: 19–20). They are, in effect, forced to perform a lie – or, at least, a half-truth that hides dimensions and complexities of their experience that are literally 'unthinkable' within dominant cultural logics. Spaces, and the patterns of relationships that prevail in them, make disabled bodies visible inside the dominant order, but, in doing so, deny their specificity.

This pressure to 'lie' to have any position at all in public space comes out most clearly in the compulsion to pass. For people with disabilities – particularly concealable, or potentially concealable, disabilities – telling half-truths or lies through stories, coping strategies or the somatic fictions set up by prostheses is, as Tobin Siebers says, an all-too-frequent feature of daily life (2008: 96). It is something that is encouraged, even celebrated, by family, friends and medical professionals, and the dominant discourses of a culture discomforted by disclosure of difference. 'Passing' hides what David Mitchell and Sharon Snyder call 'the "visible" and fixed evidence of a violated bodily wholeness' (2000: 125). Many commentators have noted how well the benefits of passing – creating a socially acceptable impression through some sort of subterfuge – are embedded in private, public and medical discourses. In her examination of the experience of learning disabilities, for example, Sheena Brown talks about a woman who taught her son 'to behave and appear normal' (2000: 78) by lying – saying he needed to sharpen a pencil, or seek a book, to give himself time to task-switch during classes, concealing difficulties doing this from teachers. Similarly, in her examination of advertisements for prosthetics, Lorraine Thomas (2001) shows that they are sold on their ability to replicate supposedly 'natural', 'normal' functions such as walking, and, in the advertisements' mode of address, set up an assumption that people should, and should want, to do this. Kimberly Myers, discussing chronic medical conditions, argues that even when people do, for whatever reason, have to come out as disabled, they 'nevertheless feel compelled to mimic healthy people, [and] to be a "stoical", "brave" or "cheerful patient" whose illness isn't really debilitating' (2004: 265). Passing as normal, or at least presenting an acceptable image of the abnormal, allows others to interact with disabled people in predictable ways in public spaces and places. Passers-by can be confident they are 'doing the right thing', 'helping', and so forth.

Passing, and the performative tricks, techniques and prostheses that support the 'lie' of passing, uphold a social contract in which a closeting-as-cure approach accommodates discomfort with difference, both for people with disabilities and people interacting with people with disabilities. If, as Erving Goffman says in *The Presentation of Self in Everyday Life*, 'normal' people see 'abnormal' or 'stigmatized' people as deficient, then concealing the source of stigmatization – even if it takes lies, deceit or duplicity – makes sense in terms of impression management (Goffman, 1973; cf. Goffman, 1963; cf. Myers 2004: 257). The lie can, as Goffman says, hide facts and information that don't accord with the ideal images of the self (Goffman, 1973: 40–1, 58–66, 141, 209). This may be the ideal of the normal person, or, more insidiously, the ideal of the normal disabled person, who stoically suffers his or her afflictions without imposing too much on the rest of us. Clearly, these deceits do have personal and social benefits of the sort Brown (2000), Thomas (2001) and Myers (2004) described. They do allow people to take pride in their ability to overcome, be productive, and 'fit in'. Which, as Myers (2004: 257) says, is desirable for everyone in social terms, and keeps socio-spatial mechanisms – and the power systems in them – working smoothly, and invisibly. It can, though, be very difficult for people with disabilities to live with. These deceits are productive, in a Foucaultian sense, in that they perpetuate power relationships – privilege one reality and prevent the emergence of other potential realities – whilst leaving people with disabilities to cope with difficult, displacing, alienating encounters in their daily lives. Encounters which might, for example, include a sense of falsity, a fear of being caught out, a litany of anecdotes about moments when they have been told off for doing the wrong thing, or tripped up by well-meaning passers-by who tried to 'help' them in the most unhelpful ways. In this context, it is little wonder that artists like Shannon, Araniello, Williamson and others should want to re-engage and re-envisage this aspect of their life experience.

For Foucault, of course, space, spatial relationships and the power regimes that subtend them can be subverted by people – like the artists I consider in this chapter – who make tactical interventions in public spaces and places. Tactical interventions can produce patches of struggle and resistance where ideas about ability, gender, race or class are contested from within the system that supports and perpetuates them. This is precisely what Back to Back's *Small Metal Objects* (2005), Bill Shannon's *Regarding the Fall* (ongoing), and Katherine Araniello and Aaron Williamson's *Assisted Passage* (2007) do.

In their work, Back to Back, Shannon, Araniello and Williamson deliberately re-inhabit social spaces and places in subversive ways. The work is characterized by a desire to disrupt the scopic, discursive and ideological regimes that prevail in these spaces, and thus the modes of subjection these spaces make possible. Whilst these performances are not site-specific – they can be transferred between streets, squares or shopping malls in a range of cities – they are site-based, infiltrating specific types of spaces, and drawing spectators into perhaps unfamiliar relationships in these most familiar of spaces. In each of the performances considered here, the roles, relationships and scenography of the space is isolated, manipulated and intensified in some way. The focus is on the idea that disabled people are not useful, productive citizens, and thus either need to be 'helped' to use these spaces, or hidden so they do not disrupt the rest of us as we use these spaces – a common issue, inflected differently in practices from Australia, the United States, and the United Kingdom. The desire to 'help' poor disabled people is, for these artists, the sort of ready-made response to their disabled body they find a burden. This, then, is exactly the type of encounter they re-engage and re-enact as part of their effort to make spectators think about the way disabled people, and non-disabled people, negotiate their identity, power and perception of self as efficacious in public spaces and places.

When the artists considered in this chapter reperform their everyday encounters in public spaces and places as a sort of invisible or guerrilla theatre, they bring hidden assumptions about how disabled people should act and interact in public space to the brink of visibility. Their work confronts passers-by with their complicity in dominant cultural logics by forcing them to reperform their own spontaneous response to people with disabilities. Yet it can, of course, also be (mis)read by passers-by, who fail to realize they are part of a deliberate, duplicitous recitation of already deceitful discourses about ability, disability, and the benefits or drawbacks of 'fitting in'. This makes this sort of practice – in which social spaces become a stage on which bodies perform and potentially contest culturally determined ideas about others and the Other – complex, challenging and uncertain in its outcomes. This sort of practice is not about a majoritarian politics that tries to rid the public sphere of pejorative stereotypes and provide alternative, affirmative images of 'other' bodies. It is about a far riskier politics, based on re-inhabiting stereotypes with a difference. The blurring of fact, fantasy and fiction can be so complicated that they almost completely merge. In some cases, the stereotypes recited are not exaggerated enough to be easily distinguished from daily life, so the already fraught question of whether such recitation can create uncertainty, questions, and the conditions of possibility for an ethical encounter can become even more fraught. The uncertainties here are very uncertain uncertainties. Indeed, the effects of this sort of practice may be more marked in secondary spectators who see documentation of the work than its primary spectators. This is, though, a level of uncertainty many of the artists feel is vital to their aesthetic and political agenda, regardless of any ambivalence or anxiety they might feel about it.

'I want to be a full human being' – Back to Back Theatre's *Small Metal Objects*

Back to Back Theatre is an ensemble of Australian artists with what they, in their Australian context, characterize as intellectual disabilities (cf. Hickey Moody, 2009), although, of course, such cognitive differences are now characterized as learning disabilities in many other countries and contexts. The ensemble works with non-disabled director Bruce Gladwin, their collaborative model being that which Anna Hickey Moody describes as 'reverse integration', or 'the practice of people without intellectual disabilities "integrating" to fit in with the styles of people with intellectual disabilities' (Hickey Moody, 2009: xv).

Back to Back Theatre have long been recognized in Australia and around the world for their aesthetically and socially innovative work, often characterized by unconventional forms, spaces and performer-spectator interfaces. They are, after years of practice, one of relatively few ensembles of artists with disabilities that have made their way almost entirely into mainstream professional practice in performing arts centres and, more importantly, festivals where they can be part of the programme without being in a theatre space, in Australia. Their interest in unconventional spaces is, according to Gladwin, influenced by the fact that 'not all of our actors ha[ve] a classically trained voice or studied at drama school' (Gladwin quoted in Logan, 2007), a fact which is hardly surprising given the difficulties drama school practices continue to pose for disabled people (cf. Auslander and Sandahl, 2004; Lewis, 2006). Accordingly, Gladwin says,

> the whole notion of what an actor is, how they use their voice and stand on stage, is slightly irrelevant to us. Eventually we found ourselves asking, 'why try to meet the needs of a given architectural space? Let's try to create our own spaces from scratch.'
>
> (Gladwin quoted in Logan, 2007)

This has, over the past decade, included inflatable theatres, streets, railway stations, shopping centres and food courts (*The Democratic Set*, 2009; *Food Court*, 2008; *Small Metal Objects*, 2005), installation spaces (*Soft*, 2002), as well as performances in more conventional theatre spaces (*Ganesh versus the Third Reich*, 2011; *Cow*, 2004).

In *Small Metal Objects* (2005), a title referencing coins or small change, Back to Back uses performance in public spaces as a platform for restaging the way some people find themselves excluded from social and economic systems. The performance is, as Andrew Templeton says, about 'how we put value on things and people' (2008). When I saw the work in Brisbane, Australia, it played in the

Queen Street Mall, the main open-air shopping mall in the city centre, on a Sunday afternoon in summer. It has also played in streets, railway stations and other shopping malls around the world, with the days, dates, times and locations shifting slightly depending on the public traffic patterns in the city or countries. The content of *Small Metal Objects* is conversations, actions and interactions that spectators over-hear through headsets as they sit in a stand, watching the street-scape, mall-scape, or station-scape in front of them. It is, Brian Logan says, 'an elliptical slice of barely-glimpsed life, unfolding at its own pace, striking no compromises with drama or narrative conventions' (2007).

As the performance begins, spectators overhear two men talking – about what they are doing tonight, dinner, DVDs, finding love, sex, the death of a pet, crime, and hope. It takes a long time to connect the conversation to Steve (played by Simon Laherty when I saw it), a skinny man in a singlet, and Gary (played by Allan V. Watt when I saw it), a large man in a loud shirt. Almost all commentators describe how difficult it is to know who is speaking at this point of the per-formance, and how they listen and look for visual, audio or verbal clues as to who it could be, until the moment the two performers

Figure 4 Simon Laherty and Allan V. Watt in *Small Metal Objects*, Flinders Street Station, Melbourne, 2005 (Photo: Jeff Busby)

'come out of nowhere. The invisible made visible' (Templeton, 2008; cf. Logan, 2007). In the end, it was Steve and Gary's stillness that singled them out from the rest of the crowd for me. As the performance progresses, spectators overhear a call to Gary's phone. It is Alan (Jim Russell), a property lawyer after drugs for an awards night. 'Gary's response to Alan has such a fantastic, child-like blankness that you're sure there's been a mistake', Templeton says (2008). But, thinking about it, Templeton wonders who might be better to be in the drugs business than these two socially invisible beings. Whether Steve and Gary are dealers or not, what is clear is that there's some sort of miscommunication playing out here, with the potential to put a dampener on Alan's party. Accordingly, Alan and his corporate psychologist friend Carolyn (Genevieve Picot) enter the scene, playing out a scenario in which they become increasingly frustrated by the fact that the men do not appear interested in the deal, and the fact that Gary will not leave Steve, amidst the passers-by.

> Alan and Carolyn's impatience with the dealers is palpable and their ability to quickly increase their offers through terms that they understand – money, social acceptance and ultimately sex – do not work with Steve or, because of his undying loyalty to his friend, Gary [...] Alan and Carolyn cannot fathom the dealers they have been forced to deal with.
>
> (Templeton, 2008)

The action plays out against a musical score in the headsets, and pedestrians provide the other activity – improvised, unpredictable and ever-changing – around which the slice-of-life performance unfolds. There have, Gladwin says, been things like fights or medical emergencies, and there are almost always people who want to talk or perform to what they see as an audience without a performance to watch (Gladwin quoted in Logan, 2007). On the day I attended, this included a small child doing a dance, a pair of 'emo' girls disappointed their kissing display only drew a laugh, and old people asking the actors for directions, amongst other things.

According to its creators, *Small Metal Objects* is '[a] subtly comic fable of identity and invisibility' (Back to Back Theatre, n.date). Steve and Gary are, they say, 'the kind of men who normally escape notice' (Back to Back Theatre, n.date), 'a quiet, lonely pair who exist on the fringe of society' (Performing Lines, n.date). In commentary on the work, many spectators talk about whether or not they were aware that the performers had an intellectual disability (Abell, 2007; Hawthorn, 2007; Richardson, 2005), though it is fair to say that some of this might be based on awareness that they are seeing a performance by Back to Back, and there will therefore be performers with disabilities involved. This, according to Owen Richardson, is where spectators' assumptions are first questioned. 'What am I looking for?', he says, 'What does someone with an intellectual disability look like?' (2005). The difficulty seeing the actors is central to the performance. It is, Tim Milful says, 'the point [of the performance]. The actors are invisible, just as intellectual disability is often not visible in our everyday world' (2007) – physically, discursively or economically – as long as it is attached to the pervasive stereotype of a sweet, simple but socially unuseful set of people (cf. Hickey Moody, 2009: 7). Steve and Gary's stillness, their conversation, and their friendship, differentiates them from the productive 'busyness' of the city space, and the productive 'busyness' of Alan and Carolyn. It positions them as outsiders who fail to display the right sort of functional, socially serviceable docility in social spaces and places. Most critically, as the plot unfolds, it raises questions about Steve and Gary's visibility, their worth, their worthiness of respect, and what they contribute to society (Milful, 2007). 'I want people to see me', Steve says at one point. 'I want to be a full human being' (quoted in Abell, 2007; quoted in Low, 2007). Through Steve and Gary's story, Back to Back aims to investigate 'how respect is withheld from outsiders – the disabled or the unemployed – who society deems "unproductive"' (Back to Back Theatre, n.date). '[A] person's value is determined by their productivity', Gladwin says, and this 'is a question that's pertinent to people with disabilities. But it's increasingly pertinent to everyone in society' (quoted in Logan, 2007).

In *Small Metal Objects,* spectators are asked to react to and reflect on the way 'others' – the unemployed, the unuseful and the disabled – are positioned in the public sphere. '[T]he impact of *Small Metal Objects* is', as Templeton says, 'directly related to how the audience experiences the show' (2008). Throughout the performance, spectators sit in a bank of seats, in a public space, watching something passers-by cannot see, which makes them the point of focus. 'The actors wear small head microphones and move freely through the crowds who are generally oblivious to what's going on. If the public notice anything, it's the audience sitting on a raised platform, wearing headphones' (Templeton, 2008). The spectators are, in this sense, far more isolated, individuated and surveilled in the space than the performers (Milful 2007). As Lucy Hawthorn said, narrating her sensations as spectator, 'I am [the] spectacle' (2007; cf. Abell, 2007). The staging of spectatorship in *Small Metal Objects* isolates, complicates and intensifies the usual ways of seeing and looking (Milful, 2007). According to Hawthorn, it 'challenges notions of community and judgment in society' (2007). And, according to Owen Richardson, '[i]t creates a special sense of solidarity with your fellow audience members and the cast' (2005). By 'unmistakably' positioning the act of seeing itself as a 'performance', a spectacle, which constructs, perpetuates and potentially contests ideas about disabled bodies, *Small Metal Objects* questions subject positions in social spaces and places. On the one hand, the performance asks spectators to re-enact conventional ways of encountering the Other, as a non-productive, non-participatory anomaly in social spaces and places. On the other hand, by showing us how the unpleasant Alan and Carolyn engage the Other, and staging our own engagement with the Other for a street full of passers-by, the performance puts our conventional ways of encountering the Other in question. There is, at least potentially, an opportunity for us to both experience the encounter and experience an increased consciousness of the way dominant symbolic, social and spatial systems define the terms of this encounter, and draw us into complicity with the terms of the encounter. In many cases, spectators suggested, this – the story, the spotlight on how they respond to the story, and the questions, reactions and reflections that come from it – creates a sense of greater closeness with fellow performers and spectators. A sort of non-violent communion Lévinas (1996a) might call 'religion' or Jill Dolan (2005) might call the 'utopian' moment in performance.

Watching *Small Metal Objects*, I am not certain I myself felt precisely – or only – this sort of utopian community or communion with fellow spectators-as-performances that some critics celebrate. There was, certainly, a sense of being part of a group of about a hundred people, which made the situation less anxiety inducing than it might have been for a solo spectator-as-performer. We were all experiencing something out of the ordinary, but, in a sense, experiencing it within a social net of spectatorial togetherness that encouraged a sort of bond to emerge. There were, though, also moments where some of our readings of the 'yuppie' characters, or the passers-by-as-characters such as the 'emo' teens, could not really be classed as a non-violent, vulnerable, community or ethically oriented readings. Our laughter was, at times, linked primarily to a sense of superiority available to us as a result of the solidarity and special perspective of the spectator group – which, in a sense, made us feel comfortable to sneer at some of the others, such as the 'emo' girls, in front of us in a way we might not normally have done.

This did not, however, typify our reading of the central characters, Steve and Gary. With these central characters there was a sense of a non-violent, responsible and respectful connection with an other we could relate to, without wanting or being able to make them the same as us. This came primarily from the way the performance positioned Steve and Gary, as 'particular' (small o) others, between ourselves as spectators and our understanding of the 'general' (big O) Other that subtends the Western cultural imaginary and collapses people like Steve and Gary into a generic group that serves its own logic (Lévinas, 1996a: 5). The staging, and the struggle to find, identify and listen to Steve and Gary as specific others in a space populated by so many representatives of socially othered groups was what made this possible. By inviting spectators to respond not simply to an example of a general category of 'Other' in the crowd, but to Steve and Gary as specific, idiosyncratic, unique 'others' in their own right, *Small Metal Objects* invited spectators into a more complex relationship with these strangers to our selves. Seeking out these strangers, engaging with their story, empathizing with their struggles, in a situation where thousands of passers-by watched us do this, a sense of Steve and Gary as people we could like and respect without ever completely knowing begins to emerge. A sense of Steve and Gary in particular, rather than in general, begins to emerge. In a society where disabled people often feel they are subject to generalization that overrides the nature, nuance and specificities of their embodied experience, the opportunity to engage with Steve and Gary on these out-of-the-ordinary terms in *Small Metal Objects* became a valuable one.

The weight of empathy – Bill Shannon's
Regarding the Fall

Being addressed as a type, instead of as a unique, idiosyncratic individual with an identity that may or may not align with what society would assume a disabled person's identity to be, is also an issue for US artist Bill Shannon. A dancer, performance artist and provocateur, Shannon is well known for spectacularly athletic performances in public spaces and places in which he works with crutches, skateboards and other elements of the environment to showcase his unique modes of dance and movement. He has, in fact, been featured in an advertisement for US credit card company Visa that showcases his unique sort of street dance for the widest possible public, and worked with companies like Canada's Cirque du Soleil, a very unusual showcase for an artist with a disability who began his artistic life working primarily in popular, street and public space forms.

Much of Shannon's work uses his own specific techniques of 'Performative Sociological Anthropology' to investigate the way his identity is defined, redefined and redefined again by the reactions of others in public spaces and places. In particular, Shannon is interested in reactions to the level of visibility of his disability in public spaces and places (Shannon, 2009a). Born with a hip condition that makes it difficult for him to walk, Shannon – mainstreamed from his childhood – has found he needs to adapt to function in day-to-day life, and that this has fostered in him both an interest in the way people respond to him, and, at the same time, a creativity he applies to the whole spectrum of his arts practices as readily as to his self-performances. 'I feel that being mainstreamed had a significant impact on me', he says.

> When I noticed my own alternative solutions to everyday task[s] such as carrying books while climbing stairs or picking up a cup without bending over I instinctively realized that thinking creatively and looking inwardly for answers was the way for me to survive. I lived in a world with no peers to follow. I believe this type of daily creativity and self-reliance cultivated creative problem solving without looking to others for answers.
>
> (Shannon, 2009a)

This experience of living with a disability has led Shannon to produce a series of guerrilla-style interventions in public spaces – he has called them his 'public works' – in which he performs tasks, including tasks considered difficult for people on crutches, to see how passers-by respond. In tandem with these performative interventions in public spaces, Shannon has produced a distinctive lexicon of terms that name the specific events, phenomena and relationships he encounters in public space, providing a set of handles by which he can discuss his interventions and investigations with those of his audience members who share – or share an interest in – these experiences.

According to Shannon, when he goes about his day-to-day life in public spaces and places, he is all too often burdened by what he calls the 'Weight of Empathy' of strangers and passers-by. The term 'Weight of Empathy', one of the terms in the lexicon he has created to describe, define and provide handles to help address the phenomena he experiences, is designed to give as practical as possible a name or designation to a phenomenon that is a pervasive part of the disability experience. To clarify what 'Weight of Empathy' means, Shannon gives the experience of being on a crowded subway train one afternoon as an example. Initially, he says, there were no seats, so he sat on his skateboard, which signalled his disability, and prompted a man and his wife to free up a seat. For a variety of reasons, Shannon did not want to take the seat – partly because of the pain and effort to transfer from the skateboard to the seat, partly because he was comfortable on the skateboard, and partly because of other factors, including, for instance, his experience that it is often those in most need of seats who give them up first, because they understand what a seat means. In this apocryphal situation, as so often in Shannon's life, though, this led to an awkward scene in which strangers press him to take up their well-meant offer of aid:

> they both stared at me along with seemingly the whole car full of people as in disbelief that I was still refusing their kind empathy. The seat remained a gaping empty [space] as time began to crawl and all eyes were on me. I was expected to fall into line, graciously stand and take the seat... The WEIGHT OF EMPATHY at this moment was crushing me. [...] they are staring at me as if there is something the matter with me for not reciprocating. I realize that this is a situation where I am now expected to explain myself.

I now owe the kind man and his considerate wife an explanation. I am supposed to announce my logic to them. However, I have to point out here also that I am expected to explain myself to perfect strangers in a multitude of contexts on a cumulative basis all day every day and that even the act of explaining in time becomes a burden.

(Shannon, 2009b, original emphasis)

The 'Weight of Empathy' encounter, as Shannon's exemplifying anecdotes such as this one indicate, is one of those tricky situations that become all too familiar for people with disabilities as they negotiate public spaces and places. It is characterized by a complex, time-consuming set of negotiations with bystanders that can be almost as much of a barrier to smooth progress through public spaces and places as curbs, stairs and other physical obstacles. Samaritanism, and the gesture of help in which a non-disabled person projects a need for help that may not be there onto a disabled person, is something Shannon finds a burden in day-to-day life. He is, he says, verbally, visually and physically asked if he needs help almost constantly, asked what is wrong, and thus asked to define his identity in intimate detail that would never be expected from a person marked by their gender, race, ethnicity or class.

The difference with my disability is [that it is] treated as a temporary trauma, my use of a skateboard is looked upon as an invitation to point and laugh and my medical details are open for pointed questions and ultimately expected to be validated on some level before I am accepted as 'real'.

(Shannon, 2009c)

Shannon, of course, understands why these 'Weight of Empathy' encounters happen, and draws on anthropological, sociological and phenomenological thinking to help describe the factors underpinning the phenomenon.

Goffman defines interaction as 'performance', shaped by the environment and audience. The performance exists regardless of the intent of the individual, as persona is often imputed to the individual in spite of the individual's lack of intent to perform.

The persona is defined by the 'front' – a vehicle for standardization that allows others to understand the individual on the basis of normative character traits. Because [I], in effect, break this collective representation in [my] everyday life, [I] elici[t] sociological phenomena that [are] a break from the norm.

(Shannon, 2009d)

In effect, Shannon's non-normative 'front' is read in terms of a standardized cultural script that sees disability as a problem for others in the social field. When Shannon's disability becomes apparent, he says, people need to find a way to react to the non-normative 'front' he – albeit unintentionally – appears to be presenting or performing to the world. They all too often do this by turning to what culture has taught them about ways to respond to people with disabilities, without pausing to wonder whether or not this standard script might apply in Shannon's case. As a result, Shannon has had all too many opportunities to identify regular ways in which people respond – or, in his terminology, 'phenomenologically intend' – towards his body in public spaces and places again and again and again.

Shannon harnesses these patterns of response in public spaces and places in his performances. Each of the performances investigate, work with, and pursue alternate possibilities to the 'Weight of Empathy' encounter or phenomenon. In perhaps the best known work of this series, a set of public space interventions and performative lectures Shannon calls *Regarding the Fall*, Shannon performs his 'realtime Performative Sociological Anthropology', investigating and analysing the 'Weight of Empathy' phenomenon via performance, performative lectures and the distinctive lexicon he has developed to unpack the engagements taking place in public space encounters with people with disabilities. Shannon makes a move to pick up a bottle off the pavement to see how passers-by will respond to him doing this on his crutches. He later combines footage of the passers-by's responses, anecdotes, and his own views on the 'Weight of Empathy' into a performative lecture for a secondary group of spectators. In these lectures, Shannon says, he 'treats the subject matter of events within the street performances on video as a form of verifiable proof to his invented lexicon that defines phenomenology apparent within the videos' (Shannon, 2009e). In other words, his public space interventions become a sort of fieldwork, and his lexicon helps him report his results to a wider audience, in specific, detailed and rigorous terms. In one sequence, for example, Shannon's footage (Figure 5) shows an elderly passer-by making a small unconscious gesture with her bag, as though herself picking up the bottle, or providing assistance to Shannon in picking up the bottle, in a sort of somatic sympathy whereby she wills him to succeed in what she – via projection – sees as a difficult task for him (Shannon n.date). In his later performative lecture, Shannon points to the way this passer-by assigns him the burden of having to live up to a social script which positions him as needing help – having to play his part, so she can play hers, and they can both uphold the limited and limiting social script or contract mentioned so many times already throughout this book. 'Every simple utilitarian task in public is turned into this spectacle', Shannon says, 'where someone is [...] staring at you. Think about it. Imagine going through that everyday. So these [performances] are tools, and it's not just a question of what's happening, but what to do about it' (Shannon, n.date).

In the *Regarding the Fall* interventions, Shannon highlights a daily burden people with disabilities deal with. His interventions highlight how hard it is to get the balance between closeting, disclosing and calling for help with his disability 'right' in cultural terms, to play

Figure 5   Bill Shannon in *Regarding the Fall*, Various, 1994–Date (Photo: Bill Shannon)

out a role of dependency, and, of course, highlight the fact that this leads to frustration, displacement or disintegration in his own sense of self as a result of 'goodwill' gestures by passers-by who have been taught they are 'doing the right thing'. Understood this way, Kuppers says, 'Shannon's street actions are not performances of disability, but a performance of the readings, visceral effects, social embodiments, and public nets surrounding the meeting of different bodies' (Kuppers, 2004: 64).

The problem with these readings of disability, for Shannon, is that they are ready-made responses that prevent passers-by from knowing him, and prevent him from knowing passers-by, in specific terms – as a unique, specific, singular other – rather than in terms of a universalized Other.

In other words, while I may be interacting with 'Fred', Fred's behaviour fits into pre-existing phenomenological patterns that I have interacted with many times in the past, labelled and developed strategies for. This is important to take into consideration because I want to be clear that Fred is not a victim that I am tricking, he is not being used for my own entertainment. Fred represents the cumulative presence of a phenomena that I am forced to engage in public space whether I choose to or not. Fred is approaching me everywhere I go every day even though he might know himself as the only one in the moment he inhabits. I imagine that for Fred, its me and Fred, and I know that for me its me and Fred and Fred as Phenomena beyond Fred. I respect Fred but I cannot relate to Fred as Fred if he falls into the many patterns strangers tend to inhabit in relation to my public presence.

(Shannon, 2009c)

Works like *Regarding the Fall* are not just about investigating the daily drama or spectacle of disability, and the part both performers and passers-by play in constructing it. They are also about investigating – and expanding – possibilities for action within the daily social drama of disability, including more ethical interactions between disabled people and passers-by, so they can relate to each other in less predictable or at least less disempowering ways. The performances demonstrate the phenomena. The performative lectures prompt discussion around the demonstrated phenomena. The lexicon – including labels like 'Weight of Empathy' for the demonstrated phenomena – at once characterizes the phenomena in a way that is readily, viscerally recognizable to those who encounter them in daily life, and, at the same time, shifts the emphasis from a single person's personal problem to a whole group of people's social problem. Together, these aspects of the work are designed to empower Shannon, and others, to manage their identities in new ways, and make meaningful interventions in the public sphere.

The challenge in Shannon's work is, of course, the fact that some of his work – including work like the *Regarding the Fall* interventions – is not easily differentiated from daily life. Although there is a certain amount of extrapolation, exaggeration and theatricalization in Shannon's actions in his public space performances, it is still more subtle than the theatricalization seen in a work such as Back to Back's *Small Metal Objects*, and it remains possible therefore that passers-by may not realize that the gesture, glance or action they encounter is both a reality and a representation of a broader reality. As a result, it is possible that passers-by may not experience the confusion, uncertainty or interruption to the communicative flow that might force them to reflect on their ideas about disability. This means Shannon is taking a risk in his public space performance – a risk that passers-by will misread his actions as part of the phenomenon Shannon is actually trying to challenge. Shannon's body seems well-suited to the role it plays. Accordingly, unless there is some specific reason to stop, reflect and think further about the action – what Petra Kuppers (2004: 2) describes as 'the visible, tangible scene of a show' in 'a bracketed framed format' that makes spectators suspect the action may be more than what it seems – spectators may simply fall back on familiar, efficient and easy mechanisms of recognition and reception. In fact, the risk of misreading is perhaps particularly acute for an artist with a disability like Shannon, partly because spectators in public streets will not necessarily have the theatre-going experience needed to spot the fairly subtle framing he is using here, and partly because spectators in public streets will not necessarily see his disability as a political problem, around which people might be expected to stage political protests, rather than an unfortunate personal problem. In Shannon's work, as in Jones's *Portraits by Proxy* work, it may in fact be secondary spectators seeing the situation unfold in Shannon's performative lectures who are more likely than the passers-by themselves to experience this encounter as a call to engage a specific other, step into the shoes of a specific other, and recognize, respect and reflect on their relation with that other. Indeed, given the guerrilla nature of Shannon's work, it might seem to some of the passers-by that Shannon has forcibly co-opted their image, body and behaviours into his performances to serve his own agenda. Just as Jones has done when she reclaims her spectators' words to create a rescripted summary of people's struggle to speak about her appearance. In Shannon's work the passers-by enact – or, at least, are presumed to enact – established ways of seeing the disabled body as tragic, hopeless or helpless. They are, in a sense, set up to perform supposedly standard responses rather than surprisingly idiosyncratic responses. The work could, therefore, be accused of 'playing pranks' on passers-by.

Shannon is certainly all too conscious of the potential for ethically problematic co-option of his own or others' identities that his public space interventions present. He has, in fact, spent considerable time thinking through the risks of his own practices. Shannon is not, he says, playing a prank or using passers-by as part of his own agenda, but building specific 'strategies' to re-engage, re-envisage, rescript and thus subvert some the encounters that are so ubiquitous in his everyday life. He is, in effect, experimenting with strategies, with tactics, with small episodes of struggle and resistance, in the hope of finding ways to shift the way these encounters usually unfold. The process, he says, requires that he 'remain open to the moment and neutral to the momentum of events' (Shannon, 2009b). With increased experience, Shannon says '[m]y interactions with pedestrians and random individuals in public space [are] constantly evolving and changing over the course of time' (Shannon, 2009c). In this sense, whilst Shannon is aware that prompting passers-by to recite their habitual reaction to his body as part of a political performance practice may be seen as using them, this clearly is not his intent. He is, rather, trying to open a pathway or opportunity for more ethical engagement on both his own and his passers-by's side of the encounter – that is, both his and 'Fred's' side of the encounter – in which both he and his passers-by make themselves vulnerable to a specific other instead of the usual universalized Other. The potentially reifying step of noting, naming and defining phenomena is, in fact, a necessary first step in enacting strategies that empower people to try, step by step, day by day, encounter by encounter, to move past present relations to a more liveable set of relations. To rebalancing power relations. Shannon is keen to engage others in conversation about his work, and the issues it raises, at any opportunity. 'I would love nothing more than to debate the merits of this strategy of engaging strangers in public space', he says (2009c). Ultimately, it seems, he is hopeful that the work will – in its challenges and failures as much as its successes – lead to more ethical outcomes, even if the nature of these outcomes remains unpredictable.

Guerrilla tactics – Aaron Williamson and Katherine Araniello in The Disabled Avant Garde's *Assisted Passage*

UK performance artists Aaron Williamson and Katherine Araniello are also interested in guerrilla-style performances in public spaces and places that fall somewhere between prank and political statement. As noted in the Introduction, Williamson and Araniello, when work-ing individually, and when working together under the title of The Disabled Avant Garde, are both all too conscious of the problematic ways in which their bodies can be read by social spectators in public spaces and places. Though embodied very differently – Williamson is hearing impaired and Araniello is a wheelchair user – both find these readings to be a burden in day-to-day life. Indeed, for Araniello, these readings are more than merely a burden. A small woman in a wheelchair who looks different to the dominant norm, Araniello is all too well aware that passers-by who read her body as pitiful or impossible to bear may, in fact, go beyond making her life difficult to menacing it, particularly when they start to suggest people like herself might be 'better off dead'. This, of course, is why Williamson and Araniello use a range of ever-evolving live, performance and public art strategies to highlight, investigate and intervene in the daily social drama of disability.

Their work displays a great deal of diversity. Williamson, as I noted in the Introduction, has done everything from installations where he puts himself on display in a glass case in a museum, naked, and proceeds to paint the glass so people can no longer see him, to public interventions where he puts construction tape and signs up in public streets to show passers-by what it feels like when movement partners are restricted, to the assisted suicide work with Araniello I discuss here (cf. Williamson, 2008). He has also created far more conceptual lyrical, photographic and performance works about the hegemony of hearing culture (cf. cf. Davidson 2008; Williamson, 2008). Araniello has made performances from the lists of all the (to her) ridiculous questions about her disability she gets asked on a daily basis (cf. Disability Arts Online, 2008), acted as a guide shepherding people into the afterlife in her *Terminal Services* performances (Araniello, n.date), and posted mock suicide messages on YouTube (Araniello n.date). Williamson and Araniello also work together under the title The Disabled Avant Garde, creating films, performances and performative interventions in the public sphere that, in Williamson's words, 'farcically play up the stereotyping we encounter' (2008: 12).

In *Assisted Passage* (2007), one of their best known public space performances, Williamson and Araniello set themselves up amongst a line of protesters outside Birkbeck College. Williamson asked passers-by to sign a petition supporting an at first ill-defined cause – something to do with airlines. It was ill-defined because, in the beginning, spectators saw only a 'banned from the clouds' sign at the desk (Figure 6), and could not see the petition or hear the performer's speech to clarify the specifics of the situation until they came closer to them, not because the problems that airlines, their policies and their practices present to people with both visible and invisible disabilities are not well known. Araniello, though primarily playing the speechless 'charity case' stereotype (Araniello, 2010), asked people as they came closer to help her. 'Behind the fictional protest against the airlines' treatment of disabled people', Williamson explains, it gradually unfolded that '[...] the public was actually being asked to support Araniello's right to purchase a flight to attend her assisted death [in Switzerland]' (2008: 94). In this narrative, disabled people are again positioned as needing help – albeit, in this case, help of a more controversial ilk than a body like Shannon's might seem to demand. In this case, disabled people are cast as needing help to end their less-than-human lives. In the United States and United Kingdom in particular, as Siebers (2010: 23) notes, there are philosophers such as Peter Singer, politicians and members of the public who genuinely contend that people with pain, impairment and disability above a certain level of severity are not really living a life of the standard a reasonable person would consider human, worthwhile or worth suffering through, and should therefore by euthanized by a humane

Figure 6 Katherine Araniello and Aaron Williamson in *Assisted Passage*, Birkbeck College, London, 2007 (Photos: The Disabled Avant Garde)

society. This is the for many disabled people frightening opinion and narrative position Williamson and Araniello engage in *Assisted Passage*.

In presenting *Assisted Passage*, Williamson and Araniello were not necessarily taking an anti-euthanasia stance. 'I'm not here as a campaigner trying to stop people from ending their lives', Araniello says (2010). The concern with assisted suicide in this and other works, she clarifies, is not necessarily with assisted suicide per se, but with the idea that people might choose assisted suicide because they have been taught to fear the loss of control over one's own life illness, disease or disability can bring and it is the fear, not the life, that is intolerable. The fear, for example, that illness, disease or disability will render a person reliant on others for day-to-day grooming. 'I can't do any of that', Araniello says. So, '[y]ou can see why it is so hard for me to leave that subject alone. It really isn't a problem. You know, who cares if you need somebody else to comb your hair [or cut it, or wash it, or cloth you, or feed you, and so forth]' (Araniello, 2010).

Basically, Araniello says, 'I don't think people should go on the basis of fear' (2010). It is this fearful perception of what it feels like to be disabled that underpins the euthanasia debate that Williamson and Araniello take issue with. Williamson and Araniello, like most disabled artists, see other people's perceptions, and their tendency to project a need for help, tolerance or sympathy onto the disabled body, as a burden, or an obstacle. These projected narratives present, they say, more problems than the impairments themselves. Both are highly critical of 'the "medical model" (with its emphasis on affliction and cure)' (Williamson, 2008: 12). From their point of view, then, *Assisted Passage* 'adopt[ed a] tactic of sustaining irony to draw out a response from the public and thereby reflect the depth of "normal" prejudices about (or pity for) disabled people' (Williamson, 2008: 93). It enacted what Williamson calls '[a] politicized sensibility (which turns the spotlight onto socially normative forces since "being normal" is something we may have no wish to perform even if we could)' (2008: 12).

Williamson and Araniello admit, though, that they were 'frankly shocked that a significant proportion of our audience took all of this "protest" at face value, either missing the dark twist in our ostensible cause, or choosing to agree with it anyway' (Williamson, 2008: 95). Whilst there were a few passers-by who looked, double looked and laughed, Araniello says, 'the majority just happily signed my life away' (Araniello, 2010). There was, she notes, one woman 'starting to talk about putting it [the petition] on Facebook' (Araniello, 2010). Others made even more condescending efforts to 'help' this charity case – one man, for example 'waved a five pound note and said, "Here you are. I don't need it, I don't need it just treat yourself"' (Araniello, 2010). When documentation of the work was later put on YouTube, some after-the-fact interlocutors proposed possible reasons as to why passers-by were so ready to sign the petition. 'Strikes me that those who signed didn't need to be pro-assisted suicide', one said. '[I]f that's what you're trying to say [it] is horrific if true [...] [but] they may well have signed on just because they disagree with the idea that airlines could bar certain types of people from travelling by plane' (kingofaikido quoted in Araniello and Williamson, 2007). Others noted that, even if 20, 30 or 40 did sign, many must have still walked past without signing (mrribes quoted in Araniello and Williamson, 2007). Which might be taken as a positive. Or, of course, might be taken to mean that people made choices – whether to sign, pass by without signing or otherwise – to take a simplest, easiest, less embarrassing route to dealing with the people or the issue. A way, in other words, of avoiding engagement that might draw people into difficult conversations. Either way, there clearly were passers-by that took the performance to be real, signing the petition even as the performance itself pushed into farcical 'She's Got a Ticket to Die' songs (Williamson, 2008: 95).

Though prankish in some ways, the point of this performance, for Williamson and Araniello, was not to make fun of a passer-by's potentially troubling assumptions about disabled people. '[I]t's not like candid camera', Araniello says (2010). '[W]e are not inviting them to make asses of themselves' (Araniello, 2010), even if it seems that some of them do. It was, rather, to investigate – and creatively investigate – whether stereotypes about the disabled might potentially be dealt with differently in public spaces and places. A risky prospect for Araniello in particular, who worries people might take her work on assisted suicide too seriously, as well as spectators who might seem foolish to anyone seeing the documentation of the work after the fact. Although Araniello has, as she has gotten older, become more and more resilient in the face of the attitudes others can display toward her, she does note that this type of work is personally rather risky. 'One of my concerns was that some nutter might come along', she says. '[...] You know, that somebody would think "Oh, put her out of her misery right now". So that is one fear I do have. That is a fear that I have had. Nevertheless, I will continue to make work' (Araniello, 2010). The risks in this type of work – the personal and the physical risks in this work – may, as Araniello indicates here, be greater than commentators, critics or spectators-become-performers typically imagine when they dismiss it with sarcasm or suspicion. But, in some respects, because these are risks people with disabilities are always already taking in their everyday social performances, Araniello and Williamson – like Shannon – seem to feel that they do need to continue these investigations. They are, it seems, part of the process Garland Thomson (2009) describes whereby people work at managing, addressing and potentially altering the dynamics of the daily drama of disability to see if they or their spectators can, in fact, discover different ways of engaging in these day-to-day encounters.

Uncertain uncertainties

Like the work I analysed in Chapter 1, the work I have analysed here in Chapter 2 begins with some basis in autobiography, or, at least, in specific events, encounters and forms of stereotyping the artists experience in their own everyday lives. It does, however, depart from the format we would typically expect of staged autobiography, heading in a direction that may in the end prove even riskier for artist, spectator and society.

At the heart of *Small Metal Objects*, *Regarding the Fall* and *Assisted Passage*, there is a rather literal re-enactment of the stereotyping people with disabilities are subject to in daily life. The performers play painful social stereotypes across their own supposedly suitable bodies, and, in one way or another, ask passers-by to respond to these stereotypes. Obviously, the theatrical techniques and tactics Back to Back Theatre, Shannon, Williamson and Araniello use in their performances are still more complex than simply setting a disabled body in itself before passers-by to see what will happen. The performances operate in the paradigm of the 'explicit', a term Rebecca Schneider (1997) coined just over a decade ago to describe the practice of women performers who literally, explicitly play the sexualized, animalized or otherwise subjugated roles women are assigned in Western culture across their own corporeally suitable bodies. Like Schneider's women artists, these artists exaggerate and make explicit the traits associated with disability in the Western cultural imaginary (cf. Hadley, 2008). They merge their identity with that of the charity case, sufferer or suicidally depressed disabled person. They allow spectators to inhabit the pity or sympathy these figures provoke. Yet, for all that they start with a basis in autobiography, these artists do not play these figures as a reality that exists outside the order of representation. If we apply Jean Baudrillard's (1984) discussion of the different orders for representation, we can see that these artists are not just presenting an originary order of reality (playing themselves), or a copy of an originary order of reality (as they might when playing a disabled person in a main stage play), or even a false or counterfeit copy of an originary reality (dogged as they are by a corporeal specificity that makes it clear they are not simply playing a part). Instead, these artists play their assigned roles as hyperreal – representations which are, for all their recognizability, so much more extremely drawn than any real life referent that they become simulacra that escape the complication of any authenticating referent.

The artists attempt, in this way, to present their body as a ground that fails to ground the culturally recognizable figure of the charity case, sufferer or suicidally depressed person. They make the relation between signifier and signified, person and persona, other and Other so literal that it starts to seem constructed (and in some cases down-right ridiculous), showing these figures to be symbolic constructs and thus, for Schneider, following Walter Benjamin, threatening the symbolic order with collapse (1997: 22–3). These artists attempt to show that, for all that they have real effects, these figures are just part of the representational system, formed at the moment when people look at their disabled bodies on the stage, in the street, or in other public spaces and places. In this sense, while disabled bodies are not commodified or even clearly visible in the Western scopic economy in the same way Schneider's women artists are, they are using related strategies to reclaim space for what Schneider calls a postmodern politics of transgression (1997: 4), exposing 'the sedimented layers of signification themselves' (1997: 21) rather than establishing 'an original true or redemptive body' (1997: 21) beneath.

The artists' aim in these performances is not to eliminate stereotypes – to enact some sort of truth beneath or beyond the disconcerting, deceitful or hurtful narratives embedded in the daily social drama of disability. It is, rather, to draw attention to the 'dirty work' of these lies, and the way the 'dirty work' of these lies shores up a social contract that controls, conceals or excludes the 'commotion' disabled people cause from the public sphere. In doing so, these artists draw attention to the ready-made readings, reactions and responses to disabled people – in particular those that position disabled people as needing help, support or sympathy – they personally find to be burdensome. They bring the 'lies', the hidden assumptions about how we should do disability and do relationships with disabled people embedded in the social contract, to the very brink of visibility. They challenge passers-by, who become unwitting co-performers, to reperform the response to people with disabilities that has become embedded in what Pierre Bourdieu (1977) would call their bodily *habitus*, and thus confront their own complicity in deceitful discourses about disability by forcing them to spontaneously reperform their own relations to disabled bodies.

Where *Small Metal Objects, Regarding the Fall* and *Assisted Passage* differ from the work discussed in Chapter 1, of course, is in the way they commandeer actual public spaces and places as sites for subversive repetition of the events, encounters and stereotypes they seek to challenge. These works reperform daily personal actions and interactions as a sort of guerrilla theatre. They do use theatricality and theatrical frames to create uncertainty, confusion, and the chance that spectators who do not (or do not immediately) know how to deal with the situation will stop and reflect on what is happening. They focus, for example, on awkward, embarrassing or anxiety inducing moments that are easily exaggerated. In *Small Metal Objects*, it is the stillness of the unemployed and unemployable that is exaggerated. In *Regarding the Fall*, it is the struggle to pick something up off the ground. In *Assisted Passage*, it is the signs, the songs and the charity shop clothing. The theatrical framing, though, is much more subtle than the framing present in Cunningham, Lakmaier or Jones's work discussed in Chapter 1. As a result, Back to Back Theatre, Shannon, Williamson and Araniello offer performances that for many spectators may be almost indistinguishable from daily life unfolding in front of them. The strength of this approach lies in the power it holds to engage spectators in an encounter with specific, rather than universalized, others. The work has real potential to open performer and spectator-as-performer alike to challenging questions about each other's way of being in the world, and, in the process, a relationship characterized by something other than immediate transportation into Lévinas's (1996a) 'horizon of knowledge' or of 'the known'. It asks the spectators, and the performers, too, to put themselves in a risky position, where they may be witness or party to a reductive reading of an Other, as a necessary condition for creating an encounter in which new relationships with specific others rather than a universalized Other might be negotiated. Still, because this sort of public space performance is less exaggerated – or, more accurately, less metaphorized – and less engaged with anything beyond the everyday moment, the commentary, counter-positions, sudden shifts in perspective and sense of being in the spotlight that might prompt spectators to reflect on the encounter is less present in some of these works. This makes it more difficult for the artists to anticipate what people's response might be, and whether they will become conscious of the way they personally can be complicit in the dominant cultural logic of disability (cf. Williamson, 2008: 9).

These differences mean passers-by may (mis)read the encounter these performers create, mistaking a deliberate, deceitful recitation of an already deceitful discourse about ability, disability and dealing with disabled people for part of the phenomenon it is trying to challenge. This, of course, may not be for want of effort on the performers' part to complicate the framing of the work. In Williamson and Araniello's *Assisted Passage*, for instance, the 'She's Got a Ticket to Die' songs might understandably have been assumed to be enough to encourage spectators to be in the encounter and begin reflecting on the encounter at the same time. It does, though, increase the likelihood of unproductive relations and recuperations emerging during the encounter. For, as I have suggested in Chapter 1, if spectators see performances as just fact, or as just fiction, they are far less likely to feel the uncertainty that sets an ethical encounter in motion. Without framing – or more critically, multiple frames of reference – there is far less chance that spectators will forsake their ready-made readings of disabled bodies in favour of a full reflection on what they see. In this sense, the risk that performer or spectator-as-performer will misread, mistake or otherwise reduce the meaning of the Other, their other, is an inherent, unpredictable but unavoidable part of these performances.

Shannon, Williamson and Araniello are all alert to the danger of reductive, recuperative or downright dangerous readings of their interventionalist performances. They acknowledge the unpredictability of the form, and, of course, the need to work at the encounters that unfold in this form of work – the exaggeration, interaction and activation of the audience – constantly. Even so, the fact that each passer-by brings their own habits and histories to the encounter means there is never any guarantee that it will not cause rather than challenge problems. Still, as great as these risks are, these performers all seem to feel compelled – at least to some degree – to continue using the guerrilla-style intervention in public spaces and places as part of their politicized arts practices, even if the results are unpredictable and open to problematic recuperations.

One reason artists persist with this form of practice is, as I have suggested in the Introduction, that these potentially risky renegotiations of relationships in public space are part and parcel of the artists' daily lives. These risky negotiations and renegotiations of relationships are always already part of the process by which disabled people work at managing, addressing and potentially altering the dynamics of the stare in daily life. In this sense, if the phenomenon is going to happen anyway, it may as well become part of their work. It becomes a way of managing, and taking back power over, daily identity and impression management processes.

Another reason, I think, is that the improvisational nature of the interventions allows for the possibility that new ideas, new ways of relating and interrelating, and thus new identities may emerge. Improvisation always carries with it the potential for creativity, innovation and new ideas. It is, however, an intimidating prospect for many people, as Dan Diggles notes. In actor training contexts, Diggles argues, improvisation teachers almost always ask their actors to say the first thing that comes to mind – even if might seem unoriginal, ordinary or obvious – instead of planning, preparing, self-censoring, or preparing something more clever or meaningful (2004: 7–24). They acknowledge that this is a difficult thing for most people to do. This, Diggles says, is because 'we live in a society of templates' (Diggles, 2004: 11), and performing our selves usually means trying to perfect our performances of one of these types or templates so we can say or do the suitable thing for a man, woman, friend, lover, worker and so on. People are 'judged', as Diggles puts it, on their ability to do this (Diggles, 2004: 13). As a result, people hesitate or suppress their first impulse if they are not sure of it, fearing it will not be clear, acceptable or successful. What makes improvisation difficult, then, is that people are scared they will not live up to the template, or scared that they will seem dim, dull or 'a little crazier than everybody else' (Diggles, 2004: 15). 'Open your mouth, say the first thing that comes into your head, and you could say something stupid – or, worse, personal and revealing. You're on display, giving yourself away' (Diggles, 2004: 24). You could, in other words, find yourself blocked, ill-at-ease or embarrassed. Accordingly, many people prefer to deploy a socially acceptable response rather than try to act and react with whatever words or movement come in the moment.

Understood in Lévinasian terms, avoiding improvisatory moments might be understood as an attempt to avoid vulnerability. For Lévinas, as I have said, encounters with the Other always automatically ask us to recognize, respond and thus make our selves vulnerable to others at a pre-ontological level (1996a: 7). In an effort to avoid this vulnerability, though, we often impose culturally determined codes, categories and labels on the Other – an imposition that occurs in the ontological realm, and is informed by our social scripts. Avoiding improvisation is, in this sense, a way of suring up one's own identity and ideas, instead of opening ourselves up to something new, surprising or outside our social norms. For artists like Shannon, Williamson and Araniello, improvised public space performance is important precisely because it puts pressure on our ability to apply social scripts to sure up our identity in this way. It puts pressure on our ability to apply culturally (if not always consciously) pre-planned performances to avoid the possibility that something surprising might emerge in the course of a social or communicative encounter. It allows performer and spectator-as-performer alike to engage with the specificities of each other's experiences in ways they might not in the normal flow of daily life. This, for these artists, makes the risks involved in this sort of work worthwhile. It is not a perfect, predictable process – but the challenges, and the failures, may teach performers, spectators-as-performers and society as much about possible futures as the successes.

Yet another reason these guerrilla practices appeal, I think, is that most of these artists re-represent their guerrilla-style encounters in secondary performances – descriptions, documentations, performative lectures, multimedia packages and so forth. This means that, no matter what happens in the moment itself, there is still potentiality in the deferred performance. There is still the deferred moment where a new set of spectators see the artists' documentation, and the primary spectators' range of (potentially) reductive, habitual responses in the documentation, and thus a chance that these secondary spectators may start to reflect on their own habitual responses. The role remediation plays here is potentially quite productive. Normally, the illusive nature of live performance – its ability to disappear, allowing decontextualized descriptions and documentation to dominate the ongoing debate about it – allows it to be co-opted into the mechanics of controversy as a receding centre, around which combat between opposing ideologies can be played out. Normally, this enables us to remove the encounter (pre-ontological) and replace it with explanation (ontological) to deal with the Other on our own terms. This is, though, a characteristic of the part performance plays in negotiations in the public sphere that artists can co-opt into their own agenda. In structuring their performance so that a primary spectator participates in an encounter, and a secondary spectator then participates in a new encounter re-engaging the first encounter, the artists considered here invite the secondary spectators to step into the shoes of the first spectators in a way that makes them think about how they apply their own culturally ingrained explanations to deal with the Other. In effect, the artists co-opt the mechanics of commentary, continuing debate and controversy – as critical parts of public sphere negotiations of ideas, ideologies and identities – for their own ends.

The dangers, ambiguities and unpredictabilities of their work can, as a result, still lead to broader debate that the artists find very valuable. This is something I have seen in action as I have described these artists' works at conferences, symposia and seminars (cf. Hadley, Rajak, Filmer, Caines and Read, 2010 for a colleague's summation of reactions to my reading of these artists' work in one such context). Occasionally, people will be offended, feeling that these disabled people have 'used' able people, who were only trying to 'do the right thing', to create their critique of what they see as an able-oriented society. Offended, in other words, that able people have been 'used' in service of someone else's cultural agenda. As though disabled people have not been 'used' in service of someone else's cultural agenda in freakshows, medical schools and the media for centuries, and the inversion that takes place here is not useful in highlighting how uncomfortable being called into such service can be for anyone. Though relatively few, these people have expressed real anxiety at the way their own view of Others, in particular disabled Others, which they had usually thought very compassionate and politically correct, has been seen by disabled people as problematic. The concern ripples out from primary, to secondary, to tertiary sets of spectator groups hearing my accounts of the practices. The artists, therefore, have in some cases seen this debate emerging from my discussion of their work as a useful expansion of the influence of their improvised public space performance into new sectors of the public sphere – an expansion that allows further interaction, improvisation and negotiation of exactly the sort they hope to see.

These ideas about the reasons why artists engage in risky performance practices notwithstanding, it remains difficult to track the ways in which the encounters – or the expanding sphere of influence, discussion or debate about the encounters – impact on specific spectators. This, as I have said, is because it is always challenging to capture information on what a given performance's impact on spectators might be. In the last two or three years, though, a great deal of interest in cultivating the internet as a forum for capturing spectatorial responses has emerged, for disabled artists and for a range of other artists too. Many have expressed a real desire to experiment with how the internet, and in particular social media sites, can enact, expand or shift the terms of the debate about a particular performance, or the ideas canvassed in a particular performance. In Chapter 3, then, I consider the way disabled artists have begun to work with this relatively new forum for engaging spectators.

3

'That you would post such a thing...': Staging Spectatorship Online

It is difficult to determine what drives spectators' responses to disability. The ready-made responses culture provides – or, at least, the process of improvising or riffing off these ready-made responses – are undoubtedly a factor, as is the spectator's own identity position, history and habits. As, of course, is their level of literacy with performance practices, and the signs, symbols and stories performance practices invoke. To gain a glimpse, scholars can study what spectators say in comment books, critiques or reviews. Scholars can observe what they do. Nevertheless, whether any given instance represents a ready-made response, an improvisation concealing a challenge to ready-made responses, or some sort of individual, idiosyncratic sensibility towards what the spectator is seeing is not necessarily easy to establish. A lack of comment books, critiques or reviews by mainstream critics of the practices considered in this book – positioned, as they are, outside the mainstream performance practices that garner this sort of media attention – makes it even more difficult to gather the documentation, discussion or analysis that might indicate the potential of the practices to have an impact in the public sphere.

In the twenty-first century, however, social media – interactive internet-based applications that allow people to express and debate ideas such as Facebook, Twitter, blogs and so forth – has started to provide another channel by which we might access material to support this sort of analysis.

For many artists with disabilities, the internet is an important part of the public sphere. At a minimum, many find it is worth posting ideas, information or documentation of their practices as part of their interventionalist agenda. At an extreme, some artists feel it is worth creating works specifically for online public spaces and places, including guerrilla-style interventions that have the potential to re-envision the encounter between disabled and non-disabled people. Indeed, given that the internet is at once a highly accessible public 'space' (given the availability of adaptive technology), and a highly contested public 'space' (given the power networks, communities and examples of inclusion and exclusion that permeate it), it is little wonder that a number of artists with disabilities have engaged with the internet in one way or another.

Online performances, or offline performances which acquire a mechanism for online responses such as a blog or a 'like' button, provide a unique platform for spectators to perform their response to the disabled body. They provide a unique platform for spectators (bystanders, passers-by, or whatever we might call people passing by on the web) to participate in debates that shape public perceptions of disability, reflect on their own role in perpetuating dominant discourses about disability, and, therefore, reflect on their own role in producing a public sphere that is or is not inclusive of people with disabilities. Clearly, online platforms do not provide the same theatrical, architectural or technological devices to prompt spectators to perform their response to a disabled body as the stage, performance installation or public space intervention practices I have considered here. To post comments, challenges or contests via online mechanisms – be it via a comment thread beneath a review or a video, a blog, Facebook, Twitter, or other social media mechanisms – is not the same as accepting the invitation to enter the mirror boxes in Cunningham's *Mirage*, interact with Lakmaier's weebles, provide a portrait by proxy for Jones, or improvise a response to Shannon, Araniello or Williamson on the pavement. It is a textual or written performance of a spectator's response rather than a visual, physical or verbal performance of a spectator's response. It may be more or less immediate. It may be more or less anonymous. Moreover, while online public performances are just that – very public – there is a sense that some people are not fully aware that they are performing in a forum where they are visible to others when they post comments online.

There are also other, more critical, issues. Precisely what a spectator is responding to – a performance, the press about a performance, or conversations other spectators are having about a performance rather than the performance itself – may not be clear in this context. Precisely what identity position a spectator holds may not be clear, and, of course, may not be performed truthfully. The nature of the community, and the roles, rules and relationships within the community, can also be unclear or differ quite markedly from one online space to another. Often, as David Kociemba notes, the people present online may be but a vocal minority within a much larger group (2010a). They may engage with other posters well, but, equally, they may display bad 'netiquette' – for instance, ignoring or abusing those that hold contrary views. Examining the sometimes cringe-worthy, conflicted or confused responses to performances by people with disabilities online is, though, still very useful to a study of this sort. These responses provide glimpses or traces of trains of thought that – whilst not necessarily a more stable, dependable indicator of what a person thinks than what they might say to you in a foyer at the end of a performance – can be useful in investigating how individuals, and groups of individuals, negotiate a response. Online responses can in other words provide indicators of the narrative, dramaturgy and, perhaps most importantly, negotiations, by which attitudes towards disability and disabled people are constructed. Precisely the sorts of negotiations that do – if not necessarily in a direct or directly predictable way – have the potential to have an impact in the public and political spheres.

Clearly, performing a response to an online performance, or to a performance with an online response mechanism, does not involve the physical co-presence of performers and spectators that, for many commentators, is critical to the political and ethical potential of performance. There is still, as Helen Freshwater (2009) again reminds us, an 'orthodoxy' that suggests that the short-lived, sensory and social interactions of performance – the co-presence of performing and spectating bodies struggling to improvise new relationships here, now, together – is what makes it a privileged site for contested citations of dominant cultural narratives. There is truth to this, at least insofar as the co-presence of different bodies can assist in creating the layers of fact, fiction, fantasy and cultural frames that, according to Hans Thies Lehmann (2006), create uncertainty, and thus create the conditions of possibility for an ethical encounter (even if it is not the only way to create this encounter). But the ephemerality of performance may also be critical to the way it intervenes or has lasting effects in the public sphere. The ephemerality of performance means it is able to disappear, allowing decontextualized descriptions and documentation to dominate memory, meaning-making and media debate about its ethics, politics and impact. It means, as John Houchin (2008) and Miriam Felton-Dansky (2008) say in an issue of *Theatre Journal* on 'Censorship & Performance', and controversies like the Janet Jackson 'wardrobe malfunction' illustrate, that performance can be co-opted into the mechanics of controversy, as a receding centre around which combat between opposing ideologies can be played out. They cite the phenomenon of people misreading a performance, or denouncing a performance on the basis of what they have heard about it, as examples of this sort of co-option. Here, the original encounter in which – at least according to Emmanuel Lévinas (1996a) – we engage with something or someone other (at a pre-ontological level) disappears. The other is translated into something readable (at an ontological level), and readings are informed by cultural histories, habits and memories. This phenomenon, in which a performance becomes a receding centre around which a new performance, a new negotiation of ideas, ideologies and discourses takes places, undoubtedly characterizes responses to disabled artists work in online spaces and places as much as it does in offline spaces. Their work becomes a receding centre around which spectators' performances, spectators' negotiation of ideas, ideologies and discourses take place.

Yet, as I have argued in Chapter 2, many disabled artists seem to think this may in fact assist their performance in having an impact on individual and public perceptions about disability. The initial performance – online, or live with online responses – is one opportunity for citing, reciting and challenging ideas about disabilities. As this initial moment of encounter recedes, new performances amongst responding spectators may provide new opportunities for citing, reciting and contesting ideas about disabilities, in a sort of expanding circle of effect. These new performances are influenced by cultural narratives, and the histories, memories and meaning-making habits of those who choose to participate – but here, again we can see performers, co-participants and spectators improvising or 'riffing' off these influences to create new chains of thought, confusion, uncertainty or changes of perception. In this sense, the fact that the initial performance recedes in these online contexts might, instead of being seen as a problem, be seen as an opportunity to create cascading series of new performances, new uncertainties, and new reactions that in the end may (or may not, or may not predictably) effect changes in the public sphere. Clearly, each encounter, and each expanding chain of consensus-building, confused or conflicted responses, is individual, idiosyncratic and unreplicable. Examining these chains of response – these chains of performances – can, though, provide insight into the way these encounters impact on individuals, groups of individuals, and the way these improvised reactions build or block new points of view emerging. It may, in other words, be precisely what is needed to shed new light on the features of risky, unpredictable performance practices in which performers and spectators alike engage their Other.

In this Chapter, then, I consider the performance of spectatorship in and through social media, in the hope that it can indeed provide insight into the features of these performance practices. I track the way spectators' performance of meaning-making plays out in social media forums, and the ways these encounters at the interstices of performance, memory, public history, private history and technology negotiate ideas about disability. I draw on four diverse examples – Rita Marcalo's offline *Involuntary Dances*, Liz Crow's offline/online *Resistance on the Plinth*, Katherine Araniello's online *Suicide Messages* clips on YouTube, and *Cast Offs*, a TV show about disabled people coping with nature *Survivor*-style available on YouTube – to examine how spectators respond via social media. I cite spectators' comments, in their own often highly idiosyncratic shorthand, precisely as posted on public websites where they were, at the time of writing, available for all web users to read and respond to (as opposed to semi-public or private sites that can only be read by 'friends' or 'followers', which have not been included in this study precisely because posters on those sites would have had some expectation that their correspondence was private rather than publicly available to anyone on the web). Whilst the four works in focus in this chapter differ in style, tone and structure, and what the spectators are responding to is different – in some cases it is live work, in others it is webcast work, in others a combination of the two – they share some of the features of the performance practices discussed throughout this book. Indeed, responses to them via social media demonstrate some distinctive features. In each case, responses demonstrate confused, conflicted and consensus-building negotiations about reality, representation and appropriate ways of performing (or performing a response to) disability. In each case, the social media forum that supports the responses becomes a platform not just for recording memories of an original performance (which posters may or may not have seen), but for new performances, new encounters and new negotiations, which go well beyond remembering or remediating the original. Trends in the way experience, memory and meaning-making play out in these performative forums – which typically move from clarification of the original act's parameters, to claims of disgust, insult or offence, to counter-claims confirming the comic or political efficacy of the act, often linked to disclosure of personal experience of disability – start to emerge. In doing so, these spectatorial performances start to reveal as much about the politics of disability, and the ethics, politics and efficacy of subversive restagings of disability, as the initial acts.

'She should work on that' – Rita Marcalo's *Involuntary Dances*

The highest profile example of a performance by a disabled artist causing controversy online in recent years is the response to Rita Marcalo's *Involuntary Dances* (2009), a 24-hour durational piece in which Marcalo stopped taking her epilepsy medication, took stimulants such as tobacco and alcohol, and subjected herself to triggers such as strobe lighting, in an effort to induce a seizure. 'At any point in the event', publicity materials state,

> Marcalo might have an epileptic seizure. Whenever this happens, a loud alarm will sound, lights will brighten, music will stop and a series of cameras will start recording her seizure. Audience members will be encouraged to record it on their mobile phones.
> (Bradford Playhouse quoted in Norfolk, 2009)

'[E]pilepsy is often an invisible disability', Marcalo says.

> If I don't reveal to someone I suffer from it, most people in my life will never know. They will know that at times I might leave a meeting or an event and spend more than usual time in a toilet,

and that I will come back looking tired and may give an excuse and leave [...] But they might never know this means that I just had a seizure.

(Marcalo quoted in Verrent, 2009)

Managing this invisible disability, and this invisible identity as a disabled person, is a constant challenge, as are decisions about concealing or disclosing the condition to the public (cf. Norfolk, 2009; Marcalo quoted in Tracey, 2009). 'As a performer my work is about "exposure"', Marcalo says,

> but as an epileptic I constantly work very hard at 'hiding' my condition. For once in my life I was interested in exploring what it would mean for me to 'expose' my epilepsy, instead of hiding it away.

(Marcalo quoted in Verrent, 2009; cf. Marcalo
quoted in Stokes, 2009)

A theme Marcalo wanted to pursue in a planned trilogy – *Involuntary Dances*, followed by a piece about Marcalo's health maintenance called *She's In Control* and a piece about anti-epileptic medication called *Sem Corpo* (Marcalo quoted in Tracey, 2009).

Marcalo's work, in contrast with others considered in this chapter, is not at the time of writing available online except in media releases or reviews describing it – but, and perhaps because of this, has drawn a range of heated responses from online commentators. For Marcalo, the decision to create this controversial work came from her day-to-day experience of epilepsy. When the publicity material for *Involuntary Dances* went out, the press and newspapers in the United Kingdom immediately began citing experts from the National Society for Epilepsy, or Epilepsy Action, or other similar associations, expressing concern about the performance (cf. Norfolk, 2009; cf. Verrent, 2009). One blogger, a woman who said she herself has epilepsy, in a blog she had (somewhat ironically) started because she was frustrated with her employer's unwillingness to accept her largely invisible impairment as a disability, said that while she admired the lengths Marcalo was willing to go to, she 'fail[ed] to see the entertainment factor in watching someone have an epileptic fit' (Roy Williams, 2009). She had YouTubed to watch some fits, and found them underwhelming, if still personally upsetting, insofar as they conformed to her expectations of what they would look like. This blogger mused on whether spectators would be morbidly fascinated, underwhelmed or overwhelmed, decided it was in bad taste to turn something real into a 'strange' sort of art, and that she was worried it would sensationalize rather than normalize the condition (Roy Williams, 2009). This blog captured the themes common to many of the comments responding to Jo Verrent's review of Marcalo's work on Disability Arts online. A lot of posters started by saying they were epileptic, or knew an epileptic, and were worried by what Marcalo was doing. One said, 'As a person who has had seizures since the early 80s that have been under control with increasing doses of medication, the idea of inducing an uncontrolled seizure in a steel basket scares me' (Brian Newman quoted in Verrent, 2009). Another said:

> [T]he reason I am so angry about this work is that it threatens my identity. Rita Marcalo may have delighted a well-established disability arts community, albeit a tiny audience, but has alienated the mainstream E-Type community to which I belong. [...] [I]t bloody hurts.
>
> (Richard Johnson quoted in Verrent, 2009)

A number of posters suggested that if she was contemplating this, Marcalo's condition must not be that authentic, or that severe. 'It seems this young woman only has two seizures a year', one put it. 'I have already had two seizures in the past three days. I would not wish one on my worst enemy, and if I had any warning I would go to a safe place, not a public toilet' (Anna Kennedy quoted in Verrent, 2009). Another poster was even more explicit in querying the nature, severity and authenticity of Marcalo's condition and her act.

> I'm still waiting for one of the spectators to make an affirmative statement about the experience of not seeing one of the visible types of epileptic seizures.
>
> I would also like to know how many minutes Rita spent in total, actually trying to trigger a see-able seizure, and hear from somebody who can guarantee she did not take her medication.

Once one subtracts the romanticism, and the words-base of the performance, one is still left wondering if this was authentic.

(Richard Johnson quoted in Verrent, 2009)

Some posters suggested that it is Marcalo's own fault that she fears negative public perception of her fits (and tries to hide them by running to a public toilet or other ruses), and that she should work on that rather than creating this controversial sort of performance piece.

The real disability is not the visible or invisible effect of the seizures themselves. Mine is the vulnerability I feel during them, and sometimes after. Rita's is her inability to cope with her perceptions of what others might feel. It is Rita who locked herself in a cage – not us. [...] I have a sad feeling that any negative reactions from the spectators would have had the effect of justifying her own negative viewpoint about public reactions and not given her an opportunity to focus on her own issues.

(Laura R quoted in Verrent, 2009)

Whatever the case, most of these posters thought Marcalo was not really making any legitimate comment on her condition. Many called *Involuntary Dances* a 'circus act in front of a crowd looking for blood' (Brian Newman quoted in Verrent, 2009), or 'humiliation as entertainment' (John Brett quoted in Verrent, 2009), saying 'anyone who went to watch it should be ashamed of themselves' (Cat Watson quoted in Verrent, 2009), because Marcalo was 'portray[ing] the victim-figure most of us reject' (Richard Johnson quoted in Verrent, 2009). For these posters, it seems, Marcalo was recasting herself as a monster, mutant or freak, or as an object of pity who will not let the medical profession and the public help her, and submitting herself to the exploitative gaze of those who would be shameful enough to want to go and watch this restaging of what Marcalo feels her daily life as a disabled person is like. The comments often focused on the fact that in doing this, rather than doing something that could be clearly defined in terms of the conventional value of art – authenticity, aesthetic quality, audience engagement and entertainment – the value of her work was unclear. '[T]he review did not mention any of the usual aspects of art. Like talent. Or quality. Or the strength of the artist's ability to communicate' (Richard Johnson quoted in Verrent,

2009). Some posters worried that Marcalo was only reinforcing the negative view held by many people (including, perhaps, that first blogger's boss) that epileptics are malingerers who will not do the right thing.

> This performance has reinforced the negative view held by many people, who think E automatically means psychiatric problems.
>
> It has gone even further. It has reinforced the view held by some police and health professionals, that E can be faked, that people with E don't work as a part of the healthcare team demanded by the NICE Guidelines, that they are not to be trusted.
>
> (Richard Johnson quoted in Verrent, 2009)

Other posters came to Marcalo's defence, arguing that hers was a legitimate perception or interpretation of the experience of being epileptic. 'Marcalo is drawing attention to public perceptions of epilepsy and asking us to examine our responses' (Colin Hambrook quoted in Verrent, 2009). '[T]his performance wasn't actually about Rita. It was about the fact that we are often seen as objects of fascination when we fit' (Joe Shann quoted in Verrent, 2009). '[P]eople are afraid of epileptics because it is this thing of no-one being in control' (Peter Street – Poet quoted in Verrent, 2009). As these posters indicate, the medical model asks epileptics to hide, conceal and control a condition that cannot be cured, so people like Marcalo do still feel a compulsion to fit in private, to go to a public toilet to make sure the fit stays behind closed doors for example, and feel a lot of pressure to follow doctor's advice. 'Everyone felt it should be addressed through a medical model approach. They were keen to take away rights, take away choices' (Rich quoted in Verrent, 2009). In this sense, as one poster (also a regular reviewer of disability arts in the UK) notes:

> She's evidently raised a lot of issues about our right to make our own decisions. Why should not following the doctor's orders be such a transgressive act? 'Epileptic eats chocolate' is hardly a front page story. Why should we not make our own decisions on such things? What right does anyone else have to tell us what to do with our own bodies?
>
> (Sutherland quoted in Verrent, 2009)

What Marcalo's performance captures, at least for Allan Sutherland, is the way having to hide, or having to have doctors, charities or do-gooders tell us what is good for us, may be more horrific than the condition itself. Accordingly, as Sutherland says in his own full-length commentary on Marcalo's work:

> What Marcalo's piece highlights is that adults with epilepsy own their own bodies and have a right to choose what to do with them. It illustrates that we are able to speak for ourselves, and don't need charitable organisations to step in on our behalf. (It's extraordinary that this is still an issue).
>
> She is also saying that there are worse things than having an epileptic fit. Several hundreds of thousands of us in this country live with epilepsy in one form or another, and our lives are not blighted. But it is nevertheless a feared condition. The ancient idea of possession by demons still lurks beneath the surface of people's awareness. But those who are most afraid of epilepsy are those who don't have it. I've lived with the condition for half a century, and I've lost count of the number of times I've had to calm some gibbering bystander who was distraught at what they saw. Marcalo's performance will implicitly say: 'It's just a fit. Get over it.' She speaks for us all.
>
> (Sutherland, 2009a)

Views, however, remain mixed, with others suggesting that

> Talking about not following the doctors' orders entirely misses the point. People who have acquired confidence in managing an often-dismissed medical condition have done so with teamwork, not by blindly following instructions.
>
> It is usual for such people to know as much in general, and more in particular, than the most eminent of E specialists.
>
> (Richard Johnson quoted in Verrent, 2009)

By restaging her seizures in *Involuntary Dances*, Marcalo demonstrates the damage the medical model, which tries to normalize disability, can do, and, at the same time, the non-normalizability of the reality of fits, fatigue and pain. Indeed, the uncontrollability and uncertainty of her condition was emphasized by the fact that she did not, in fact, fit during the work. In this sense, for Verrent, the work seemed to challenge both medical and social models of disability, and, she says, the Disability Arts Rulebook which suggests: 'Thou shalt only produce work that relates to your experiences as a disabled person according to the social model of disability; Thou shalt not produce work that relates to pain or fatigue or anything that speaks of disability in a way that could be interpreted as weakness' (Verrent, 2009). For the most part, fellow performers and critics (as distinct from members of the public with, or with an interest in, epilepsy) typically praised both what Marcalo sought to do and how she sought to do it here – that is, the way the work captured disability, responses to disability, and the conflicted dialogue around disability, disclosure, medical demands, and the individual versus the community view of how best to deal with this medical condition. Positioning the work within the live art tradition (Colin Hambrook quoted in Verrent, 2009; Rich quoted in Verrent, 2009), they said they understood why the paradoxes and tensions the work played with – secret versus spectacle, visibility versus non-visibility, and control versus non-control – would be important and interesting to a dancer like Marcalo (Colin Hambrook quoted in Verrent, 2009; Allan Sutherland quoted in Verrent, 2009). For these posters the work was, therefore, a legitimate artistic provocation. 'Rita Marcalo's performance was about the convention whereby the "spectacle" of epilepsy, as it is viewed in the public eye [...] It was an experiment in asking an audience to reflect that perception back to her' (Colin Hambrook quoted in Verrent, 2009). Amidst the commentary, counter-commentary and claims about the work's impact, people noted that it did at least get a debate started, and suggested that the fact that there are not many forums for such a debate might explain the excesses of emotion in some of the posts. 'I guess it's to do with the fact that, as people with epilepsy, we tend to be very isolated', Sutherland says, 'and therefore don't get the chance to share experiences very much. So when a public event such as this occurs, a whole flood of emotion comes welling up to the surface' (Allan Sutherland quoted in Verrent, 2009). Liz Crow agrees, saying:

> The more disabled artists explore the body and its relationship to the world around us, the more we represent our selves and bring the

wider world face to face with the presumptions, misunderstandings and controls that have dogged us through history. Sometimes, this relies on provocation. Rita has provoked and – look – we're talking! Whether or not she had a fit to order was never the measure of whether the performance worked.

(Liz Crow quoted in Verrent, 2009)

This, indeed, may have been exactly what Marcalo most hoped for. 'I like to generate debate', Marcalo herself says, 'and whether people agree or not, I've seen more written about epilepsy in the last few weeks than I've ever seen before' (Marcalo quoted in Tracey, 2009). Whatever the range of views, there was an acknowledgement that tensions that exist within the public sphere were being played out, not only in Marcalo's performance, but in the remediations of it online – effectively a new performance – even if the editor did in the end start cutting out some of the more extreme attacks in a very passionate set of responses to the work.

'Perhaps we should be looking to the future' – Liz Crow's *Resistance on the Plinth*

British storyteller, artist, filmmaker and activist Liz Crow – amongst those who celebrated Marcalo's work's ability to generate discussion and debate about disability – is a disabled artist best known for her portrayal in films of women with disabilities such as Helen Keller and Frida Kahlo (Ouch Team, 2009; cf. Hadley, 2011). Crow's work 'covers the gamut', and has included 'themes of identity, resistance, survival, [and] finding a place in the world [that] apply to being human' (2010). These themes are linked to a disability perspective because that is part of Crow's own lived experience. For Crow, 'the term disability arts may include explicitly politicized work about disability. However, it may also include work about daily lives which happens to engage a disability perspective because that is part of the artist's lived experience' (Crow, 2010). Like many artists with disabilities, Crow feels that the narratives projected onto disabled people's bodies can be more disabling than the physical impairments of their bodies (Crow, 2009b).

In 2009, Crow's interest in challenging the cultural narratives projected onto people with disabilities, and challenging dominant culture to be more inclusive of people with disabilities, led her to nominate herself to be part of Antony Gormley's *One & Other* public art project in the United Kingdom.

Gormley is a British sculptor best known for a series of works emphasizing the human body, and the way the human body relates to a range of spaces in the material and social worlds (cf. Engelen, 2010). His early works include the Turner Prize winning *Field for the British Isles* (1994), which featured 40,000 clay figures created by volunteers facing the viewer from the floor of a large room, and *Angel of the North* (1994), a 20-metre-tall figure of a man with wings installed in Gateshead, England. More recent works include *Asian Field* (2006), which featured 180,000 clay figures created by villagers from China; *Waste Man* (2006), a 25-metre-tall figure made of household waste burned as part of Exodus Day in Kent, England; *Another Place* (2006), which featured 100 cast-iron figures of Gormley's body facing out to sea at Crosby Beach near Liverpool, England; *Time Horizon* (2006), which featured 100 cast-iron figures of Gormley's body placed amongst olive trees in Calabria, Italy; and *Event Horizon* (2007), which featured 31 iron and fibreglass casts of Gormley's body displayed atop buildings along London's South Bank. Gormley's sculptures use transfigurations of the body, scale, proximity, distance, separation, and – in his later works – interventions in public space, to call viewers' attention to their own ways of being in the world.

In 2009, Gormley was commissioned to create *One & Other*, a public art project for the Fourth Plinth in Trafalgar Square in London. Gormley described *One & Other* as an attempt to 'make a portrait of the UK now' (Gormley quoted in British Sky Broadcasting, 2009), or, more precisely, a 'lens through which [to] see what the UK is like now' (Gormley quoted in Sutherland, 2009b). It gave 2400 people, selected at random via a lottery, a chance to do whatever they chose for an hour on the vacant Fourth Plinth in Trafalgar Square over 100 days in July, August and September 2009. At the time, Gormley characterized *One & Other* as 'a celebration of our national diversity, an extraordinarily precarious mixture of those who just wanted to do something fun, and those with a burning cause for which they wished to serve as a living representative' (Gormley quoted in M. Kennedy, 2009). In this sense, whilst *One & Other* had its supporters and its detractors, it did, to a greater degree than Gormley's prior work, engage with the workings of the public sphere as a space for negotiating ideas about the identities, roles and relationships later adopted as authoritative by the state. *One & Other* experimented with definitions of the public, who performs it, when, and how, and thus – at least potentially – offered 'Plinthers' a chance, or a platform, to play with the way ideas of identity, community and culture are performed in a very public space.

In practice, of course, what people chose to do on the Plinth was broad-ranging, and sometimes bizarre. It ranged from considered performances, and people promoting causes, to people pleading for jobs via placards (*The Guardian*, 2009b), and even one person pleading to the British Government to help her get a reprieve from a death sentence in the United States via a cardboard cut-out of herself (Batty, 2009), as well as those looking to make a spectacle of themselves by means of stripping or silly behaviour.

Throughout its 100 days, *One & Other* was the subject of constant media commentary. Some commentators, like *The Guardian*'s Alex Needham suggested it 'created a real and virtual community' in 'a very short space of time', as an 'incredibly varied group of people' engaged Plinthers 'either by heckling and applauding in Trafalgar Square, or by posting online' (Needham, 2009). Others, though, saw it as simply a new version of *Big Brother* (Brooker, 2009; Jones, 2009), as it became a 'surprise hit' for its media sponsor Sky TV (Holmwood, 2009). In effect, in *One & Other*, Plinthers were engaging two intersecting components of the public sphere – one live and one mediatized. There was, as a result of the Sky TV sponsorship and web-streaming, a media-fuelled pressure to perform or 'do' something in public space (Eshun quoted in British Sky Broadcasting, 2009; Dowse, 2009). Yet, as commentators like Patricia Bickers and Jonathan Jones pointed out, the intersection of the live and the mediatized in play in *One & Other* often resulted in a situation where the web-streaming offered what Bickers calls a 'privileged view', while the live performance left Plinthers and spectators with 'a depressingly foreshortened view from above or below' (Bickers, 2009: 12), as Plinthers struggled to communicate from atop a tall platform in a public space at all times of the day and night, passers-by coming and going, looking and lapsing in their attention. 'The camera', Jones noted, was 'far, far closer to the participants than any spectator [could] get' (J. Jones, 2009). As a result, Jones felt the live performance presented 'a diminishing, isolating of the individual', which, paradoxically, 'remove[d] the performers from the social world' (2009). 'If *One & Other* [was] an image of British democratic life in our time', he argued, 'it was a pessimistic one. It [was] a portrait of a society in which people will try anything to get their voices heard, even stand on a plinth, but where no one can hear what they are saying' (J. Jones, 2009) amidst the chaotic, channel-switching hubbub of contemporary life.

Participating in *One & Other* presented a lot of challenges for a professional artist like Crow – and not just because using the immediacy of live art to interrupt the narratives culture projects onto her body is something she has only become interested in relatively recently (Crow, 2010). The complexity of *One & Other*'s attempt to construct a portrait of the British public and intervene in public perceptions of identity, community and culture via an extremely visible platform left some Plinthers, particularly the professional artists who participated, with a sense of trepidation as they considered their contribution. As one participant, Jill Dowse, has rightly argued 'this was not an easily manageable context for any kind of presentation' (2009). It was difficult, Dowse argues, to create 'a dramaturgically sound piece for an audience whose presence would be so unpredictable', and 'the live coverage threatened a *post hoc* call to account for anything I might say or do, leaving me open to misinterpretation and criticism from the public or media' (Dowse, 2009).

In *Resistance on the Plinth,* the title Crow gave the piece she created for Gormley's *One & Other,* she presented an image of herself in her wheelchair in a Nazi uniform. She too faced a risk of misreading, misrecognition or misinterpretation of the culturally recognizable image she chose to present in this charged, unpredictable context. The Nazi uniform is a meaningful image for Crow and one she has used on a number of occasions. Indeed, *Resistance on the Plinth* is one of four pieces Crow has produced as part of the *Resistance* series over the past few years, a series which also includes a 30-minute moving-image installation, a film and a documentary about the making of the film. The *Resistance* series examines the Nazi regime's Aktion T4 programme during World War II, which resulted in the mass murder of a quarter of a million people with disabilities. This atrocity is, for Crow – who creates work in a British context, where public debate about the eugenics of genetic testing, euthanasia and assisted suicide is prevalent in the media – still rich in confronting imagery, resonant and relevant in a contemporary context. The Nazi uniform used in

Crow's plinth performance was designed to 'draw attention to a hidden history and the message it holds for us all today' (Crow, 2009a). This is a theme Crow returns to again and again throughout the *Resistance* series. For Crow, the uniform represents the way disabled people are subjected to discrimination, their plight relegated to private and medical realms. A recognizable historical narrative, which, for Crow (2009b), is 'still really contemporary' in a UK context where debate about assisted suicide is contentious (and, of course, mobilized by artists such as Williamson and Araniello as well as Crow).

> Seventy years ago, the Nazis instituted their first official programme of murder. It targeted disabled people and became the blueprint for the Final Solution to wipe out Jews, gay people, gypsies and other social groups. Today, the development of pre-natal screening and a rush to legal rights for newly disabled people to assisted suicide, show that disabled people's right to life still needs to be defended. With a rise in hate crime, disabled children still excluded from mainstream schools, and over 340,000 disabled people (more than the population of Cardiff) living in institutions, disabled people still experience those historical values as a daily threat.
>
> (Crow, 2009a)

Crow says 'had people openly spoken out at the very first stage where disabled people were murdered, had they thought disabled people's lives were worth saving or speaking out for, then the rest of that history would also be different' (Crow, 2009b). Yet, for Crow, as for other artists with disabilities, it is clear that popular cultural and political discourses continue to characterize disabled people as sufferers, in need of cure, or to be 'pu[t] out of their misery' (Crow, 2009b) so they are not a burden to themselves, their families or their nation. As Crow says, 'I've been congratulated by a complete stranger for not having committed suicide' (Crow quoted in Ouch Team, 2009). This, for her, demonstrates just how deeply entrenched the notion that disabled people suffer intolerable pain that should not necessarily be allowed to continue is in contemporary society. 'If [it is taken as self-evident that] our lives are supposedly intolerable', Crow says, 'then isn't it second nature that everybody will [want to] help us on our way, instead of actually looking at what makes our lives intolerable? (2009b). For Crow – as for most artists, activities and scholars who situate their work in a social model that sees these narratives projected onto disabled bodies as more problematic than the pain and impairment itself – the fact that people assume rather than ask questions about the ideologies beneath their assumptions is problematic. What if people support the idea that the concrete logistics of living with disability are so difficult that a caring society would put disabled people out of their misery without delving deeper into the cultural ideologies that cause them to think the difficulties are insurmountable in the first place? Crow is, therefore, very concerned about the absence of disabled people's voices in the debate about these issues in the public sphere – or, at least, the dominant public sphere, determined by the mainstream press and politics – and the *Resistance* series speaks to that concern (Crow, 2009b). Disabled people, as the group of people best able to challenge these cultural discourses, need to be heard.

Crow felt strongly that disabled people should have a presence as part of *One & Other* (Crow, 2010), so they would not again be excluded from public spaces, democracy and discourse. Accordingly, when selected, she felt a responsibility to present a powerful image (Crow, 2010). Her commitment notwithstanding, Crow did feel the pressure surrounding her hour on the Plinth on Saturday 8 August 2009. Crow planned her hour on the Plinth in detail, and tested her image prior to it. Still, the situation, including the media coverage, naturally left her somewhat nervous. It was very important to Crow that people did not simply see this as a Nazi on the Plinth, and did not simply see this as a comedy performance by a woman who looked like a bad band leader in an oversized Nazi uniform (Crow, 2010). Her concern about potentially reductive readings of the recognizable image she was reciting meant she did not actually commit to going ahead with the project until she tried on the uniform in Bristol about four hours before taking the train to London for the event (Crow, 2010).

Crow's performance on the Plinth was based on what Allan Sutherland has characterized as 'a series of memorable images, carefully choreographed to take advantage of space and time' (Sutherland, 2009b). Crow was lifted onto the Plinth in a white sheet. She took it off, revealing herself in the Nazi uniform (Figure 7). After that, she raised a flag, with words from Martin Niemöeller's famous anti-Nazi

Figure 7 Liz Crow in a publicity photo for *Resistance on the Plinth*, Trafalgar Square, London, 2009 (Photo: Kevin Clifford, Arts Council England & Roaring Girl Productions)

statement which begins: 'First they came for the sick, the so-called incurables and I did not speak out – because I was not incurable.' After that, she took off the Nazi uniform, and flew the flag again (Crow, 2009a; cf. Sutherland, 2009b). Crow's performance was characterized by simple gestures, interspersed with long periods of stillness and silence, carefully constructed to have an impact in a context where, as I have said, it was always going to be difficult to communicate with an unpredictable spectator group, watching live, as well as via the webcams.

The key to Crow's piece was the counter-position of two images – the wheelchair, and the Nazi uniform, associated with eugenics, euthanasia and a desire to eliminate people who do not accord with the Aryan 'norm' – which do not make sense together (Crow, 2010). For Crow (2010), there are two options in presenting politicized works which raise questions about the inclusivity of the public sphere and public spaces. The first is to present a very controlled work – although Crow doesn't use the term, what Mikhail Bakhtin would call a monologic text – which dictates its own stable, singular reading. The second is to present an uncertain work, which, due to undecidability, and a resultant deferral of meaning-making, becomes what Bakhtin (1981; 1984a; 1984b) would call a dialogic text, drawing spectators into a dialogue, rather than dictating a single, socially sanctioned reading almost immediately. For Crow (2010), the latter is more likely to draw people's attention – indeed, they may not have a choice if it is in public space – and more powerful in encouraging people to 'stop, look and think', and thus to reflect in the longer term.

In *Resistance on the Plinth*, the framing device Crow used to create this uncertainty was not so much confusion between fact and fiction – though there may of course have been confusion for some spectators about whether Crow really was a Nazi, whether Crow really was a wheelchair user and so forth – but rather the incompatibility of the two images, which made it difficult for spectators to process what they saw. The incompatibility of the two images made it difficult for spectators to reconcile conflicting realities. Spectators were asked to interpret, then reinterpret, then reinterpret again. The counter-position of images thus forestalled passers-by from attributing a single, stable, socially sanctioned meaning to the image. Instead, it invited them into a more difficult meaning-making dialogue in which the irreconcilability of the contradictory images, ideologies and cultural logics that Crow embodied encouraged them to continue thinking and talking about these logics after the encounter itself.

Though Crow did not have a lot of opportunity to look at what was happening below whilst she was on the Plinth, she did see groups at the edge of Trafalgar Square trying to decipher the image, decipher the words on the flag, and determine their meaning (Crow, 2010). Apparently, spectators did see that the image did not immediately make sense, though different spectators were more or less well equipped to work out why, depending on the frames of history/ *habitus* they brought to the encounter, and their familiarity with the historical implications of the image (Crow, 2010).

Having created this uncertainty, Crow felt a need to provide a platform for spectators to work through it after the encounter (Crow, 2010). In this case, it was via the presence of about 50 supporters on the ground, handing out flyers which provided the full quote from Niemöeller, and the rationale for the performance (Crow, 2010; Crow, 2009b).

In the days following *Resistance on the Plinth*, Crow's performance received attention in a range of online and offline news outlets. Crow called her local newspaper, *The Bristol Evening Post*, and the national newspaper *The Guardian*, to alert them to the work and the reaction to it (Crow, 2010). Her local paper published images of the work the following week, and, whilst *The Guardian* did not cover the work at the time, they did cover it at the conclusion of *One & Other* when they announced their 'Fourth Plinth Top Ten' (*The Guardian*, 2009a), and included *Resistance on the Plinth* amongst it.

The reaction to Crow's work registered on the *One & Other* website, and on other websites, blogs and social networking sites such as Facebook and Twitter, gave a sense of how spectators responded. According to Crow (2010), the first response on Twitter was 'WTF' – what the fuck. This was followed by conversations in which spectators worked out the meaning of the image, drew links to their own experience, their family and friends' experiences, and their own art or activism. Spectators inserted additional information, identifying Crow as an artist, and pointing others to the *Resistance* installation and film websites. For Crow (2010), the sense of community amongst these secondary spectators, engaging with *Resistance on the Plinth* via the web, was important because it had the potential to broaden the work's value as activism.

The tone of the reaction to *Resistance on the Plinth*, particularly on the social networking site Facebook, was positive and celebratory:

> It is very moving to watch you sitting there. You have just taken off the shawl and there you are in the Nazi uniform It is shocking and humbling and very emotional.
>
> (Jan Fairley quoted in Artichoke et al., 2009)

> when you put on ya hat, and i thought, jeez, what's happenin' here? at first i was a bit shocked. then i realised, this must be some kind of statement. then i read why ya there [...] and it all became clear. i've checked the plinth out a lot, and you're the most powerful image i've seen. gormley's come in for a lot of stick about what he is doing, but by doing this, i hope, is someway gonna open and improve peoples minds, about art, and comment and reaction.
>
> (Martin Morris quoted in Artichoke et al., 2009)

Interestingly, though, one spectator did not see disability as oppressive – or, at least, not anymore.

> Where is the evidence for a rise in hate crime against people with disabilities? Or do you mean hate crime in general? It's the perpetuation of the myths of fear released by the press that causes these misguided beliefs in society. In all of my work in Social Work

and through my Social Work studies, the evidence clearly shows
a move to more acceptance of disabilities of all kinds. The institutions are closing down and people are being introduced back
into the community. All have now closed in Scotland. Perhaps we
should be looking to the future rather than the past?

(Stephen Social Work quoted in Artichoke et al., 2009)

Though this is obviously only one person's response to *Resistance
on the Plinth*, it could be seen as a reductive reading, demonstrating
this spectator's attempt to reconcile the image in terms of the ways
of being, behaving and seeing embedded in his *habitus*. In this case,
clearly, the belief embedded in this spectator's *habitus* is not the
belief that disabled people should be dealt with by removing them
from the public sphere. Rather, it is the perhaps now more prevalent
belief that as a society we have already moved past this, disabled
people are no longer excluded, and there is no value in a historical
image that looks to a past better forgotten rather than to the present
or the future.

This post drew a response from other spectators. One called him
a 'fool' and challenged him to provide 'proof and/or evidence of
the closure of ALL institutions in Scotland' (John McG quoted in
Artichoke et al., 2009). Others provided examples of the abuse disabled people are subjected to in public spaces and places on a daily
basis from personal experience (John McG quoted in Artichoke et al.,
2009; Alan Summers quoted in Artichoke et al. 2009), or published
Equality and Human Rights Commission research reports (Kai
quoted in Artichoke et al., 2009). Another reiterated the relevance of
the Niemöeller quote in light of contemporary political debates (Bob
quoted in Artichoke et al., 2009). Yet another told him that Crow's
performance 'perfectly supports Pastor Niemöeller's words that if
you ignore history you are condemned to repeat it' (Kai quoted in
Artichoke et al., 2009).

As with online responses to Marcalo's work, these responses to
Crow's work created a new performance, in which participants negotiated the meaning of Crow's piece, Crow's disability, and contemporary
ways of dealing with disability, amongst themselves. Although posters did not necessarily query the authenticity of Crow's performance,
they did still seemingly need to begin by negotiating the nature,
intent and parameters of the act. This done, the participants – using

tales of personal experience with disabilities – articulated agreement or dissent with the perspective Crow seemed to present, leading to discussion, debate, conflict and even name calling. This new performance, it was clear, was about whether disabled people are still excluded, and whether there's value in a work that looks to a past better forgotten. As with Marcalo's work, naysayers suggested the problem might all be in the artist's perception. They provided 'facts' to dispute this perception. These were, in turn, disputed by others with their own 'facts' that they felt were relevant to the debate. This being the case, the debate was at the level of 'facts', at the level of the concrete logistics of dealing with disability, rather than the level of the cultural logic of disability underpinning current cultural practices and views.

This emphasis on facts rather than deeper ideological forces notwithstanding, by courting uncertainty *Resistance on the Plinth* did, in turn, seem to court continuing dialogue and debate. It demonstrated the ways in which spectators bring their 'self' – the usually unconscious modes of being, behaving and seeing that are embedded in their own bodily *habitus* – to this dialogue. The responses highlighted both the challenges, and the potentials, of public space performance as a vehicle for encouraging spectators to reflect on their own ideas, their own ideologies, and their own contribution to the construction of discourses and ideas about disability. Whether the debate was at the level of fact, or feelings, or ideologies, it did embody an extended reflective engagement with a work whose meaning could not be fully processed in the moment of encounter, making it a productive intervention in the public sphere in which the spectators themselves took primary responsibility for the interpretative labour involved in processing the meanings of the work. The discussion prompted by *Resistance on the Plinth* did draw attention to a range of pressing, concrete problems associated with discourses about the eugenics of genetic testing, euthanasia and assisted suicide in the United Kingdom. As a result, it did draw attention to public assumptions about what it is like to live with pain, impairment and disability – including what it is like to be told constantly that this is intolerable. In this sense, it did draw a community of disabled and non-disabled people together to perform views about the 'tolerability' of disabled people's lives that come up again and again in the United Kingdom.

'Look deeper' – Katherine Araniello's *Suicide Messages*

As discussion of Araniello, Williamson, and their work together under the umbrella of The Disabled Avant Garde in Chapter 2 demonstrated, Araniello in particular shares a lot of Crow's concerns about eugenics, euthanasia and assisted suicide debates in the United Kingdom. She, too, sees the tendency to think or talk about disability in terms of burden, suffering and unbearability as a really contemporary concern, because she, too, shares the confronting experience of having people constantly tell her that her life seems too horrible to live. For Araniello, having people project this sort of narrative onto her disabled body – whether via condescending 'if I were you I would kill myself' style comments or the back-handed 'your capacity to cope is amazing' style compliments – is, of course, personally affronting. These comments display no understanding at all of the fact that pain, impairment or the presence of caregivers in one's day-to-day life, though challenging, may be less problematic than people think, and certainly far less problematic than constantly being told one's life is unfruitful, futile and worthless. '[T]he reality is, if you are disabled in this world, I am not saying it is terrible, I am just saying it is pretty shitty', Araniello says (2010). The negative attitudes are 'pretty shitty'. 'My work', she says, 'is [...] driven by these sort of negative attitudes that people have towards me [in particular,] and disabled people per se or people of difference' (Araniello, 2010).

In this context, it is hardly surprising that Araniello sees a need to challenge the discourses that describe her life as unliveable, and the moments in her day-to-day life where these discourses come up, through her practices. This topic comes out in live public space performances like *Assisted Passage*, and in other live public space performances such as *Terminal Services* (2008) at the Tate, where she adopted a tour guide persona across a variety of digital print, video and performance pieces in gallery spaces and approached people asking them some of the ridiculous comments and questions she gets from passers-by on a daily basis – 'Are you lost?', 'Can I help you?', 'It's great to see you out!', 'I've been specially hired to help people like you', 'Can you move so this man can see the film?', and so forth. It also comes out in a series of mock suicide messages Araniello has been posting on YouTube over the past five years. In *Suicide Message on Valentine's Day* (Araniello, 2007a), Araniello talks about how being disabled is terrible and how she would rather be dead. In *Suicide Haircut* (Araniello, 2007b), Araniello has her hair cut for a trip to Zurich so she can look nice as she exits the world, and tells us about last-minute arrangements she still needs to make to get to Zurich to do this. In *Last Dance* (Araniello, 2007c), Araniello dances on her own and with her dogs before the trip. In *Suicide Interview* (Araniello, 2007d), a regular viewer of Araniello's YouTube messages asks her what is happening with the trip, and then asks to come along to celebrate Araniello's last goodbye with her (Figure 8). In a later piece, *Suicide Mission* (Araniello, 2008), Araniello assures us she still has an ambition to terminate her life, it is just that there are problems getting through Heathrow Airport at the moment, so the trip is on hold until she can be sure it will go smoothly. In still later works, parody, satire and silliness start to come through more strongly. In *Why Do You Want To Die* (Araniello, 2009a), Araniello sings about silly reasons for dying in a drag persona. In *Our Time To Die: A Satirical Look at Assisted Suicide* (Araniello, 2009b), a jazz song

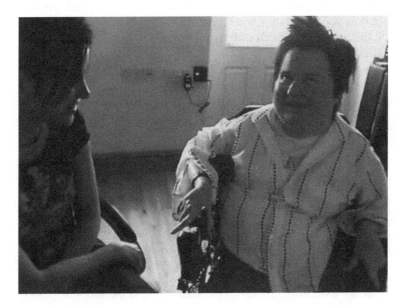

Figure 8 Katherine Araniello in *Suicide Interview*, YouTube, 2009 (Photo: Katherine Araniello)

about the euthanasia blues runs beneath a slideshow and a series of snippets of public discussion and debate how bad being disabled is and how natural it is for people to want to end their suffering.

These *Suicide Messages* – pieces Araniello has created specifically for online spaces – clearly constitute a series of guerrilla-style interventions in one of today's most contested public spaces, the online space, in which networks, community relationships and negotiations about cultural norms are constantly playing out. In these performances, as in her live performances, Araniello is trying to re-engage, reenact and re-envision the encounter between disabled and non-disabled people by drawing passers-by – googlers-by? posters-by? – into a recitation of attitudes that typify the daily social drama of disability, at least from her own perspective as a physically disabled person. The aim, again, is to draw people's attention to the part they play in perpetuating specific ideas about disability (as a burden, shame or unbearable). 'I think personally that I am in a unique position', Araniello says, '[...] I can really string along the public, and that sounds as if the work is only about stringing along the public, which of course it is not' (Araniello, 2010). It is, Araniello says, 'about reinventing a world and then, in a sense, turning it upside down and creating different parameters and different structures for people to operate in' (Araniello, 2010).

As the *Suicide Messages* examples suggest, Araniello's performances are typically more guerrilla in their style than Marcalo's or Crow's. They are difficult to distinguish from the daily life – or the daily online life – they intervene into. Certainly, Araniello does use a range of performance strategies to blur the boundaries between fact, fiction and cultural fantasy in all her live and online interventions in public spaces and places. She uses parody in the imagery, clothing and songs she chooses to include in the performances, exaggeration and absurdity. In particular, she typically pushes to an extreme the stereotype of the poor suffering disabled person who produces a 'bad' self-expression poem, song or performance we still have to applaud to be polite. It is, though, fair to say that the relationship between the actuality of the artist's disability and the artifice of the activist strategies the artist uses are – at least in some of this work – less than clear to spectators. There is, for some spectators, less uncertainty over whether they are seeing actuality or artifice, which, as Lehmann (2006) would suggest, makes it less challenging for them to apply a ready-made response to this image of a disabled woman wanting to die. '[T]he idea was to do it absolutely deadpan so the viewer wouldn't really know what it was', Araniello says, but 'to me it's so obvious that I'm not in any way thinking about contemplating suicide' (Araniello, 2010), because there is so much exaggeration, parody and pushing stereotypes to extremes going on in the later *Suicide Messages* in particular. Still, she says, 'many people didn't catch the irony' (Araniello, 2010), even in some of the silliest of the works. '[T]o me it's a really hilarious piece. To a non-disabled audience, it becomes a very serious piece because they do not know how to receive it' (Araniello, 2010). It is almost as though, although there may be a suspicion that Araniello is taking a stereotype too far in these clips, which might normally create uncertainty, confusion and a challenge to meaning-making, some people find it so difficult to believe a woman as severely disabled as Araniello would make fun of her own assigned identity position in this way that they can dismiss this possibility and take the clips as real. The severity of her disability does, as she put it earlier, seem to make a difference in the degree to which she can bring people to believe in the reality of the stereotype she presents. This being the case, Araniello says, the responses to the *Suicide Messages* series ran the spectrum from the unsympathetic, to the sympathetic, to 'Jesus freaks' telling Araniello that she had 'everything to live for' (Araniello, 2010) and should never consider this sort of action.

As Araniello's comments indicate, a closer analysis of actual online responses to her *Suicide Messages* shows that at least some people do seem to mistake the YouTube clips for real clips. Accordingly, some begin their comments by telling Araniello not to commit suicide in the way she says she is planning to. ':(DONT DO IT', as one poster puts it (thefantasticrolster quoted in Araniello, 2008a). Others then point out that it is satire, that Araniello is an artist, and that this work blurs the lines between art and artifice to create debate. '[C]razy lady is not going to kill herself this is 8th video I have seen', one says (havefunhere quoted in Araniello, 2007d), although here the tone does still seem to leave it a little unclear whether the comment-maker is casting this as satire or as simply the actions of a crazy woman that should not concern us too much. 'Okay, people do you realize she's not serious. This is her art, her expression', another says, more clearly casting the work in the realm of artistic representation (TomWings09 quoted in Araniello, 2008a). 'Of course she's not going to do it... It's satire...', still another says, 'Get a sense of humor, people' (imatroll5 quoted in Araniello, 2007d). Some posters do acknowledge that it took time for them to register that it was satirical. 'I gotta tell you, you had me going for a minute, I was ready to dispute everything you said', one says,

> then... it hit me... (Ok ok, I'm not the coldest beer in the fridge, or the brightest bulb in the lamp, or the sharpest knife in the drawer, or the brightest crayon in the box..)well you get the idea... Anyway, I love your humor, and I give you much credit, you are a GREAT actress... lol you got me good... Love it, and hope to see lots more of your vids, umm well before your trip to Zurich, that is...:)
>
> (Cbaz2 quoted in Araniello, 2007a)

Still others start to play along with Araniello. 'Stop making such a scene and get on with it! No seriously, this is deliciously subversive and I hope you inspire others to rethink their lives before doing something very very foolish', another said (knightyknight quoted in Araniello, 2007a).

Although the flow of commentary around Araniello's *Suicide Messages* shares similarities with that around Marcalo and Crow's work, in this case there is less debate about deploying a real disability as art (as in the responses to Marcalo's *Involuntary Dances*) and more debate about the issue itself (as in the responses to Crow's *Resistance on the Plinth*). Some people, though seemingly aware that the *Suicide Messages* series is satirical, suggest that there may still be sensible reasons for contemplating suicide even if these reasons are not:

> I absolutely cannot agree with anything that is being sung here. People want to die for MORE than just their hair being a mess and so on and so forth. I've been suicidal in the past because my parents hat[e] me, my da[d] has abused me emotionally and s—ually, some physical, along with other things that come up in life. Look deeper, it's not about the lifestyle – its about the life that they've been dealt.
>
> (TheBrokenSoul101 quoted in Araniello, 2009a)

Some suggest that even if Araniello is not serious, it may not be a good idea to joke about it because suicide, or thinking and talking about suicide, whether as an attention-seeking strategy or something more, is a coping strategy for some people:

> I know what you mean :/ I think this is more related to euthanasia/ assisted suicide as it says in the description...but still. I've been suicidal but I think this isnt meant to be taken seriously and I find it kinda amusing...but maybe its not fair to joke about something like suicide, when there are people hurting from it? I don't know. I joke about suicide all the time, but that's just a way of coping with staying alive.
>
> (Suikoden26 quoted in Araniello, 2009a)

Indeed, one says suicide isn't always irrational in Araniello's situation – or in situations where people also look like they are functional, but do not seem to have much to live for:

> Also how can people judge whether someone is suicidal because of 'depression' or because of... well, its always depression...but when is it 'justified depression' that is apparently enough to justify assisted suicide? I've been suicidal and people told me my feelings were irrational and that I have things to live for. That's only because I look normal and look like I should be able to function properly and keep myself alive.
>
> (Suikoden26 quoted in Araniello, 2009b)

> I've never known exactly what to think of euthanasia. Seeing people being treated badly/abused/degraded by nursing staff and carers, if I couldn't do anything to get out of that situation then I'd want to die.
>
> (Suikoden26 quoted in Araniello, 2009b)

The notion that disability brings suffering is here aligned with assumptions about that suffering, and even about other sorts of suffering, to argue that wanting to die is rational in some circumstances. Indeed, it is as though this poster is in a bizarre way jealous of Araniello – because Araniello is visibly different her dysfunction and suffering is unquestionable, but the poster is not visibly different so her dysfunction and suffering is questionable. For one of Araniello's interlocutors, at least, the curable have been cured, and it is not illogical for the incurable to want to be dead if they have 'justified depression', or are 'badly treated/abused/degraded' by those around them. The posters do not necessarily advocate for assisted suicide, but they do, in a sense, advocate for some of the cultural logics surrounding the concept – logics that, for many disabled people, are more the issue than the act itself.

The online commentary on Araniello's messages raises issues around self-determination, response to disability, disease, illness and depression, and responsibility (or otherwise) for our own responses to others facing these situations in their daily lives. These issues are complex, and in drawing them out I do not think Araniello is advocating for or against the act of assisted suicide in itself, as much as advocating for a deeper consideration of some of the cultural assumptions and logics that come up when considering motivations for this or similar acts. These motivators do seem to be the point that posters most latch on to in their comments, their performances, and their attempts to challenge, counter or convince the artist and other audience members of a view. Encountering Araniello has in a strange way, it seems, prompted at least one poster to look deeper into themselves, find moments of identification, and moments of difference, even if the worldview this poster shares is somewhat worrying for other spectators now that Araniello has set us to thinking about response and responsibility. Do we take what we read at face value? Do we post back? Do we argue for or against? Or do we argue, instead, to try to make sure that a choice – a free choice we might see as the right of any subject in any situation – is based on something other than cultural fictions that may be designed to serve society more than the individual subject in it? For subsequent spectators and posters, worry about what this poster is thinking is likely to leave us, too, feeling rather ambivalent about the sometimes idiosyncratic ideas, discourses and ideologies about liveable and unliveable lives coming out here.

'Before you come out with retarded comments...' – Channel 4's *Cast Offs*

In *Cast Offs*, a Channel 4 mockumentary produced by Jack Thorne, a group of disabled people are asked to cope *Survivor*-style on an island.

The series received a BAFTA award, and much positive commentary on its official Twitter and Facebook sites about the strength of the characters being so clear that people forgot they were disabled and simple watched. The series follows the lives of paraplegic basketball player Dan (Peter Mitchell), blind actor Tom (Tim Gebbels), thalidomide-effected disability activist and dad Will (Mat Fraser), deaf mother-to-be Gabriella (Sophie Wooley), cherubic scientist April (Victoria Wright), and career-seeking dwarf Carrie (Kiruna Stamel). Each of the six episodes in the series features the stories of one of these characters, portrayed in Will, Gabriella and April's cases by some of Britain's best known disabled artists, in a mock documentary fashion. The scenes show the characters developing relationships, fighting, falling in love, doing daily tasks like cooking round a fire, and coping with their animals and the forest environment they find themselves in. The character's task, as Carrie says when she reads a message from one of the show's fictional producers, is to 'prove differently abled people can achieve self-sufficiency'.

Throughout the six episodes, there are silly, satirical and over-the-top moments and a constant flow of crass humour that points to the relationship between the actuality of the actors' disabilities and the artistic strategies of the series. In the episode featuring the aggressive and often annoying Will, for example, we see him in a range of situations in his day-to-day life at home as well as at the camp with the other characters. There are scenes that confront us with some of our assumptions about the disabilities. In one, for example, we see Will embarrassing his son by becoming exaggeratedly loony, racing around, roaring at the camera, after scoring a goal in a street soccer game. In another, we see him punching and kicking – and encouraging son Jake to punch, kick and kill – a plastic boxing practice figure which, like Will himself, lacks normal length arms. In both cases, the character's aggression, embodied in Fraser by a martial arts expert with the ability to really let fly with the turns, kicks and thrusts, starts to go that bit too far. These moments are contrasted with scenes that show articulacy, an agenda, and a lot of anger, such as a scene where Will talks to the others to encourage them to continue the challenge, to not admit defeat, because for disabled people to admit defeat is what 'they' want. They are contrasted, too, with more poignant moments, such as the moment when April has to tell Will that the producers have just sent a message to say that his mother has died, and, quietly, all he can say is that she was sick or that he can be grateful it was not his son. There are politic moments, too, for example when Will describes Daniel Day Lewis's 'cripface' performance of disability in *My Left Foot* as 'the blacking up of the twenty-first century'. The combination of scenes at the camp, together with scenes following the characters in their lives in the year leading up to the experiment, gives the spectator a sense of the perhaps unanticipated broadness of the physical and personality attributes of the characters.

The responses of spectators who have seen clips of the series on YouTube do, however, again point to conflicted readings of, and relationships to, the images of disability *Cast Offs* depicts. Responses to *Cast Offs* again begin with debate about whether the series is or is not real. One poster says, 'I am not disabled. I haven't watched this programme. I don't watch a lot of programmes. I saw the trailers. Is it real? Or drama? I wasn't sure from the few brief trailers I saw' (wasssuppp08 quoted in Channel 4, 2009b). Some people say the series is real. 'I love these kinds of programs; it is great to see disabled people putting their issues to one side and trying to get the most out of their lives!' (New European Tigress quoted in Channel 4, 2009b). 'Its 10000 % real life! Its a documentary of how they all can work together and cope out in the out doors with out any aid except for relying on each others help and support' (New European Tigress quoted in Channel 4, 2009b). Others clarify, suggesting the series is not real, but is based on the real lives of real disabled people. 'It's not documentary but it is based on real disabled people' (dervish2173 quoted in Channel 4, 2009b). Still others say that the series is not real and, in doing so, show a real condescension to people who may have thought it was:

It's a comedy drama. It is not real. The way you can tell is when the credits at the end display the actors' real names. This happens surprisingly frequently in programmes which means that everytime it happens, the people on your television are actors, they are not taking part in a documentary. This might mean that a lot of other 'documentaries' you watch on Channel 4 aren't real life – Peep Show for example. Sorry to break it to you, but you need to know.

(Toobecks quoted in Channel 4, 2009b)

The reason for some of this confusion may, Fraser says, be the fact that the producers had in developing the series decided to interview the actors selected for each role to learn more about their lives. This was, in the end, used in the writing process. Accordingly, Fraser says, it may have caused a 'blurring' of character and actor – a 'blurring' perhaps greater than the blurring that always already arises as a result of a disabled actor's corporeal suitability to the roles they are typically asked to play. '[M]y character Will is a sad older guy with an alcohol problem who didn't do very well in relationships', Fraser says, 'and as a result is really bitter about women. A misogynist and old school. He expresses all those opinions in no uncertain terms' (Fraser, 2010). In fact, the character expresses these opinions to the point of crassness in overly sexual, offensive and vulgar comments about men, women and sex which might seem to point to the satirical status of the mockumentary. Still, Fraser says, '[T]he next day I got onto Facebook and there were people saying "oh I didn't know you were like that"' (Fraser, 2010). Casual acquaintances had put the character in the performance together, perhaps, with Fraser's long history of interest in examining the sexuality of people with disabilities, engaging with forms like burlesque, or something from their own experience and expectations not connected to him at all, and come to the conclusion that the character was real rather than a representation of a type. There were, Fraser confirms, plenty of flags that the performances in *Cast Offs* were not really real – if not in the exaggeration in the roles, then at least in the camera movements, editing and other conventions. However, these clearly were not enough for some spectators to be clear about the status of the work. 'I didn't know whether to be offended or flattered', Fraser says, '[...] Randoms, fans, I don't have a fan page, but randoms, fans and um... you know, light acquaintances [were making these types of comments]. I was like, hello folks, it's called acting' (Fraser, 2010).

In the social media conversations about *Cast Offs*, disagreement about this point leads to arguments – both about the show's status as representation or reality, and about the show's depiction of disabled people. A number of people applauded the series for showing disabled people trying to be normal, but, ironically, attempted to make their point by calling other posters 'dumb' or 'retarded' or other terms pejorative to disabled people:

> You don't know a thing at all! badpenguin talking shit; this program is not a drama... it is REAL!!! Dumb ass.
> (New European Tigress quoted in Channel 4, 2009b)

> Your so thick; it is a reall life issue on disabled people trying to survive on each others support! Your so fucking thick; do your research before you come out with retarded comments like that! I hate it when people like u think that they know every thing! Dumb ass hole!
> (New European Tigress quoted in Channel 4, 2009b)

Amongst those who did accept that *Cast Offs* was not real, or not altogether real, a number of people said the series would have provided a better depiction of disabled people trying to cope together if 'better' non-disabled actors had been cast in the series. According to one:

> I actually know someone who was asked to audition for the role of Dan. He, like the guy who ended up playing him, has no acting experience at all so he turned it down, thinking it was like a disability project rather than a serious production, with disability taking precedence over talent. He was absolutely right. I know a lot of people think it's un-PC to have able bodied actors playing disabled parts but I'd much rather have seen that than genuine disabled people who can't act.
> (thelovepigeon quoted in Channel 4, 2009b)

Again, others argued the point – but, it seems, more because the disabled actors are 'nice' and 'great people' and are good role models than because the disabled actors are or could actually be good actors.

> Cant see why people like dervish2173 have to write such hurtful comments about the cast. I have actually met the man which dervish2173 is being prejudiced against and he is a great person in real life. Someone who is a great role model and disability advocate. Clearly people like him and Victoria Wright who played April are great in raising awareness of disabilities.
> (fraserkatie quoted in Channel 4, 2009a)

Indeed, some people say they are downright disgusted that people might post anything negative about the disabled actors in the series. 'Having met the actress in real life', one says, 'I have to say that she is very nice. That you would post such a thing implies that you are a despicable human being' (nashertheatheist quoted in Channel 4, 2009a). Another says, 'You are disgusting! I can't believe Channel 4 let filth like you post here!' (3862wilfred quoted in Channel 4, 2009a). This said, still other posters suggest the series is offensive and disgusting regardless of whether or not it was real, whether or not it was using real people as actors, or whether or not these real people were nice, talented, and so on. '[M]y dad is a care worker and works with the mentally ill/disabled honestly this offends', one says, 'i know what it is really like and this is taking the piss tbh. Its not fun and games nor should it be played out to be. (masterchiefx2 quoted in Channel 4, 2009a). At this point, posters' comments on *Cast Offs* seemed to come full circle, back to the concerns about presenting disability as art – particularly as satirical, subversive live art – that came out so strongly in Marcalo's work, if not as strongly in Crow's or Araniello's work. For such posters, it seems, disability might be a theme, topic or motivator for theatre workshops in the 'helping and healing' paradigm, but not for funny, confronting or controversial performance in either mainstream or more experimental formats. By re-engaging and satirically re-enacting stereotypes about disabled people, *Cast Offs* caused confusion, conflict and a need to negotiate between different points of view, some of which seem to some posters to downplay the seriousness of disability. It became, at least for some of these spectators-become-performers, another example of why disability should not be played out as subversive performance on stage or on screen.

Scripts of spectatorship?

Although responses to these YouTube clips, commentaries, media releases and reviews of performances by Marcalo, Crow, Araniello and others differ, the commonalities are also somewhat striking. In each case, the online platform becomes a place not just for recording memories of an original performance – which posters may or may not have seen – but for a new performance, which goes well beyond remembering or remediating the original. In each case, the posters perform a debate about disability politics. Indeed, there is a surprisingly common dramaturgical structure and characters in the different debates about Marcalo's, Crow's, Araniello's and Thorne's work. In most cases, posters start with a claim about their authority to perform a role in this debate, linked to disclosure of personal experiences or memories of disability – I have this condition, I know somebody who has this condition, etcetera, so I have authenticity, knowledge and authority. This is followed by clarification of the parameters of the original act, and the uncertainties or potential uncertainties this has or may have created in the minds of those who have encountered it. Posters argue about whether the acts are authentic, whether the acts are art, and even, paradoxically – with *Involuntary Dances* and *Cast Offs* – whether the acts are authentic enough and/or too authentic to be art. Posters debate the relationship between reality and representation. Should real lives, real traumas and real people's predicaments ever be seen as art? Some say making disability into art – subversive art, satirical art or live art – denies its seriousness. They say these artists are turning their disability into something comic, controversial or a circus for the media. In some cases, posters claim disgust, insult or offence because the work counters or trivializes their own identity claims. In other cases, posters take offence because the work confirms the idea that some disabled people simply won't do the right thing, follow doctors' orders, take advantage of cures and inclusivity, and thus overcome their own problems. In still other cases, posters take offence because they think these problems have largely been overcome in a contemporary, politically correct society. This leads to debate about how people should or should not deal with disability. A debate which, ironically, can sometimes even embody implicit prejudice as posters label those with contrary views 'retards', or tell them they're projecting their personal psychological problems onto others, or judge people in terms of very conventional definitions of art, theatre and talent. In some cases, the phenomenon Davidson (2008: 6) has observed, whereby people find it difficult to observe art made by people with disabilities outside a medical or therapeutic model, which is more about supporting, healing or advocating for people with disabilities than about aesthetic or political agendas, pops up at this point. As the debate unfolds other posters offer counter-claims, confirming the validity of the artist's views, and the comic or political efficacy of the artist's work. There is, in some of the more cohesive communities (such as the Disability Arts Online community), acknowledgement that the typically 'private sphere' status of the conditions now being debated in public is bound to make emotions run high, and acknowledgement that the work has at least got us talking about the issues. There is, in other words, acknowledgement that the negotiations occurring here do need to happen if dominant attitudes towards disability are to be confirmed, challenged or changed, and this in itself makes the dialogues unfolding here worthwhile.

Although responses to these works differ, then, they do clearly capture some common anxieties. A number of the posters raise concerns about acts which blur the boundaries between fact, fiction and fantasy – acts that cause confusion, uncertainty, a need to think about how oneself, others and one's society ought to respond. These acts, this social media commentary seems to confirm, can challenge the identity positions, cures and inclusivity mechanisms that some of the posters want very much to believe in to bolster their status as a politically correct person who deals with disability well. The challenge draws posters into a dialogue, a debate between different cultural logics, of varying depth or length. Occasionally, the dialogue gives a glimpse of one poster thinking through their perspective, grasping their similarities, differences and upsets with others, and other perspectives, as they try to articulate their own view. Even if this is not characteristic of each and every post. And even if, as in some of the comments around Araniello's *Suicide Messages*, the poster's developing perspective is likely to leave later participants, posters or readers even more worried about the worldviews people find their way into than they initially were – or, indeed, worried about whole new issues. This being the case, these encounters – these re-enactments of the daily social drama of disability – do offer performers and spectators-as-performers at least some opportunity to participate in contesting the ideas about disability that currently circulate in the public sphere.

How productive are these encounters? Are they really, as scholars like Peggy Phelan (1993) might suggest, an example of how performance draws us into an ethical encounter? At one level, analysis of these encounters demonstrates that disabled artists' recitation of the daily social drama of disability does appear to create the conditions of possibility for an ethical encounter, even if the spectatorial responses, and the results, are predictably unpredictable. The unconcluding dialogue between a range of different worldviews that for Conquergood (1985: 9) characterizes the ethical encounter is clearly developing in at least some of the discussions in these online platforms. There are examples of people dealing with questions they do not necessarily know how to answer (Ridout, 2009). Indeed, this is presumably what prompted at least some of the posters to take the time – be it a moment, a minute or more – to write a post and become part of the discussion with performers and fellow spectators-as-performers. The decision to participate creates an opportunity to consolidate or convince others of one's own viewpoint. But, at the same time, it also creates an opportunity to become open or vulnerable to the viewpoints of others, who they may never be able to categorize, control or comprehend as fully as they would have liked to. At another level, though, it is striking how often the debate in these online platforms operates at the level of facts, proofs and positively verifiable examples of whatever point a poster is trying to make. This comes out, for example, in the authority claims in so many of the posts – I have this condition, I know somebody who has this condition, my parent/partner/friend works with people who have this condition, if you look at the literature on this condition, and so forth. For a lot of posters, it seems, this dialogue, debate and negation about different attitudes towards disability hinges on a desire to try to prove particular facts, which might provide answers to heretofore unanswerable questions, and thus shut down the confusion, uncertainty and ethical challenge experienced here in one or another side's favour. Whether the posters return to the social media platforms to check if their facts have shut down debate or been deterritorialized again by the comments of others is rather variable.

The longer term impact of a dialogue that operates on this level – a dialogue that concentrates on facts without necessarily broaching the more insidious ideological beliefs that underpin any argument based on facts – is worth considering. This level of dialogue does allow for argument, and ambivalent responses, if not fully fledged reflection, in particular posts or chains of posts. But it also allows for recuperations in which dialogue at the interstices of performance, history, memory, habit and technology ultimately reinforces an individual poster's belief that their ideas about disability are the right ideas. Accordingly, these online performances, and the cascading circles of new performances that come from them, still present the same risks seen in the live performances considered in Chapters 1 and 2.

Looking at the comments on Marcalo's, Crow's, Araniello's and Thorne's work, the balance between reflection and recuperation possible in the discussion platforms seems to have something to do with the nature of the community operative on the particular platform. Some platforms lend themselves to single state-my-opinion and go performances. Others lend themselves to more to-and-fro performances. In the latter, there seems to be more potential for dialogue to go longer and deeper, and thus more potential for developing, challenging or changing participants' points of view on particular issues. In the debate about Marcalo's piece on Disability Arts Online, for example, one poster finished a rather scathing remark with the words 'Please continue talking' (Richard Johnson quoted in Verrent, 2009). Here – the level of the debate, dialogue and perception change notwithstanding – is a clearly expressed desire to continue performing, continue negotiating. Indeed, this particular poster did seem to be improvising or 'riffing' off his existing views, and adapting, expanding or altering some of those strongly held views (or, at least, the range of views he felt relevant to the debate) as the debate unfolded. As part of this process, language and points raised by other posters became part of this poster's own performance. This indicates that these online performances offered some marginalized people an opportunity to perform, improvise and participate in interpretative labour that is valued and appreciated. Not always comfortable, as long-held habitual views are challenged, but nonetheless valued and appreciated by members of a minority community who have not always had opportunities to participate in the negotiations that figure and reconfigure the public sphere. These online performances – not just rememberings or remediatings of an original but themselves new citations of contested cultural logics – raised passions, tempers and anxieties for many of those who participated. Particularly for those who did not want to think that their politically correct attitudes towards disabled people were not appreciated. But, at the same time, they also offered a voice to people who might not otherwise have an opportunity to participate in the debate that was, in at least some cases, considered worthwhile.

4
Same Difference?: Disability, Presence, Performance and Ethics

The meaning of the body emerges through acts of seeing, looking and staring in daily and dramatic performances – acts in which social performers and social spectators play, improvise or 'riff' off socially scripted parts. In Western culture, the daily social drama of disability has historically cast the disabled body as a source of fear, deficiency or pity. The artists discussed throughout this book seek, via subversive repetition of the stories, roles and scenography that underpin daily and dramatic performances of disability, to destabilize stereotypes from within. They do this in productively live spaces and places, sometimes in theatres, galleries or installation spaces in which the fourth wall no longer exists, and sometimes in the very public streets, shopping malls or social media in which the stereotypes circulate. Although Cunningham, Lakmaier, Jones, Shannon, Araniello, Williamson, Crow and the other artists considered here create very different types of performances, they do seem to deploy some distinctive performance strategies. They play out a more or less exaggerated, abstracted or absurd image of the role society assigns them in public spaces or places. In doing so, they prompt spectators-as-performers to replay their own socially assigned role in response. They use commentary, counter-position or other devices – characters, staging, proliferation of shifting perspectives or calls for specific sorts of spectatorial responses – to position their performance as a reality, and a representation of something more than its own reality, at once. The blurred boundaries between performance and social process make it more difficult for spectators to respond to the drama unfolding before them. This, combined with the fact that

148

the spectator-as-performer is often on the spot and in the spotlight in these practices, raises the stakes of the spectators' responses. The dual framing, and the confusion, undecidability and uncertainty this creates, can result in an uncomfortable deferral of meaning-making. It can, if the right conditions come together in the moment, result in a liminal moment in which spectators start to think about how their own interpretative habits, and the ways of looking, seeing and being seen that underpin these interpretative habits, contribute to the construction of disabled and non-disabled identities. There are, as analysis of social media responses to artists with disabilities in Chapter 3 demonstrates, scripts for both performing and spectating in the daily social drama of disability that are so prevalent they can be played out repeatedly with recognizable plot points, twists and turns in their dramaturgy. To contest, negotiate or renegotiate these usually unconscious interactions can be confronting, but, at the same time, very worthwhile – particularly for performers, spectators, and spectators-become-performers who do not feel they have histori-cally had much of a voice in the contestation of ideas, discourses and ideologies that characterize the public sphere.

Though it may not in and of itself be enough to create the condi-tions of possibility for an ethical encounter in a performance context, the presence of the disabled body in productively live spaces and places is – or, at least, on the surface appears to be – a significant part of the performance strategies and potential for impact in the works discussed here. It is part of what makes the dual framing, the dual awareness of fact, fiction and fantasy, and thus the uncertainty about how to respond to the questions the work appears to be asking, possi-ble. Certainly, dual consciousness of the reality and representational significance of Lakmaier's disabled body in her living installations, Marcalo's disabled body in her involuntary dances, or Araniello's disabled body in her suicide messages, is part of what potentially prompts reflection in these works. This is perhaps why spectatorial responses to this sort of work in social media platforms – which show negotiations that usually go unseen – so often start with queries about the authenticity, knowledge and authority of artist and specta-tor alike, and about the relation between authenticity and artifice in the artist's work. The state, status and meaning of the disabled body is, at least in part, what makes frames fuzzy and meaning-making fraught in these works. It is, at least in part, and at least potentially, what prompts spectators-become-performers to start thinking about their beliefs, attitudes and behaviours.

Clearly, though, the process remains unpredictable. Different spectators bring different histories, memories, habits of interpretation and perspectives, and it is thus difficult to predict the images or moments that may complicate meaning-making for a given spectator. Still, whilst there is no way of guaranteeing the emergence of the uncertainty that creates the conditions of possibility for an ethical encounter – and there are always going to be spectators who reterritorialize what they see with a reductive ready-made responses – the presence of the disabled body does seem to impact on the performance's ability and approach to cultivating ethical encounters. It may not be the only way of encouraging such an encounter with the Other. It may not even be the privileged way of encouraging such an encounter with the Other theorists like Peggy Phelan (1993) or Hans Thies Lehmann (2006) suggest it to be. It is, though, a strategy that appears to be harnessed with regularity in the practices considered here, and one that is pivotal in creating undecidability, dialogue, and a long space – a long period of interpretative anxiety and what Helena Grehan (2009) would call ambivalence – between seeing the work, processing the work, and making meaning of the work.

Over the course of this study, though, one of the things that has interested me is the fact that disabled artists do not have, and have never had, ownership over experiences, images or motifs of cognitive or corporeal difference. It sometimes seems that almost everyone feels they have had some experience of having to perform their own identity as Other at some stage, in some situation, somewhere along the line – even if it is as an able, white male who wishes they did not have to live up to some of the expectations society lays out for that identity that they find personally difficult. Indeed, some of the artists discussed here deliberately invoke an ambiguous image of difference, difficulty fitting in or difficulty functioning to encourage spectators to relate emotionally if not literally to the experience of Otherness. Lakmaier, for example, does exactly this in works like *We Are for You Because We Are Against Them* when she puts people in the large spherical balls she calls weebles, making their movements strange and difficult. She is deploying a sense, if not a literal situation, of difference and the difficulty of fitting in that participants, spectators-become-performers and passers-by might relate to.

That images, motifs and metaphors of disability can become broadly relatable is, on the whole, a positive thing. Making disability more relatable may make it more difficult for spectators to interpret experiences of Otherness as personal problems which, as noted in the Introduction, tend not to be seen to have anything to do with broader social or political concerns. Although physically, psychologically or socially confronting, then, work which makes disability more broadly relatable may aid in drawing spectators' attention to the way they – like disabled people – are unconscious, unwitting or unwilling performers in the daily social drama of disability, albeit in different roles. It may highlight difficulties with well-intentioned politically correct responses to disabled people, including helping them, acknowledging their humanity and accepting that they would be different if they could. It may even be validating or community-building as disabled and non-disabled people come to new understandings of each other as Other and of many specific others.

As a result of the work of scholars, activists and artists such as those considered here, there has undoubtedly been some level of shift in dominant discourses about disability in the past decade or so. Ideas about controlling, curing and overcoming disability persist. But there are also now some discourses that suggest that the differences disability so readily signifies are in fact a positive, productive thing. These discourses go beyond the idea of emotional, if not literal identification, with a range of different differences invoked in works like Lakmaier's. They return in a strange way to some of the initial power and productivity people associated with fairs, sideshows and freakshows as public spectacles of provocative corporeal differences with the power to shift what it means to be a human being. These discourses are, for example, seen in efforts to reclaim, validate and valorize the experiences of Otherness in modern cultural practices such as the phenomenon of voluntary enfreakment. In this phenomenon, able-bodied people deliberately differentiate, modify or queer their body with folk surgery, implants, tattoos and the like, to break free or get beyond the average. This is part of a distinctively postmodern desire to break free from the constraints of culturally condoned identity categories altogether. It is a phenomenon some of the artists I have discussed in this book have remarked on. As Mat Fraser says in his documentary *Born Freak*, when he finds out that a company of self-created freaks is competing with his show *Sealboy: Freak*, which places the historical reality of sideshow performer Stanley Berent better known as 'Sealo' against the contemporary reality of disabled actor Tam, for audiences at the Edinburgh Fringe Festival, '[t]he irony is, these days, everyone is trying to get in on our act' (2001).

In these and similar situations, Carrie Sandahl claims, the signs, symbols and somatic idiosyncrasies of the disabled body are increasingly being transported or translated into cultural narratives in theatre, film, literature and other media as metaphors for expressing every body's experience of – or desire for – Otherness (2004: 579–602). They are being mobilized as a potent metaphor or 'master trope' (2004: 583) for imag(in)ing bodily difference in Western culture. This means symbols associated with the disabled body are being reappropriated and recontextualized not just by disabled artists, but by other artists, too, as positive symbols of difference, self-determination and sovereignty over one's own mode of being. They are becoming a preferred way of representing, and (ostensibly) valorizing, a broader spectrum of different differences that have very little to do with the realities of (pain and impairment that are part of) being disabled. In contemporary culture, and contemporary performance culture, this reappropriation of the disabled body becomes part of a move from a coalitionist identity politics to a queer politics concerned with diverse mobilizations of difference. Or, indeed, a move from what Eve Kosofsky Sedgwick would call a universal, majoritarian politics to a specific, minoritarian politics (1990: 91). A whole range of non-disabled artists operating in this paradigm appropriate the images, motifs and performance strategies identified as distinctive in the work of the disabled artists discussed in this book thus far. This happens in performance art – for example, Guillermo Gómez Peña's use of a wheelchair in combination with a plethora of other pop cultural signifiers to create a more extreme or shocking representation of racial otherness in works like *Museum of Fetishized Identities* (2000) or *Chamber of Confessions* (1994). This happens in performance – for example, Marie Chouinard's use of crutches, canes and walkers in *bODY rEMIX / gOLDBERG vARIATIONS* to explore and represent dancers' experience of becoming different or mutant during dance training. This also happens in pop culture – indeed, in the most popular of cultural performances, and in a perhaps surprising inclusion in a study that has so far focused on the other end of the spectrum – for example, characters on canes, on walkers or in wheelchairs in television programmes such as *Glee* or *House*.

In this chapter, I chart some of the changing representations of the disabled body in these contexts, and consider what happens when non-disabled artists co-opt images of the disabled body to draw attention to, affirm, and even exoticize, eroticize or beautify other modalities of, or desires for, difference. What is it about cultural concepts of the disabled body that lead artists like Gómez Peña, choreographers like Chouinard, or creators of thoroughly over-the-top programmes, like *Glee*, or *House* or others, to see images of the disabled body so apposite to their own representational agenda? Why would non-disabled artists want to invoke the material, embodied experience of disability as a metaphor in service of what the choreographer Chouinard calls her own 'exercise of freedom' (Brisbane Festival, 2008)? What are the pleasures, perils and implications of non-disabled people's desire to metaphorically transpose the trope of disability onto their own experience of corporeal difference as Otherness? What does it say about a broader politics of embodiment? What does it say about presence, liveness, and the physical specificity of the disabled body as components deployed in creating the conditions of possibility for an ethical encounter? What effect does a decision to use disability to express one's own fascination with or celebration of 'dis' or 'diff' ability have on spectators? Do spectators identify with these fragmented, augmented or alien bodies? Do they see the emergence of once repressed Others, no longer silenced, censored or negated? Do they enter into uncertain, conflicted meaning-making encounters of the sort discussed in the previous chapters? Do they engage with their own sense of Otherness? Perhaps most critically, does it make any difference if it is able or disabled bodies deploying or sparking debate about Otherness in these ways? Do the performance strategies identified in this book hold just as much potential to create the conditions of possibility for a productive, political or ethical encounter whether deployed by abled or disabled artists? Or is this just an example of what theorists have called 'disability drag', 'cripdrag' or 'cripface' (Anna, 2009; Kociemba, 2010a; Siebers, 2008:114; Smith, 2010a)?

The reclamation of disability as a metaphor for a range of different differences in what Gómez Peña calls the 'mainstream bizarre' spectacle of daily life (2004: 287–98), in theatre, film and television practices, and in theoretical figurations of feminist philosophy that favour the grotesque, monstrous and mechanical (Haraway, 1991;

Braidotti, 1994), certainly raises real questions for scholars like Garland Thomson (2002: 9) and artist scholars like Sandahl (2004: 581–3). When a disability motif becomes a metaphor for a range of different differences, Sandahl says, it loses its currency as a politically useful category around which materially specific subjects, with materially specific personal, social, economic and political issues, can mobilize their own interventions in the public sphere (2004: 583). The concern for scholars like Sandahl, then, is that deploying disability as a signifier for a range of different differences – or for the idea that we can all be together in different differences that are somehow the same difference – has the potential to usurp a trope by which disabled people can and currently do generate an activist aesthetics and politics that speaks back to dominant culture. Petra Kuppers has expressed similar concerns. We have, she says, reached 'a point in modernity when extraordinary bodies have currency as lifestyle accessories, when alienation value is eroded by the ubiquity of difference that is consumed and repackaged' (Kuppers, 2004: 3). But '[w]hen nondisabled people don disability paraphernalia or masquerade as disabled, the results rarely offer interesting insights to disability scholars looking for resistance to dominant images of disability', she says:

> [...] As a long time wheelchair, crutch and cane user, I know the sensuous and choreographic potential of chairs and other mobility paraphernalia onstage, but as a disability-culture activist and scholar, I am also aware of the negative stereotypes and narrative shortcuts a chair often provides.
>
> (Kuppers, 2007: 81)

In voicing these sorts of concerns, disability artists, scholars and activists are not necessarily arguing that these motifs and images are for them alone to use. As Fraser says, 'the early disability movement did that, they told everybody they were not allowed to do stuff, and I am anti that, I think anyone can talk about anything' (Fraser, 2010). It is, rather, the lack of interesting, expansive and ethically engaged encounters with others that emerges in a lot of this sort of work that can be a worry. Fraser, for example, considers the differences between seeing a contemporary dance company using disability to develop an 'innovative', 'new' or 'interesting' movement vocabulary, and seeing disabled dancers work creatively with their own movement vocabulary. '[I]t looked like a party at the mental hospital for people with cerebral palsy', he says of one work he saw where able bodied dancers were spasming and spatisticating their bodily movements. It was, Fraser says, 'really apparent to me when I saw it that they were borrowing physical movement from disability heavily to impress audiences with their "wow, new", choreography', and whilst that is okay, 'it all got a bit much towards the end' (Fraser, 2010). The work offered no engaging, uncertain cultural negotiations with the idea of disability, the idea of disability in dance, or the idea of dance movement itself. 'A lovely juxtaposition to that would be Claire Cunningham's show', he says. 'Claire Cunningham uses crutches and does a crutch-heavy-floaty dance piece, a good piece' (Fraser, 2010). As these comments attest, it can be frustrating to watch, and watch other spectators watch, a work which is simply another recuperation of disability in service of someone else's aesthetic, cultural or political agenda – particularly for artists, scholar artists and scholars familiar with the broader possibilities for this sort of work.

In this concluding chapter, then, I want to consider practices in which able-bodied people reclaim disability – this time not as a metaphor for negative character traits, or for something flawed, corrupt or pitiful, but as an example of human problems, human potential and the human capacity to overcome. I want to ask if, and if so how, the distinctive performance techniques identified in the work of artists with disabilities can be effective when employed by artists without disabilities. Doing this does, I think, deepen understanding of if, when and how the types of work I have considered throughout this book work. In this sense, examining this cultural shift is an important part of analysing how active, interactive encounters with materially distinctive disabled bodies in public space performance create the conditions of possibility for the face-to-face ethical encounter with the Other that philosophers like Emmanuel Lévinas describe.

Guillermo Gómez Peña – *The Museum of Fetishized Identities*

One of the best known examples of a non-disabled live or performance artist appropriating images of disability would be the Mexican American artist Guillermo Gómez Peña. In provocative, confrontational performance pieces about fear of the racially Other, Gómez Peña and his collaborators in the La Pocha Nostra company use wheelchairs, along with a whole host of other colonial and pop cultural signifiers of otherness, to draw attention to the problematic ways of seeing, imaging and imagining their 'brown' bodies that dominate in mainstream America. 'Gómez-Peña is', as Kuppers explains, 'interested in exploring fantasies and cultural stereotypes, in particular Anglo visions, desires, and fears of Latino/Latina embodiments' (Kuppers, 2007: 82). He and his collaborators create a bizarre collection of characters that capture the traits Latino/Latina Americans are associated with in the US cultural imaginary. They replay these characters across their own corporeally suitable bodies, in combination with commentary, proliferation of artefacts, and interaction with audiences. In this sense, Gómez Peña's performances use strategies similar to those used by women and disabled artists who work with extreme, exaggeratedly literal and in Rebecca Schneider's (1997) terms 'explicit' remobilization of stereotypes across their own corporeally suitable bodies (Chapter 2; cf. Hadley, 2008).

In *Two Native Amerindians Visit* (1992), for example, Gómez Peña and his collaborator Coco Fusco make the symbolic association of Native American peoples and animals clear by placing themselves in a cage filled with mock native artefacts and the detritus of commodity culture (Goodall, 1999: 127). In *The Museum of Fetishized Identities* (2000), Gómez Peña and his collaborators present themselves as ethnocyborgs, outlaw characters and other museum exhibits there for the education and amusement of audiences (2004: 97). He has even asked spectators to feed their own ideas into the construction of the freakish characters by sending in surveys or 'images, sounds and texts about how [they feel] Mexicans, Chicanos and Native Americans should look, behave and perform' (Gómez Peña, 2005: 57; Gómez Peña quoted in Giannachi, 2004: 145). In such works, Gabriella Giannachi says, 'the performers solicit the viewers' racist and prejudiced opinions and act them out in a courageous act of political confrontation' (2004: 148). They give spectators a perverse sort of permission to inhabit their most racist beliefs about other bodies.

> My colleagues and I have explored the multi-screen spectacle of Other-as-freak by decorating and 'enhancing' our brown bodies with special effects make-up, hyperethnic motifs, hand-made 'low-rider' prosthetics and braces, and what we term 'useless' or

'imaginary' technology (that is, with special, ritual or performative purpose). The idea is to heighten features of fear and desire in the Anglo imagination and 'spectacularize' our 'extreme identities', so to speak, with the clear understanding that these identities have already been invented by the surgery of the global media.

(Gómez Peña, 2004: 297)

As Kuppers notes in her analysis of Gómez Peña's work, disability is one of the tropes he deploys in his works (Kuppers, 2007: 82).

In *The Museum of Fetishized Identities* (Figure 9) and other performances, Gómez Peña takes on a character called El Mex Terminator, a character with bionic arm, who sits in a wheelchair in leather chaps smoking, twitching with 'various spastic movements' (Kuppers, 2007: 82), and having collaborators and spectators help him with tasks like feeding. 'In the figure of El Mex Terminator', Kuppers says, 'a number of these fantasies [about Latino/Latina bodies Gómez Peña

Figure 9 Guillermo Gómez Peña in *The Museum of Fetishized Identities*, The Performance Space, Sydney, 2001 (Photo: Heidrun Löhr)

replays in his work] coalesce, exposing configurations of difference ordered around a figure of disability' (Kuppers, 2007: 93). Kuppers analyses the way the wheelchair, and the activities Gómez-Peña and his collaborators are involved in around the wheelchair such as rituals of helping him, work as a 'meaning maker' (2007: 81) in the work. 'In *Museum*', Kuppers says, 'disability aligns easily with various forms and fantasies of difference' (2007: 82) in interesting ways:

> [F]or Gómez-Peña, redeploying a wheelchair-using character as herald of difference is a 'natural' step, given the dominant significations in popular culture of disabled characters as secondary or weak. The wheelchair operates as a sign of 'other than the norm' aligning itself with the Latino in opposition to the Anglo 'norm.' [...] In his mobilization of the wheelchair, Gómez-Peña brings together two contradictory images that merge, leaving spectators with a sense of cultural unease: the independent and strong tough guy and the wheelchair user.
>
> (Kuppers, 2007: 82)

As Kuppers suggests, Gómez Peña's performance invokes conflicting images, just as Crow's *Resistance on the Plinth* wheelchair performance invoked conflicting images spectators could not easily reconcile. In this case, though, Gómez Peña invokes – metaphorically – cultural narratives that characterize Latinos/Latinas as at once less powerful, less productive or a threat to American jobs on the one hand, and powerful, threatening and responsible for things like gang violence in America on the other hand (Kuppers, 2007: 83). These narratives are, for those who participate in American culture, as familiar and recognizable as the narratives about monsters, corrupt characters with flaws, concealment, cures and overcoming are for people with disabilities. What complicates Gómez Peña's performance even further, however, is the sheer volume of other signifiers invoked here. 'The encounter Gómez-Peña dreams, as well as what *Museum* shows, is', Kuppers argues, 'ruled by too many scripts about stages, postcolonial histories, and the functions of museums to be anything but a contact fantasy' (2007: 82) that is a conflicted, challenging to negotiate clash of desire, fear and non-truths that service specific cultural agendas. '[T]his hybrid figure in a wheelchair is only one nodal point of cultural meaning in a whole gallery full of costumed configurations of embodied semiotics' (Kuppers, 2007: 83). This, for Kuppers, means that 'the wheelchair no longer means tragic immobility but instead stands for the paralyzing effects of colonizing fantasies' (2007: 84). The projected cultural scripts that construct and constrain the racialized body and the disabled body collide in a confusing, uncertain representational structure that – though established via fictions – has real effects.

> [T]he rhetorical use of the wheelchair as a reference for disability shows its sisterhood to these postcolonial practices. Like many of Gómez Peña's props (gas masks, whips, machine guns, cyborg utensils, high-heeled shoes, crosses, angels, etc.), this standard hospital issue wheelchair projects its own history of structural power, made manifest in living people.
>
> (Kuppers, 2007: 84)

Importantly, this complicated, conflicted imag(in)ing of bodies constructed and constrained by cultural histories, memories and fantasies is deployed as part of interactions in which spectators become performers, another affinity with the work of disabled artists discussed here. 'Moving from static display to audience interaction, El Mex involved everybody in the processes of meaning making', Kuppers says (2007: 82). Here, again, spectators-become-performers are involved, implicated and spotlighted in the cultural narratives colliding in the work, aware of their responses, the meaning of their responses, and, potentially, their gaze's affinity to that of 'the colonizer and the ethnologist' (Kuppers, 2007: 82). Choosing a response becomes difficult and this creates – or, at least, has the potential to create – uncertain, ambivalent responses of the sort that typify ethical encounters.

Marie Chouinard – *bODY rEMIX / gOLDBERG vARIATIONS*

In *bODY rEMIX / gOLDBERG vARIATIONS*, French Canadian choreographer Marie Chouinard also presents images of the human body gone awry. Over the course of two 45-minute acts, ten contemporary dancers clad in tiny costumes which resemble beige-coloured bandages are repeatedly born and reborn as an increasingly bizarre series of biotechnical mutants, monsters and hybrids. We, as spectators, are transported into a mutant realm of the imagination, beyond the scope of standard human bodies, behaviours and movements, in which just about anything seems to be possible. The mechanism which drives the dancers' transformations is the unconventional use of prosthetics, including canes, walkers, crutches and harnesses, and the equally unconventional use of dance equipment such as barres and ballet point shoes as prosthetics and pseudo organs. Throughout the two acts the bodies progressively go more and more awry, pseudo organs perpetually displaced onto different parts of the dancers' anatomy – foreheads, hands, mouths, crotches. The impression is, as Alana Thain (2008: 84–92) suggests in her detailed study of the work, one of ongoing scenes of bodily transformation and transmutation.

There are scenes in which a female dancer uses a pair of very short cuff crutches to move across the stage, her legs and feet splayed out behind her. There are scenes in which a male dancer uses ski poles to launch himself into jetés across the stage. There are scenes in which a female dancer puts a microphone into her mouth, producing distorted grunts, groans and breaths. There are scenes in which dancers move themselves or others on mobile walkers or wheelboards. There are scenes in which dancers fly into each other in harnesses that hold them up off the stage. There are also scenes in which ballet shoes are worn on one foot or two, one hand or two, by male and female dancers alike, manipulated to make images of birds, herds of strange gazelles galloping across the stage, and so forth. *bODY rEMIX* ends with a striking image of a female dancer suspended above a set of the prostheses used throughout the performance hanging around her (Thain, 2008: 89). The movement is, throughout, set to a speeded up, slowed down and otherwise distorted soundtrack of Glenn Gould's 1981 recording of Bach's *Goldberg Variations*, interspersed with Gould's comments on the recording (Thain, 2008: 84, 85), and the value of variation and mutation.

bODY rEMIX is billed as

> a spell-binding performance in response to Johann Sebastian Bach's Goldberg Variations [that] us[es] different devices including crutches, rope, prostheses, and harnesses, which at times liberate th[e dancer's] movements, at other times restrict it, and at still others create it.
> (Brisbane Festival, 2008)

There is no doubt it is a spectacular piece, and since it was first produced for the Venice Biennale in 2005 (Thain, 2008: 80) it has been well received both as an example of the precise, formal movement exercises, and as an example of the engagement with the body, gender, sexuality and technology, Chouinard favours in her choreography (Thain, 2008: 89).

Watching the piece, however, two things immediately stand out – two things that make it not just spectacular but an interesting subject in the context of this scholarly analysis of disability in and as performance.

The first thing that stands out is the way *bODY rEMIX* draws heavily on symbols associated with disability, such as canes, crutches and walkers, to achieve both its effects and the questions it raises about the values accorded to these symbols in contemporary culture. In a way, *bODY rEMIX* defies established representations of disability, deformity and bodily difference. Though Chouinard's *bODY rEMIX* is populated by its share of spectacular monsters, mutants and hybrids, there is no sense that these personae function negatively as signs or warnings of what human beings should not be. These are not the monsterly narrative persona that, as noted in Chapter 1, traditionally dominate the Western cultural imaginary. These imag(in)ings of the body, like Gómez Peña's imag(in)ings of the body, seem to have a rather different and more complicated relationship to concepts of human power, potential and status. The dancers, nearly naked but for their bandage-like costumes and their appendages, do not conceal their prostheses, and they do not use their prostheses to create, or create a longing for, the more 'normal' body they clearly are not. Their differences and their difficulties are clear. But these differences and difficulties are not presented as purely negative. Instead, *bODY rEMIX* comes across as an exercise in activating and exploring what Thain (2008: 72) characterizes as new, extended, amplified possibilities for embodiment and embodied interactions with objects, people and places – what Chouinard herself called an 'exercise in freedom' (Brisbane Festival, 2008). The prostheses challenge the dancers' bodies to go beyond their normal movement habits, to find new movements, new relationships and new modes of being. As Thain puts it in her analysis of *bODY rEMIX*, the use of prostheses allows Chouinard's dancers to go beyond the material to connect with the immaterial, virtual dimension of their bodies, the dimension in which their bodies are malleable, with the ability to imag(in)e new connections, the ability to come into new assemblages, and thus the ability to become (Thain, 2008: 76, 88–90). For Thain, following Sarah Jain (1999), the piece is thus about a prosthetic imagination in which the creativity and the potential of the body comes to the fore, 'draw[ing] attention to the ways in which prostheses are simultaneously "wounding and enabling"' (Thain, 2008: 80). There is a sense of a body becoming in a Deleuzian sense – a body becoming something more, changing, transforming – that is, in the end, overwhelmingly positive. It is, for instance, far more unambiguously and unashamedly positive than the imag(in)ing of the body in becoming in works like Cunningham's *Mirage*, discussed in Chapter 1. *bODY rEMIX* juxtaposes fixed and fluid forms, restrictions and freedom, ability and disability to show how one quality is found in, through and within its other (Thain, 2008: 85). The thematic, aesthetic and affective dimensions of the work advocate in favour of difference – and, in particular, the sort of corporeal transformations and transpositions that typify the body disabled through illness, injury or disease.

The second thing that stands out is the fact that, for all the power and presence of its symbols, Chouinard's *bODY rEMIX* isn't 'about' disability. As Thain says, '[w]hile the piece uses medical prostheses such as crutches, the piece is clearly not "about" disability, and the initial meaning of these inanimate items fluctuates as they become animated in various assemblages' (Thain, 2008: 85, 86). The disability signifiers, as Thain suggests here, do immediately start morphing into something else. Whilst Chouinard has cast the work in terms of formal exercises which fabricate strong, suggestive images without necessarily telling a story (cf. Thain, 2008: 79), for me, with the history I bring to the moment, there is a clear story – a story about the dancers' bodies – told metaphorically through the symbolism of disability. Chouinard's dancers trained to work on pointe during the process of developing *bODY rEMIX* (Thain, 2008: 85), and some of the sequences with the pointe shoes as prosthetics seem to me to explicitly engage with the pain experienced by dancers – or, at least, female dancers – while learning to dance this way. In one sequence, for example, a female dancer repeatedly tries to stand on a single pointe shoe, letting out sounds of pain and stress (Thain, 2008: 92). In other sequences, dancers in the harness walk on their pointe shoe clad feed – portrayed as more or less tender, painful or pleasurable – across the hands of other dancers supporting them from below (Thain, 2008: 87). By combining the signs, symbols and tropes of disability with those of the classical dancer, Chouinard's *bODY rEMIX* becomes an extended meditation on the pain, the pleasure and, ultimately, the power experienced by the dancer who finds her- or himself becoming mutant, monstrous and mysteriously 'diff' abled during the course of dance training. In effect, a cast of able-bodied dancers is working with canes, crutches and walkers to construct a complex metaphor for their own sense of difference as their body morphs through the demanding regime of dancing training, their own overcoming, and their own reconciliation with a new, mutant, bodily state (albeit a 'more-than-normal' one more so than a 'non-normal' one). The dancers' bodies are seen to defy boundaries – including boundaries of pain and pleasure – defy expectations, develop new modes of expression, and celebrate bodily difference. The self-inflicted pain these dancers experience during training is figured as a 'disablement' that is ultimately 'enabling', a wounding that is ultimately and simultaneously enabling, to use the terms Thain deployed earlier to describe the work.

Perhaps predictably given the cultural trajectories described at the outset of this chapter, Thain – the only scholar who has considered this work in detail to date – does not see the metaphoric dimension of Chouinard's decision to use disability as a trope to express her own fascination with Otherness as problematic. Indeed, neither did any of the people I saw the performance with at the Brisbane Festival in 2008. This mobilization of mutant personae does, though, reduce the signifiers and symbols of disability it deploys to rhetorical devices. There is a superficial similarity to the work of disabled artists who dance with their crutches such as Bill Shannon or Claire Cunningham, or disabled artists who dance with an array of physical, projected and reflected imag(in)ings of their body in becoming such as James Cunningham. There is, however, no agenda that sets out to consider or convey insight into the complexities, conflicts or contradictions of these modes of embodiment, because they are neatly resolved with a representation of overcoming at the end of the work, which shows that the dancers' decision to become Other than the average human in their dance training is well and truly worthwhile in the final analysis. There is no uncertainty, confusion or uncomfortable deferral of meaning-making that might prompt us to think further here.

In this sense, Chouinard's decision to use disability to construct images of change that are not linked to the realities of disability, nor linked to the reality of any historical, cultural or political oppression – like the racial oppression as in Gómez Peña's work – in *bODY rEMIX* is potentially problematic for disabled spectators. Whilst the human desire to construct narrative and psychological contexts for traumatic, challenging or life-changing experiences – and the usefulness of disability as a metaphor in such narratives – cannot be denied, *bODY rEMIX* clearly carries the representational risks Carrie Sandahl (2004) identifies. In *bODY rEMIX*, disability is a metaphor for the self-differentiated identities of the dancers. It is readily understood in terms of the conventional literary, cinematic or theatrical depictions of disability David Mitchell and Sharon Snyder describe in *Narrative Prosthesis* (2000), where disability is no more than a useful metaphor for the problems people have to get past in life. In this case, it is a metaphor for the problems dancers have to get past in their classical dance training. The use of disability as a metaphorical, rhetorical device means spectators do not have to consider the corporeal reality of the Other. They only have to consider a simple, straightforward representation of the Other, in a singular frame of reference, and it is relatively simple to read the performance in terms of a culturally recognizable 'overcoming' narrative. Read this way, disability is relegated to a discursive and theoretical terrain that never threatens any need to engage with the lived experience of the Other.

Glee – dance, cripdrag and the Artie Abrams character

Chouinard's *bODY rEMIX* is not the only example of the disabled body entering contemporary narratives in theatre, film or television in what appears to be an affirmation of difference but, ultimately, only affirms dominant cultural narratives in which disability is a shortcut for advocating a need for human beings to overcome problems and get on with things. There is an increasing presence of characters with a disability in popular television programmes too, and many of these programmes seem to deploy disability as just this sort of shortcut. There are wheelchair-using characters in many children's and young people's television shows, such as the wheelchair-using character Stevie in the comedy *Malcolm in the Middle*. There are also characters with a range of disabilities in so-called prime-time shows;

the cane-using doctor Gregory House in medical drama *House* and the wheelchair-using character Artie Abrams in *Glee* being two of the most popular. Whilst media research suggests that such characters are still not seen regularly enough to match the proportion of people with disabilities in the general population in most countries, and that these programmes are rather unrepresentative in terms of their emphasis on mainly male, mainly white, mainly middle-class disabled characters (IAMPWD, 2010), there are enough emerging to make this a topic of interest for scholars. These characters are at one level clearly linked with a desire to bring images of the disabled body into the scope of the normal amongst some television producers. Although television is typically seen as remarkably unreflective, unresponsible or unperformative, or at least at the opposite end of the spectrum to live art when it comes to responsibility, the inclusion of these sorts of characters is, in a sense, a considered one. There is no doubt the producers of a show such as *Glee* would say they included a character in a wheelchair because the people in the target audience will certainly encounter wheelchair users in now-integrated education systems, so they are simply representing a reality in their programme. Or, perhaps, constructing an inclusive reality in their programme. This said, the characters are, at another level, linked with ongoing negotiations about ability, disability and identity in the public sphere, and, as a result, subject to criticism from scholars and activists, who suggest they do not do anything at all to advance imag(in)ings of the disabled body in Western culture.

This being the case, these images are – any good intent notwithstanding – the subject of controversy. Indeed, they are more controversial than imag(in)ings of the body in the work of Gómez Peña, Chouinard, or any of the artists discussed in this book, because of the emphasis on character, story and content rather than experimental form in popular television programmes. They are, as a result of their conventional story-based forms rather more readily accessible to many audience segments, and thus more likely to draw praise, criticism or controversy in the media.

A notable recent example of a disabled character becoming a subject of controversy is the character of Artie Abrams, played by able-bodied actor Kevin McHale, in popular US programme *Glee*. *Glee* is one of the most popular television programmes of the twenty-first century to date, in which teen self-discovery, relationships and growth plays out in the context of an American High School show choir, known in that country as a 'glee' club. The Artie character in *Glee* is controversial for a number of reasons.

First, Artie Abrams is controversial because the creators of *Glee* cast an able-bodied actor in the role. This has led some commentators to suggest that *Glee* is continuing economic and employment discrimination against disabled people, by excluding them from working in a role they would be well positioned to play. As Kuppers has noted, well before *Glee* came into being:

> Performers can perform disability, and this performance has currency, tradition and weight in the social sphere of popular culture: film actors playing disabled characters have carried off a number of Oscars, making it seem that acting disabled is the highest achievement possible [...] What we see much less is disabled people as artists and originators of artistic social texts and practice.
>
> (Kuppers, 2004: 12)

After all, as social media commentary on *Cast Offs* studied in Chapter 3 showed, some people clearly do prefer to see a non-disabled actor do a supposedly 'better' job of a disabled role than they think a disabled person could do. Critics of *Glee* tend to link their concerns to other examples of 'discriminatory' casting decisions, such as the casting of able-bodied actor Abigail Breslin to play Helen Keller in David Richenthal's Broadway production of *The Miracle Worker* (Anna, 2009; Johnston, 2012, Lewis, 2006). There are a number of popular television programmes that do use disabled actors to play disabled characters – indeed, there are even a number of programmes that are progressive enough to position disability as simply part of the character's identity, without making it or the character's struggle with it a plot point (oft cited examples include mobility impaired actor Geri Jewel as Jewel in *Deadwood*, blind actor Robert Morgan as Butchie in *The Wire*, deaf actor Marlee Matlin as Joey Lucas in *The West Wing*, mobility impaired actor Michael Patrick Thornton as Dr Gabriel Fife in *Private Practice*, or amputee Robert David Hall as pathologist Al Robbins in *CSI* (Smith, 2010b)). *Glee*, however, has chosen not to do this. The producers have decided to use an able-bodied actor to play the wheelchair-using character Artie. What is more, they have decided to make the wheelchair use of the character Artie pivotal to the plotlines he is involved in – that Artie is disabled is not there just because there happen to be disabled people in American high schools, but because the producers want to use him in particular ways in the plots they develop for the programme.

Secondly, the Artie Abrams character in *Glee* is controversial because it is a relatively minor role, and because all the other disabled characters in *Glee* (including some played by intellectually disabled people such as Robin Trocki as Jean Sylvester and Lauren Potter as Becky Jackson) are in even more minor roles, there simply to show sympathetic and human traits in the typically unsympathetic central character of cheerleading coach Sue Silvester. According to Elizabeth Smith, this means that

> *Glee*'s method of handling minorities is to devote an episode to one minority storyline, and then to shove that minority into the background. We've had the Very Special Gay Episode, the Very Special Black Episode, and now the Very Special Disability Episode, which means that we can go back to focusing on the white, conventionally attractive leads. Who are, of course, the draw, because the most common argument used to justify exclusion of minority groups from film and television is that no one wants to watch them.
>
> (Smith, 2009)

Thirdly, the Artie Abrams character in *Glee* is controversial because – although the creators of *Glee* do use the disabled characters to develop storylines about tolerance, inclusion and integration – many commentators believe the representation of inclusive cultural forms such as integrated dance in the choreography of *Glee* is rather limited. As Kuppers has noted, not in relation to wheelchair use in *Glee* but in relation to other instances of wheelchair use in film and television, '[n]ondisabled people rarely work with the exciting aspects of wheelchair use familiar to disabled performers, for instance the smooth and graceful curve that is impossible to achieve by bipedals, or the full-movement range of wheelchair athleticism' (Kuppers, 2007: 81). According to Kociemba, *Glee* is guilty of just this ignorance about the powerful, positive experience of movement

in a wheelchair in forms like integrated dance that Kuppers has
described. He says:

> Zach Woodlee's choreography shows no knowledge of integrated
> dance, which crafts distinct movements and kinetics by using
> dancers with and without physical disabilities. This genre, prac-
> ticed over the past three decades by more than two dozen dance
> companies worldwide, includes numbers choreographed by such
> movement innovators as Bill T. Jones, Joanna Haigood, Victoria
> Marks, Stephen Petronio, and Margaret Jenkins.
>
> (Kociemba, 2010a)

Instead, the wheelchair routines in *Glee* incorporate only very functional movement – nothing like that seen in the work of Gómez Peña,
Chouinard, Cunningham, Shannon or any number of integrated dance
companies in the United States, United Kingdom and Australasia. The
sense that integrated dance can deterritorialize diagnostic, medical
and social discourses about disability, challenging and changing
spectators' perspectives, discussed at length by scholars such as Anna
Hickey Moody (2009), is not developed in *Glee*. This leads commentators like Kociemba to suggest that *Glee* is continuing cultural
discrimination, by continuing to exclude a more positive, powerful
depiction of the experience of movement possibilities in a wheelchair from their programme.

These three concerns lead many commentators to suggest that *Glee*
is playing out what they call 'cripdrag' (Anna, 2009), or 'cripface'
(Smith, 2010a), in which able-bodied actors don the costume of
disability to play out cultural fantasies about bodies, bodily difference,
desire and overcoming. According to Kociemba, '[c]rip drag performances are rather like blackface and yellowface performances. They
are inherently inauthentic, [and] enact the biases and fantasies of
the majority culture' (Kociemba, 2010a). As of the time of writing,
almost every plotline involving the character Artie in *Glee* seems
to conform to this model. In the episode 'Wheels', the characters
come up with funding for a bus to get Artie and his wheelchair to a
singing competition, and choreograph a number where they are all
in wheelchairs to Ike and Tina Turner's *Proud Mary* to celebrate how
inclusive they are. The number is, though, little more than pushing
the chairs to set points on the stage and waving arms whilst singing.

In the episode 'Dream On', the characters participate in a flash mob in a shopping mall choreographed to Men Without Hats' *The Safety Dance*. In the episode's plot, Artie tells his girlfriend Tina about his desire to dance, and this transitions to a flash mob played out as a dream sequence in which Artie does leap from the chair and dance as a fully able-bodied person, though only for a moment before his desire is recuperated back into reality (Kociemba, 2010b; Smith, 2010a). The explicit emphasis on Artie's desire to overcome his disability, which *Glee*'s creators enact via fantasy moments in which Artie can walk, explains why they did not choose an actor with a disability for the role (Anna, 2009). Their reasons are the same as the reasons other programmes such as *House* choose an able-bodied actor for a disabled role – in *House*, too, chronic pain sufferer and clinical diagnostician Dr Gregory House tends to become angry, avenging and aggressive, something likely to be accepted as realistic for someone in his situation by viewers (Jarram, 2010; cf. Bolt, 2010), as accepted as the numerous dream sequences in which House is able to abandon his disability momentarily. In the later *Glee* episode 'A Very Glee Christmas', Artie's (new) girlfriend Britney expresses a Christmas wish that Artie will be able to walk, and, after much discussion amongst the characters about this, overheard by their football coach, the coach purchases an experimental exoskeleton device that does enable Artie to walk if only momentarily, this time in reality rather than in dream.

Whilst the Artie character in *Glee* comes in for the most criticism because it is a continuing character, these sorts of storylines draw criticism of other episodes in the series too. In 'Hairography', for example, the characters compete against a deaf choir, but the choir moves from signing to an emotionally wrenching vocal rendition of John Lennon's *Imagine*, and the able-bodied cast joins them to sing. Here, again, commentators lament a lost opportunity to connect with actual Deaf language and culture, and wonder why the able-bodied cast have to join in and help (Kociemba, 2010c; Phil, 2009).

Time and again *Glee*'s plotlines position disabled characters within the old overcoming narrative that the medical or diagnostic mode of seeing, imaging and imagining disability favours. The disabled characters become stereotyped examples that simply confirm for spectators how desperately someone in this situation would or should want to be able to walk or hear, and how 'inspirational' they are for pushing forward with their lives even when they cannot do this (Kociemba, 2010a; Smith, 2009). The characters prop up a cultural script in which disabled people need to be taken care of, cured, supported to overcome, and in which shining examples of this overcoming are to be celebrated as an inspiration for all of us. It is, Smith says, '*Glee*: Same shit, different episode' (2009). The disabled characters are visible, but not on their own terms, only as an example of struggle, strength and triumph over adversity which allows non-disabled characters to be comfortable with disability, and take pride in their own tolerance, a pride in which spectators seeing things through the same eyes might also share. Indeed, according to Kociemba, the only time a *Glee* episode comes even close to being confrontational or discomforting for spectators is the moment in 'Dream On' where Artie gets angry when Tina confesses she pretends to stutter only to get attention and sympathy. '[T]he creators', Kociemba says, 'fake progressive politics while reinforcing barriers for actors with mobility impairments and erasing authentic disability culture while pretending to celebrate it' (Kociemba, 2010b). In his view, then,

> Artie is a crip drag performance of stereotype written by people who erase the arts, cultures and histories of people with impairments. *Glee* does not increase the visibility of the disability rights cause or effectively convey the experiences of disability-based oppression.
>
> (Kociemba, 2010a)

Kociemba is not alone in this view, or in worrying about spectators who might be prompted to identify with *Glee*'s perspective on disability. As Elizabeth Smith says:

> [n]ondisabled viewers reacted with praise and pleasure [to the episodes of *Glee* described here], feeling that these disability-centric episodes depicted disability honestly and accurately, while some disabled viewers felt that these episodes were offensive, appropriative and wildly inaccurate.
>
> (Smith, 2010a)

The episodes, such disabled viewers felt, perpetuated the ways of seeing, talking and thinking about disability that are in fact the most problematic they encounter in their own day-to-day lives.

These issues angered commentator Kociemba enough that he looked to the blogosphere to see spectators' responses to these disability focused episodes of *Glee* and the relationship to disability they depicted. He wanted, he says, to 'see whether critics and fans of *Glee* saw what was missing' (Kociemba, 2010a) and saw the traces of spectatorial response in social media as useful in establishing this, in the way they were in Chapter 3 of this book. Kociemba found that there is a community conversing about *Glee* at sites like gleefan.com, and at a number of other fan sites like televisionwithoutpity.com, but that there is almost no discussion of disability representation in the forums for spectatorial response these sites offer. 'That short discussion is silenced when a moderator posts a "friendly" warning against discussing the representation of disability in the character thread' (Kociemba, 2010a). There is not as much community at Fox Television's official *Glee* site, and not much discussion of disability representation, at least not beyond calls to 'get over it' because it is only fiction. There are, according to Kociemba, a few more comments lamenting the simplicity of the *Proud Mary* choreography in that thread, noting that disabled people can do much more than this choreography suggests, and even comments noting the work of integrated dance companies, which is much more than in the other fan forums where comments about disability representation are moderated out. According to Kociemba, AnnieF, the one person who makes the link to integrated dance in the *Buffy the Vampire Slayer* thread (there because Joss Wheedon directed both *Buffy* and the 'Wheels' episode of *Glee*), she dislikes *Glee*'s depiction of it in the 'Wheels' episode because its choreography is poor, and she dislikes the 'Dream On' episode because Artie's desire 'makes dance a solely able-bodied experience [...] [which is] a big damn lie' (Kociemba, 2010a). 'It is', Kociemba says, 'a shame her observations were so hidden; the *Glee* recappers and the readers of the series forum need to see what she wrote' (Kociemba, 2010a). As Kociemba's analysis shows, the nature of the fan forums, and the nature of the fan interaction in them, tends to confirm that self-reflective consideration of the beliefs about disability constructed, conveyed and confirmed in *Glee* is limited to a few posters whose own personal histories, memories or worldviews led them to 'see what is missing' in the episodes. There is little in the series itself that prompts spectators to think. For most spectators, it seems, it is all too easy to take the representation of disability in *Glee* at face value, feel pride in one's own similar attempts at tolerance or assisting those with problems to overcome them, without ever needing to think further about the imag(in)ings of disability coming out in the show, in other spectators' responses, or in their own responses.

Ethical encounters?

As discussion of Gómez Peña's *The Museum of Fetishized Identities*, Chouinard's *bODY rEMIX*, and the television programme *Glee* shows, there is a lot of variability in the way artists, scholars and activists read the different representations of disability works such as these offer. Although responses to disability motifs in *The Museum of Fetishized Identities* do typically acknowledge its potential to challenge spectators to think about colonization, tyranny and attitudes to corporeal difference (if not specifically disability as a corporeal difference), responses to performances like *bODY rEMIX* and *Glee* are polarized. On the one hand, some non-disabled spectators clearly do see these as positive representations of disability, difference or inspirational overcoming. On the other hand, some disabled spectators – it seems most disabled spectators – read these freakish characters as little more than cripface or cripdrag that replays Western culture's most problematic ways of imag(in)ing disability.

The problem with use of disability signifiers for a whole range of different sorts of difference in these practices is more complex than the matter of disabled people taking 'offence' at the figure of the freak (or the cripple, or the charity case, or any other historical persona) returning to the centre of the cultural stage. The Victorian freakshow did, no doubt, play a prominent role in the project of modernity, as a pop cultural platform for staging and solidifying oppressive ideas about bodies and bodily differences (Garland Thomson, 1996: 2–15). It drew the daily social drama of disability up from homes, schools and streets onto the popular stage, turning it into an entertaining, pleasurable, even participatory social experience, in which spectators, freed from social sanctions against staring (Garland Thomson, 2009: 6), sought to make sense of bodies at odds with standard definitions of the human. Though producers sold tickets on the basis of the titillating threat of the encounter with the Other, the freakshow did, in the end, re-enact dominant ways of seeing, imaging and imagining disability. In a somewhat paradoxical cultural manoeuvre, the staging, scenography and symbolic frameworks of the freakshow unfolded according to what Lévinas calls hegemony of the same (1996b). The fat lady, dwarf, freak and geek of the freakshow in fact demonstrated degrees of difference or deviation from an illusory bodily norm. They drew spectators into performative misrecognitions that managed the difference of disabled bodies by positioning them at the far end of a continuum that, in the end, confirmed the stability of the symbolic order, and the centrality of the able, white, male self in that symbolic order. These sight-based misrecognitions allowed spectators to see the disabled body as a lesson, a warning or a worst case scenario. In this sense, Kuppers suggests, 'the psychic effects of the freak spectacle have destabilizing effects, assaulting the boundaries of firm knowledge about self, but only to strengthen them again in cathartic effect' (2004: 45).

Naturally, disabled people do need to be protected from exploitative cultural practices and producers that encourage spectators to rehearse, refine and make a habit of seeing their bodies as defective, deficient or lacking. This is what well-meaning doctors and activists who fought to shut freakshows down set out to do. Still, far from taking offense at the figures of the freak, monster or mutant, many disabled performers today in fact see remobilization of these powerful figurations of the disabled body as useful to their political agenda. Scholars have documented the work of many disabled artists who do see the freakshow and images as fragmented, confronting or ridiculous as any in the work of Gómez Peña or Chouinard, as a practice that can contest the cultural logic it enacts (cf. Hadley, 2008). Kuppers (2004) and Colette Conroy (2008) write of Fraser, who reperforms the freakshow persona Sealo the Sealboy, played by Stanley Berent who shared his short-armed stature, at Coney Island's Sideshows by the Seashore and later as part of his solo in-theatre show *Sealboy: Freak* at the Edinburgh Fringe Festival (Figure 10). Stephens (2006) writes of Fraser, and also of Jennifer Miller, who reperforms the freakshow persona of Zenobia the Bearded Lady, a historical persona who shared her hirsute physique, again at Sideshows by the Seashore. Mazer (2001) writes of Katy Dierlam, who dons a Dolly Dimples babydoll dress to reperform the clichéd fat lady figure Helen Melon, yet again at Sideshows by the Seashore. These freakshow figures are, as Fraser says, part of disabled people's history, heritage and roots, in the same way a slave is part of an African American's roots (Conroy, 2008: 344; Kuppers, 2004: 31; Stephens, 2006: 475).

Figure 10   Mat Fraser in *Sealboy: Freak*, Edinburgh Fringe Festival, Edinburgh, 2001 (Photo: Leon Steele)

These performers all replay the recognizable persona their corporeality is associated with in the dominant cultural imaginary with exaggeration, counter-position, commentary and anecdotes about the way the public sees their bodies, with a view to revealing the lack of any natural relation between the stereotype and the specific bodies it is associated with. Dierlam, for instance, counterposes Helon Melon's monstrous obesity with comments affirming her body's humanity, and quotes from feminists such as Suzy Orbach, Karen Finley and Annie Sprinkle. According to Mazer (2001: 260), Dierlam exposes herself for a gaping, gawking public who would have to look away if they saw her in the street. She 'performs her obesity' (2001: 270), telling spectators of the taunts and accusations her appearance provokes, and inviting more, to the point that '[o]ur reactions to her become transparent as clichés, our position as spectators characterized as cultural stereotypes. Her character is no longer in question but ours might be' (2001: 160).

Dierlam, Fraser and Miller's remobilizations show that the freak body is a construct, created, as Conroy suggests, 'in the moment of looking' (2008: 345). What gives these performances power is not simply the encounter with the Other. It is, rather, the exaggerated re-representation of self as Other, in combination with direct address, commentary and confrontation, in the productively live space of the sideshow where spectators are aware of each other's presence. In these practices, spectators start to become aware of the complex blend of fact, fiction and fantasy at play in the figure of the freak, and, as a result, reflect on their own habitual way of reading fat, hairy or otherwise freakish bodies. In this sense, these well-documented works are, in fact, important precursors to the interventionalist performance practices and strategies discussed throughout this study.

The problem with deployment of disability signifiers in a range of different practices is not, then, the problem of the reappearance of the freak in and of itself. It is, rather, the fact that many disabled spectators worry that the use of disability signifiers in shows such as *The Museum of Fetishized Identities, bODY rEMIX* and *Glee* do little to highlight the blend of fact, fiction and fantasy at play in the figure of the freak, or that of the monster, medical specimen, cripple, charity case, or whatever other trope the show might draw on. Instead, they draw able-bodied performers and spectators alike into some of the most well identified ethical pitfalls of performance practice.

In *Performing as Moral Act*, Dwight Conquergood identifies the four main ethical pitfalls for performers who like Gómez Peña, Chouinard and the producers of *Glee* set out to engage the Other as part of their theatrical practices – the sceptic who cops out by distancing or detaching from the Other, the exhibitionist who sells out by making the Other the subject of eroticized display, the custodian who sells out by concentrating only on curiosities that will make for a good show, and the enthusiast who falls into the trap of an energetic identification with and celebration of the Other that ends up denying and erasing the differences of the Other (1985: 5–8).

Of the three performances considered in this chapter, Gómez Peña's *The Museum of Fetishized Identities* is the only one that disabled spectators see as having any capacity to avoid the ethical pitfalls that Conquergood identifies here. In a sense, *The Museum of Fetishized Identities* does make the Other the subject of exoticized, eroticized display designed to entertain spectators with the sight of startling and even scary differences. This is, however, a deliberate re-representation of the historical form of such 'museum' displays across the collaborators' own supposedly suitable bodies with a subversive aesthetic, social and political agenda behind it. The significatory terrain of this 'museum' is so overpopulated with colliding, conflicting facts, fictions and fantasies that it is almost impossible for a spectator to latch onto a single, straightforward response to what they are seeing. The blurring of fact, fiction and fantasy, of performance and social process, and of performer, spectator and spectator-become-performer roles, complicates spectators' attempts to latch onto any single response. As Kuppers puts it:

> Gómez-Peña creates a dense web of meaning that lays the ground for many different narratives: a rich semantic field through which the audience can construct their own pathways. But this field is too rich; it clogs the act of reading. Making a meaningful path through this room of signifiers, set up in the Anglo/Latino encounter, is not easy.
>
> (2007: 83)

As spectators negotiate this tangled terrain of icons, tropes and connotations, there is a twin awareness of reality and representation – the reality of the Latina/Latino artists' oppression and the representation or re-representation of that and other oppressions in such exaggerated terms here – that leaves spectators in an uncertain, liminal space in which they cannot readily apply the responses to the Latina/Latino body their culture may have taught them. Unlike other works which are 'safely tucked up in their own fictional universes', Kuppers says:

> Gómez-Peña's performance allows spectators no space for retreat. The glass wall of the museum diorama is referenced: Gómez-Peña's performance took place in a gallery, and the tableaux were set up in scenes reminiscent of an anthropology museum's 're-creations' of the exotic Other. The anthropological gaze is made explicit in the piece's title, *The Museum of Fetishized Identities*. But this museum is alive with real bodies breaking through the glass – a far cry from the odourless, clean, divorced organization of a 'real' museum where colonial violence is coded into pristine, disinterested knowledge.
>
> (2007: 83)

The spectators' active, interactive role in, and responsibility for, how the relationship unfolds, raises the stakes of the performance even further. 'Some audience members walk out of Gómez-Peña's performances offended by his heightened stereotypes, including the maladjusted, sexually deviant cripple', Kuppers says (2007: 84). 'Some spectators give up and just 'take it in' without figuring out what it might mean to them' (Kuppers, 2007: 83). Whatever the spectators' response to this complex dialogue between different discourses, be it offence, bafflement, embarrassment or other problems relating to a work that 'denies the possibility of any single reading' (Kuppers, 2007: 84), it is on show for the performers and their fellow spectators-become-performers. Spectators are reacting and at the same time conscious of their reactions, and what their fellow spectators or society might make of these reactions. Which, as I have argued throughout this book, is just the sort of relationship that sets up the conditions of possibility for an ethical encounter in which spectators experience a relation to the Other characterized by vulnerability, responsibility, and – at least potentially – respect for an Other that can be recognized, but never reduced to the meanings we, as a society, might historically have made of it. A relation to the Other characterized not by exoticization, eroticization, commodification or complete identification, but by respectful dialogue. If, as Kirsten Valentine (2002: 280) has argued, the ethical pitfalls Conquergood identifies are a feature of spectators' as much as performers' relation to the Other – if each can read the Other reductively – then the replay of stereotypes, proliferation, counter-position and interaction of *The Museum of Fetishized Identities* pushes both spectators and performers past this reductive relationship into a more challenging, discomforting, and potentially productive dialogue.

Whilst Gómez Peña's recitation of disability, race, and the colonization of the human body by power in performances like *The Museum of Fetishized Identities* tends to both invoke and interrupt tendencies to exoticize the Other, the other performance and popular culture examples examined in this chapter do – at least according to a lot of commentators – fall into, and draw spectators into, the ethical traps Conquergood outlines.

Chouinard's *bODY rEMIX* tends to fall into the trap of overly enthusiastic identification with the Other that reduces, reifies or finalizes the disabled body's identity – in an ethically problematic way – by defining the disabled body in the able-bodied dancer's terms. The images of bodies becoming Other in *bODY rEMIX* are strange, striking and sometimes mesmerizing. Nevertheless, the bodily transformations are so complete, so committed, that the dancers – and, following Valentine's (2002) extension of Conquergood, the spectators – become caught up in a rapturous identification, and in a real-time reaction to the intensive renderings of the body on stage. The performance's form fails, as Mindy Fenske puts it in her discussion of Conquergood's take on the ethical encounter, 'to reveal the stakes of its construction' (2004: 14). There is nothing to complicate what the spectator is seeing, what the spectator is sensing, and thus nothing to set a more contemplative reflection on their own response in motion. There is, as a result, nothing to prompt the sort of dual consciousness in which a spectator reacts to what they see, and reflects on the way they are implicated in what they see, that for Fenske (2004: 8–9), as for Lehmann (2006) and others, characterizes the ethical encounter.

The disabled character Artie Abrams in *Glee* also draws criticism for its tendency to reduce, reify or finalize the disabled body's identity in an ethically problematic way. Here, again, the disabled body is but a symbol for a motivating, inspiring capacity to overcome challenges a body faces in day-to-day life. In *bODY rEMIX*, the 'disabled' bodies of the dancers are literally, concretely able to overcome their own limitations, fly above their crutches, and transform into something awe inspiring. In *Glee*, the 'disabled' body of Artie Abrams is more emotionally able to overcome its own limitations, to move, dance and make something of itself in spite of its corporeality, and thus, again, transform into something awe inspiring. There is, again, nothing to complicate the message the fiction puts in front of spectators – in this case the message, so typical of modern medical and social perspectives, that disabled people have some sort of special power to overcome life's challenges that should inspire us all to do the same. There is no critical counter-position, contrary perspective, proliferation of perspective or commentary to disrupt this stereotypical message about bodies, ability, disability and the capacity to get past obstacles in daily life. There is, as a result, nothing to prompt spectators to react, and reflect on their reaction, and thus potentially engage with the challenging questions about ourselves and others that set an ethical encounter in motion.

What these examples affirm, then, is that the disabled body, or the depiction of the disabled body, does not in and of itself create the conditions of possibility for an ethical encounter. This depiction has to be complicated by some sort of contradiction, counter-position, proliferation or commentary that creates a confusing density, uncertainty or unpredictability within the significatory terrain of the work. The depiction must, for Conquergood, following Mikhail Bakhtin, be dialogic instead of monologic. It must produce a meaning-making process in which 'different voices, worldviews, value systems and beings [come together] so that they have a conversation with one another', whilst, Conquergood says, '[...] resist[ing] conclusions' (Conquergood 1985: 9). The presence of a disabled body certainly can complicate meaning-making in this way (even if it is not the only way to do this). In *bODY rEMIX* or *Glee*, for instance, the presence of a disabled body certainly could have complicated the scenes in which the dancers or characters literally or in a dream sequence leap from their canes, crutches or chairs, both creating and creating failure in the recognizable narrative of overcoming called forth here. The presence of other bodies, signs or symbols that complicate meaning-making – such as the presence of racialized bodies, colonized bodies, and a plethora of cultural detritus in *The Museum of Fetishized Identities* – can also have this effect of creating and creating failure in a recognizable cultural narrative. In this work, Gómez-Peña does 'show the stakes' in his metaphorical co-option of different sorts of differences, and, as a result, does create a plethora of frames of reference that prompt spectators to think, and at the same time think about what they think, when they get caught up comparing modes of Otherness. The density, uncertainty and disruption of signification in this work, as in the works studied throughout this book, creates a liminal space in which fictions permeate realities and realities permeate fictions and dominant cultural logics start to come into question in and/or after the moment of encounter.

When it comes to the question of whether live, face-to-face encounters with materially specific disabled subjects have particular power to prompt ethical or political engagement, then, the terrain remains complex. It may be that, as analysis here suggests, the presence of a disabled subject is not always aesthetically necessary as a precondition of a politically or ethically productive encounter. It may, though, be that the presence of a disabled subject (or at least an other subject) somewhere in the scope of the production process is in many cases socially necessary if a piece is to develop sophistication in its deployment of disability signifiers. Because, without it, there seems to be little to forestall the sort of flights of fancy into a purely fictional world seen in works like *bODY rEMIX* and some of the episodes of *Glee* discussed here. Flights into a fictional world that eliminate the blurring of fact, fiction and fantasy that create the uncertainty that can, in turn, set an ethical chain of thought in motion for the spectator, even if the exact moment, image or mechanism that creates this uncertainty for a given spectator is never easy to establish. The presence of a disabled subject if not as a performer, then as a writer, director or producer of disabled characters may, in these situations, at least open the door to a more nuanced deployment of disability signifiers that does not instantly metaphorize the material realities of disability out of the piece – or, perhaps more precisely, force producers to make a more deliberate choice to open or close the door to a more nuanced use of disability signifiers, rather than, like the *Glee* producers, claim nuance that is not there.

Undoubtedly, there are those who see this as an unreasonable suggestion. A return to the idea that specific signifiers can be deployed with success only by subjects historically, socially and materially connected with these signifiers. This, at least, is what some of my fellow spectators have said when I have expressed anxiety about these shows. If creators cannot deploy these disability signifiers without disabled subjects present, they say, they will be stuck for images, metaphors and motifs to put in their performances or stuck with limited possibilities in their performances. Indeed, some say they enjoy the 'message' that a disabled person can learn to overcome pain and difficulty, unaware or unconcerned that this reaffirms a medical model in which disability is a defect to be overcome that has been so thoroughly problematized in disability studies over the past few decades. The absence of a disability perspective in these sorts of shows means that, for many in the audience, readings that go beyond the standard cultural script of disability come about only when fellow spectators – in the foyer, in discussion forums, in social media or in other critiques that actually constitute new performances circulating around the initial performance – raise questions or concerns. Highlighting, in a sense, the need for disabled people to have access to these foyers, as well as the stages, wings and seating banks of theatrical production spaces, as consumers, commentators and producers. This, then, shows that these shows are not altogether unuseful in sparking debate, but it also shows a need to have a mixed production and/or spectator group to make, remember or remediate the show, and to complicate its surface values for fellow spectators. This is not necessarily heartening in terms of the capacity that increased circulation of disability signifiers in mainstream performance practices holds to expand public debate about disability and other sorts of corporeal and cognitive difference.

The singular, monologic signification of works such as *bODY rEMIX* and *Glee* clearly are not complicated by the presence of a disabled subject, conflicting signifiers of disability, or conflicting signifiers of otherness. This makes it difficult to see how someone who does not bring a knowledge of disability politics, activism or arts practices to the interaction might feel or find themselves invited to question the meanings the artists seem to be trying to make. Certainly, what encouraged me to question these works was not the theatrical framing of the work, or the emergence of what Conquergood characterizes as different voices, worldviews and beings in conversation in the frame, form or content of the work. It was rather that I, as a spectator, brought my 'self', a 'self' with a history in disability studies, to the situation. This encouraged me, as an individual spectator, to enter my own liminal space in which fact, fiction and fantasy about bodies and bodily politics began to problematize, complicate and challenge each other. Plus, of course, it also encouraged me as a spectator to remember and reperform that problematization for my fellow spectators. Still, because every spectator brings their 'self' – their very different 'self' – to their responses, readings and reflections on this sort of encounter, this is unlikely to be the same for other spectatorial selves. For many, engagement with the disabled body as Other in works such as *bODY rEMIX* or *Glee* will, all too often, end up as merely another mechanism for silencing, constraining and censoring the body, the disabled body, in the guise of an apparent exercise in freedom. A mechanism that marginalizes the disabled body without even enabling – as in the historical freakshows, museums and medical schools that modern disabled artists are today remobilizing – participation, employment, and potential advocacy or subversion from within the form from actual disabled people.

Conclusion: (Dia)Logics
of Difference

'Every time a disabled person puts themselves in a performance
situation', Mat Fraser says, they are '[...] intervening in society's
preconceptions of disability to a lesser or greater degree, whatever [it is
they are] doing on stage or in public. And that's a good thing' (2010). In
a performance situation, in particular a social performance situation, a
disabled person is an unconscious-become-conscious performer with
the capacity to intervene in – confirm, challenge or change – social
ideas about bodies, bodily differences, identities and the dominant
order of things. For Fraser, as for artists like Lakmaier, Jones, Shannon,
Araniello, Williamson or Crow, this obligation to perform makes
public space performance a most tempting mechanism in the pursuit
of an activist aesthetics and politics. 'Disabled performers are', as
Petra Kuppers argues, 'often aware of the knowledges that have been
erected around them: tragic, poor, helpless, heroic, struggling, etc.
In the laboratory of the performance situation, these knowledges can
be re-examined, and questioned again and again' (2004: 3). This is
precisely what these artists do, in the laboratory of a specific sort of
performance in public space. The obligation or burden becomes an
opportunity to manipulate public perceptions of disability not by presenting alternate, more appropriate images of disability but by asking
people to reflect on how they, too, act as an unconscious performer,
how they, too, intervene in public perceptions of disability, and how
a change in their own perceptions might change the order of things.
Although not in any sense a defined aesthetic or political 'movement',
then, a desire to use public space performance to prompt spectators to
reflect on their attitudes towards disability is a recognizable trend or

tendency in disability performance today. It is done in different ways, in different stages, spaces and places. It is described in different ways. It does, though, share an emphasis on reciting recognizable images of disability, appropriation, repetition, proliferation, counter-position, commentary and an altered stage-performer-spectator relationship that puts spectators on the spot as co-performers, as a common interventionalist strategy. It is a risky practice, and, as artists' comments suggest, at times a personally, physically or emotionally confronting practice, as the outcome of the performers' and spectators-become-performers' attempts to engage each other as Other unfold in uncertain ways. It is, though, a way of using one's own body's tendency to 'cause a commotion' (Auslander and Sandahl, 2004: 2) in public space, to intervene in the public sphere in potentially productive ways.

Analysing this trend or tendency in disability performance in this book has offered me an opportunity to further the to-date fairly limited field of scholarship documenting, describing and interpreting the way artists with disabilities repeat, reclaim, reject or bypass the roles culture assigns them through politicized public space performance practices. These practices can, on the surface, seem fairly simple – particularly the guerrilla-style practices, which tend to be simple in structure, repetitive and solo. But, as my analysis has hopefully shown, these practices actually use sophisticated strategies to structure their political interventions in the public sphere. The task of analysing these practices has not necessarily been an easy one, though, primarily because of the nature of the work.

This work, like much modern disability performance, is not about identifying alternative images of disability, but about interrupting the mechanisms of imag(in)ing disability themselves. As Kuppers puts it in her analysis of other disability performance practices, '"[a]uthenticity" is not the object of these performances: the emphasis is on the new created in the encounter, not on the presentation of an essential self, or a fullness of disclosure' (2004: 2) or any of the other signs of authenticity so many spectators seem to seek in disability performance. The emphasis is, Kuppers continues, on the dialogic conversation or collaboration between what Dwight Conquergood (1985) characterizes as different logics, worlds, worldviews and voices, each contributing their own beliefs, attitudes and behaviours to an encounter that creates, or has the potential to create, some new sort of understanding. A conversation in which each party – performer, spectator, bystander and society – can be changed by an encounter with each other's Other. This means the work's value lies outside the work itself in a liminal interstitial space that exists only in the moment of engagement between performer and spectator-become-performer. This, as Lehmann (2006: 179–80) has observed, is a common challenge when analysing postmodern, postdramatic work which acknowledges that it is not the work but the meaning-making the work prompts that actually constitutes the 'performative', world-making or world-changing part of the encounter. It means, as so many of us have noted and argued of late (Freshwater, 2009; Grehan, 2009; Hadley, Trace and Winter, 2010; Ridout, 2009), that the value of the work exists or fails to come into existence in the individual, idiosyncratic experience of each spectator in and after the encounter. The spectator, improvising a response, riffing off assigned roles, has their own distinctive perspective on the encounter. The use of terms like history, memory, habit and *habitus* can help us navigate some of the factors that structure each spectator's distinctive response. The use of techniques like content analysis of social media commentary on a performance can help us chart some of the commonalities, conflicts and differences in and within a series of spectatorial responses. Nevertheless, much of the impact of the work must by necessity stay unpredictable, invisible and inferential.

This means that, though I draw extensively on reviews, critiques and commentary, much of the reading of, and response to, the works considered in this book must by necessity remain my own distinctive response to the work, based on my own history, memory and habits of imaging and imagining disability.

Throughout this book I have, in a sense, performed my spectatorship of a series of provocative, public space performance practices by artists with disabilities. I have seen, imaged and imagined the practices of these artists through a variety of lenses I have acquired as a result of my own histories, memories and habits. Histories which include my cultural location in Australia, my cultural position as an Australian of English, Irish and white New Zealand descent, my professional position as an artist, scholar and advocate, and my personal identification as a woman with a mobility disability. A combination which clearly results in a strong desire to see people with disabilities, particularly artists with disabilities, succeed in their interventionalist practices, and have an impact in the public sphere, in a way that will be positive for all of us.

As I conclude this study, then, I have to ask whether my engagement with these practices could be characterized as an ethical encounter. The truth, of course, is that I have at times struggled through my own direct response, distanced reflection and reading of these practices, and my reading of them in relation to a range of theoretical perspectives on disability, performance, spectatorship, ethics and politics. I have indeed felt confused, uncertain and conflicted. Or, perhaps more accurately, I have found my responses to be ambivalent – certain at one moment, confused the next, certain again albeit in a slightly more articulate way the next, and so on – and must acknowledge that they may continue to be so. In effect, then, I have attempted to enter into a dialogue in which, as Conquergood (1985) advocates, different voices, views and worldviews come into play. And, of course, attempted to draw readers into this dialogue too. I have often found that the most difficult thing has been to avoid reductive readings. In my case, though, it has not so much been about avoiding reductive readings of the identity, action and interaction of the performers, who I tend to identify with, respect, admire, and in some have begun continuing correspondence with, influencing both my and their work into the future. It has been about avoiding reductive readings of the identity, action and interaction of the spectators, or spectators-become-performers, who have become sometimes unwitting subjects of this study, unaware anyone has an issue with their public social performances until they hear my thoughts on them. I have often wondered how I can say what I want to say – and be faithful to my own experience, which, like the artists I discuss, suggests that pity and help may be more of a hindrance than something to (as some of my interlocutors along the way have suggested) be proud of – whilst at the same time capturing the variability of spectatorial responses. For me too, then, there has been reflection, vulnerability and a desire to develop a respect for an Other I cannot completely understand.

As I come to the end, I hope I have captured something of the way spectators 'riff' off, or improvise around, the scripts Western culture gives them to perform their own particular response to disabled bodies. Or, perhaps, of the way performers, spectators and scholars alike feel or find our way through the scripts Western culture gives us to perform our response to disabled bodies, always pushing for the change we would like to see, against a mutually acknowledged legacy of control, constraint and non-inclusion, whether or not we agree on the shape that might take. If nothing else, I think, the fact of these productive, unpredictable, improvisatory encounters – of having the will and wherewithal to negotiate these encounters – has the potential to do something in the public sphere. And that, I think, is a good, if never stable, satisfying or finished, thing.

Bibliography

Abell, Judith. 2007. *Small Metal Objects*: An Intimate Conversation and the Perfect Front. *RealTimeArts*, Special Edition: *Ten Days on the Island*, 23 March–1 April 2007. Available: http://www.realtimearts.net/feature/search/8490 (accessed 20 February 2009).

Adams, Rachel. 2001. *Sideshow USA: Freaks and the American Cultural Imagination*. Chicago, IL: University of Chicago Press.

Anna. 2009. And if this Keeps Up, there won't be Any. *Feminists With Disabilities for a Way Forward*, 5 November 2009. Available: http://disabledfeminists.com/2009/11/05/and-if-this-keeps-up-there-wont-be-any/ (accessed 1 April 2011).

Araniello, Katherine (n.date) Katherine Araniello. YouTube. Available: http://www.youtube.com/user/KatherineAraniello (accessed 1 February 2012).

Araniello, Katherine. 2010. Interview with Author, London.

Araniello, Katherine. 2009a. *Why Do You Want to Die*. YouTube, 14 April 2009. Videorecording. Available: http://www.youtube.com/watch?v7xINR0Q8Xt0&listUUfVj0ogxIZX-RqRDsPISEaw&index9&featureplcp (accessed 1 February 2012).

Araniello, Katherine. 2009b. *Our Time To Die: A Satirical Look at Assisted Suicide*. YouTube, 17 July 2009. Videorecording. Available: http://www.youtube.com/watch?vUh2KXBDKsjA&listUUfVj0ogxIZX-RqRDsPISEaw&index8&featureplcp (accessed 1 February 2012).

Araniello, Katherine. 2008. *Suicide Mission*. YouTube, 21 April 2008. Videorecording. Available: http://www.youtube.com/watch?vUHo6A3ULgcw&listUUfVj0ogxIZX-RqRDsPISEaw&index20&featureplcp (accessed 1 February 2012).

Araniello, Katherine. 2007a. *Suicide Message on Valentine's Day*. YouTube, 14 February 2007. Videorecording. Available: http://www.youtube.com/watch?v7v4ZikwYexU&listUUfVj0ogxIZX-RqRDsPISEaw&index33&featureplcp (accessed 1 February 2012).

Araniello, Katherine. 2007b. *Suicide Haircut*. YouTube, 23 February 2007. Videorecording. Available: http://www.youtube.com/watch?vCOhdTxEMaNY&listUUfVj0ogxIZX-RqRDsPISEaw&index32&featureplcp (accessed 1 February 2012).

Araniello, Katherine. 2007c. *Last Dance*. YouTube, 23 February 2007. Videorecording. Available: http://www.youtube.com/watch?v9rfms_xzctI&listUUfVj0ogxIZX-RqRDsPISEaw&index31&featureplcp (accessed 1 February 2012).

Araniello, Katherine. 2007d. *Suicide Interview*. YouTube, 3 March 2007. Videorecording. Available: http://www.youtube.com/watch?vDR8eWHtWkdU&listUUfVj0ogxIZX-RqRDsPISEaw&index29&featureplcp (accessed 1 February 2012).

Araniello, Katherine, and Williamson, Aaron. 2007. *Assisted Passage*. YouTube, 28 November 2008. Videorecording. Available: http://www.youtube.com/watch?vSvgVv-nEEIs (accessed 1 February 2012).

Artichoke, Headshift and Sky Arts. 2009. Participants, Liz_C. *One & Other*. 6 May 2009. Available: http:www.oneandother.co.uk (accessed 18 August 2009). [The comments from this *One and Other* website, Facebook and Twitter cited here were retained by Liz Crow as part of her own documentation of *Resistance on The Plinth* at the time.]

Auslander, Philip, and Sandahl, Carrie, eds. 2004. *Bodies in Commotion: Disability and Performance*. Ann Arbor, MI: University of Michigan Press.

Back to Back Theatre. n.date. Projects: *Small Metal Objects*. Back to BackTheatre. com. Available: http://backtobacktheatre.com/projects/show/small-metal-objects/ (accessed 1 February 2012).

Bakhtin, Mikhail. 1984a. Problems of Dostoevsky's Poetics. In *Theory and History of Literature*, vol. 8. Ed. and trans. C. Emerson. Minneapolis, MN: University of Minnesota Press.

Bakhtin, Mikhail. 1984b. *Rabelais and His World*. Trans. H. Iswolsky. Bloomington, IN: Indiana University Press.

Bakhtin, Mikhail. 1981. Discourse in the Novel. In M. Holquist, ed., *The Dialogic Imagination: Four Essays*. Trans. C. Emerson and M. Holquist. Austin, TX: University of Texas Press.

Batty, David. 2009. Fourth plinth appeal for government to help death row Briton. *The Guardian*, 10 September 2009. Available: http://www.guardian.co.uk/uk/2009/sep/10/death-row-woman-fourth-plinth (accessed 30 May 2010).

Baudrillard, Jean. 1984. The Precision of Simulacra. In B. Wallis, ed., *Art After Modernism: Rethinking Representation*. Boston, MA: David R. Godine, 253–82.

Bennett, Susan. 1997. *Theatre Audiences: A Theory of Production and Reception*. 2nd edn. London: Routledge.

Bickers, Patricia. 2009. Editorial. *Art Monthly*, 9 September 2009, 12.

Bishop, Claire. 2006. *Participation*. Whitechapel and Cambridge, MA: The MIT Press.

Bogdan, Robert. 1988. *Freakshow: Presenting Human Oddities for Amusement and Profit*. Chicago, IL: University of Chicago Press.

Bolt, David. 2010. The Starfish Paradigm: Impairment, Disability, and characterisation in Bobbie Ann Mason's *Shiloh*. Available: http://www.leeds.ac.uk/disability-studies/archiveuk/bolt/Starfish%20Shiloh.pdf (accessed 10 April 2011).

Bouchard, Gianna. 2009. Haptic Visuality: The Dissective View in Performance. In Alison Oddey and Christine White, eds, *Modes of Spectating*. Bristol: Intellect Books.

Bourdieu, Pierre. 1998. *Practical Reason: On the Theory of Action*. Stanford, CA: Stanford University Press.

Bourdieu, Pierre. 1977. *Outline of a Theory of Practice*. Cambridge, MA: Cambridge University Press.

Braidotti, Rosi. 1994. *Nomadic Subjects: Embodiment and Sexual Difference in Contemporary Feminist Thought*. New York: Columbia University Press.

Brisbane Festival. 2008. *bODY rEMIX: gOLDBERG vARIATIONS*, Programme. The Brisbane Festival, Brisbane, Australia.

British Sky Broadcasting/Liberty Bell Productions. 2009. *Antony Gormley's 'One & Other'*. Pres. C. Anderson, dir. P. Dick, 24 July 2009, 1 August 2009, 8 August 2009, 23 August 2009, 28 August 2009, 4 September 2009, 11 September 2009, 18 September 2009, 26 September 2009, 10 October 2009, 16 October 2009.

Brooker, Charlie. 2009. Charlie Brooker's Screen Burn. *The Guardian*, 11 July 2009. Available: http://www.guardian.co.uk/culture/2009/jul/11/screen burn-antony-gormley (accessed 13 September 2009).

Brown, Sheena Louise. 2000. *Teaching Normalcy and Learning Disability – The Risky Business of Special Education: Exploring the Retrospective Schooling Experiences by Learning Disabled Post-Secondary Students*. Unpublished thesis.

Channel 4. 2009a. *Cast Offs*. YouTube, 19 November 2009. Videorecording. Available: http://www.youtube.com/all_comments?vMS1HP71kvd4&page1 (accessed 1 February 2012).

Channel 4. 2009b. *Cast Offs*: Dan's Story. YouTube, 19 November 2009. Videorecording. Available: http://www.youtube.com/all_comments?vkuTQ loUhuGI&page1 (accessed 1 February 2012).

Chemers, Michael. 2008. *Staging Stigma: A Critical Examination of the American Freak Show*. Basingstoke: Palgrave Macmillan.

Conquergood, Dwight. 1985. Performing as Moral Act. *Literature in Performance*. 5 (2), 1–13.

Conroy, Colette. 2008. Active Differences: Disability and Identity beyond Postmodernism. *Contemporary Theatre Review*, 18 (3), 341–54.

Crow, Liz. n.date. *Roaring Girl* Productions. Available: http://www.roaring-girl. com (accessed 30 May 2010).

Crow, Liz. 2010. Interview with Author, Bristol.

Crow, Liz. 2009a. Provocation on the Plinth. *Bristol Indymedia*, 14 August 2009. Available: http://www.bristol.indymedia.org.uk/article/690845 (accessed 30 May 2010).

Crow, Liz. 2009b. *Protest on the Plinth*. YouTube, 18 August 2009. Videorecording. Available: http://www.youtube.com/watch?vEfswOExefgw (accessed 30 May 2010).

Cunningham, James, and Fuks, Suzon. 2006a. *Mirage*. Igneous.com. Available: http://archive.igneous.org.au/mirage.html (accessed 1 June 2010).

Cunningham, James, and Fuks, Suzon. 2006b. *Mirage*: Reviews. Igneous.com. Available: http://archive.igneous.org.au/mirage-reviews.html (accessed 1 June 2010).

Daily Post. 2009. Alison Jones: Portrait of the Artist by Proxy. *The Daily Post*, 10 February 2009. Available: http://www.thefreelibrary.com/'Human+mirro rs'+reflect+on+art%3B+ARTS+DIARY.-a0193326798

Davidson, Michael. 2008. *Concerto for the Left Hand: Disability and the Defamiliar Body*. Ann Arbor, MI: University of Michigan Press.

Davis, Lennard J. 1995. *Enforcing Normalcy: Disability, Deafness, and the Body*. London and New York: Verso.

Deleuze, Gilles, and Guattari, Felix. 1987. *A Thousand Plateaus: Capitalism and Schizophrenia*. Trans. Brian Massumi. Minneapolis, MN, and London: University of Minnesota Press.

Derrida, Jacques. 1995. *Gift of Death*. Trans. David Wills. Chicago, IL: University of Chicago Press.

Diedrich, Antje. 2011. Acting Out Trauma in the Theatre of Embarrassment: George Tabori's Shylock Improvisations. *Performance Research*, 16 (1), 142–52.

Diggles, Dan. 2004. *Improv for Actors*. New York: Allworth Press.

Disability Arts Info. 2009. Art, Lies and Audiotapes. *EtCetera*, 449. Available: http://www.disabilityarts.info/etcetera/archive/etc449.html (accessed 30 June 2010).

Disability Arts Online. 2008. Katherine Araniello on her Character 'Terminal Services' in Late at Tate. *Disability Arts Online*, 17 December 2008. Available: http://www.disabilityartsonline.org/Katherine_Araniello_Terminal_Services (accessed 1 February 2012).

Dolan, Jill. 2005. *Utopia in Performance: Finding Hope at the Theater*. Ann Arbor, MI: University of Michigan Press.

Dowse, Jill Francesca. 2009. 'So what will you do on the plinth?': A Personal Experience of Disclosure during Antony Gormley's *One & Other* Project', *M/C Journal*, 12 (5). Available: http://journal.media-culture.org.au/index.php/mcjournal/article/viewArticle/193 (accessed 30 May 2010).

Engelen, John. 2010. Biennale of Sydney 2010 – Antony Gormley @ AGNSW. *De De Ce Blog*, 26 May 2010. Available: http://www.dedeceblog.com/2010/05/26/biennale-of-sydney-2010-anthony-gormley-agnsw/ (accessed 30 May 2010).

Fassett, Deanna L., and Morella, Dana L. 2010. Remaking (the) Discipline: Marking the Performative Accomplishment of (Dis)Ability. In B. Henderson and N. Ostrander, eds, *Understanding Disability Studies and Performance Studies*. London and New York: Routledge, 139–56.

Felton Dansky, Miriam. 2008. Controlling the Twenty-First Century: Suppressed Theater and Global Change. In Censorship and Performance, *Theater*, 38 (3).

Fenske, Mindy. 2004. The Aesthetic of the Unfinished: Ethics and Performance. *Text and Performance Quarterly*, 24 (1), 1–19.

Foucault, Michel. 1984. *The Foucault Reader*. Ed. P. Rabinow. New York: Pantheon Books. 239–56.

Foucault, Michel. 1980. *Power/Knowledge: Selected Interviews and Other Writings 1972–1977*. Ed. Colin Gordon. New York: Pantheon Books.

Foucault, Michel, 1977. *Discipline and Punish: The Birth of the Prison*. New York: Vintage Books.

Foucault, Michel. 1976. *The Birth of the Clinic: An Archaeology of Medical Perception*. Trans. A. M. Sheridan Smith. London: Routledge.

Fraser, Mat. n.date. Live Art. MatFraser.co.uk. Available: http://www.matfraser.co.uk/liveart.php (accessed 20 April 2008).

Fraser, Mat. 2010. Interview with Author, Liverpool and New York.

Fraser, Mat. 2001. *Born Freak*. Written by Paul Sapin and Mat Fraser. Dir. Paul Sapin. Videorecording. London: Planet Wild for Channel 4.

Freshwater, Helen. 2009. *Theatre & Audience*. Basingstoke: Palgrave Macmillan.
Garland Thomson, Rosemarie. 2009. *Staring: How We Look*. Oxford and New York: Oxford University Press.
Garland Thomson, Rosemarie. 2006. Ways of Staring. *Journal of Visual Culture*, 5 (2), 173–92.
Garland Thomson, Rosemarie. 2005. Dares to Stares: Disabled Women Performance Artists and the Dynamics of Staring. In Carrie Sandahl and P. Auslander, eds, *Bodies in Commotion: Disability and Performance*. Ann Arbor, MI: The University of Michigan Press, 30–41.
Garland Thomson, Rosemarie. 2002. Integrating Disability, Transforming Feminist Theory. *NWSA Journal*, 14 (3), 1–33.
Garland Thomson, Rosemarie. 2000. Staring Back: Self-Representations of Disabled Performance Artists. *American Quarterly*, 52 (2), 334–8.
Garland Thomson, Rosemarie. 1997. *Extraordinary Bodies: Figuring Physical Disability in American Culture and Literature*. New York, NY: Columbia University Press.
Garland Thomson, Rosemarie. 1996. Introduction: From Wonder to Error – A Genealogy of Freak Discourse. In R. Garland Thomson, ed., *Freakery: Cultural Spectacles of the Extraordinary Body*. New York, NY, and London: New York University Press.
Garner, Stanton B. 1994. *Bodied Spaces: Phenomenology and Performance in Contemporary Drama*. Ithaca, NY: Cornell University Press.
Giannachi, Gabriella. 2004. *Virtual Theatres: An Introduction*. London and New York: Routledge.
Goffman, Erving. 1973. *Presentation of the Self in Everyday Life*. Woodstock, NY: Overlook Press.
Goffman, Erving. 1963. *Stigma: Notes on the Management of Spoiled Identity*. Englewood Cliffs, NJ: Prentice-Hall.
Gómez Peña, Guillermo. 2005. *Ethno-Techno: Writings on Performance, Activism and Pedagogy*. London and New York: Routledge.
Gómez Peña, Guillermo. 2004. Culture-in-extremis: Performing Against the Cultural Backdrop of the Mainstream Bizarre. In H. Bial, ed., *The Performance Studies Reader*. London and New York: Routledge, 287–98.
Goodall, Jane. 1999. Objects of Curiosity and Subjects of Discovery: Humans on Show. *Australasian Drama Studies*, 34, 123–40.
Gosling, Ju. 2010. Interview with Author, London.
Grehan, Helena. 2009. *Performance Ethics and Spectatorship in a Global Age*. Basingstoke: Palgrave Macmillan.
Grosz, Elisabeth. 1996. Intolerable Ambiguity: Freaks as/at the Limit. In Rosemarie Garland Thomson, ed., *Freakery: Cultural Spectacles of the Extraordinary Body*. New York: New York University Press, 55–66.
Grosz, Elizabeth. 1994. *Volatile Bodies: Toward A Corporeal Feminism*. Bloomington, IN: Indiana University Press; Sydney: Allen & Unwin.
The Guardian. 2009a. The Fourth Plinth Top 10. *The Guardian*, 9 October 2009. Available: http://www.guardian.co.uk/artanddesign/gallery/2009/oct/09/fourth-plinth-gormley?pic (accessed30 May 2010).

The Guardian. 2009b. Graduate gets job thanks to stint on Trafalgar Square Plinth. *The Guardian*, 2 September 2009. Available: http://www.guardian.co.uk/artanddesign/2009/sep/02/plinth-trafalgar-square-graduate-job (accessed 30 May 2010).

Habermas, Jürgen. 1989. *The Structural Transformation of the Public Sphere: An Enquiry into a Category of Bourgeois Society.* Trans. T. Burger. Cambridge, MA: The MIT Press.

Hadley, Bree. 2011. (Dia)logics of Difference: Disability, Performance and Spectatorship in Liz Crow's *Resistance on the Plinth*. *Performance Research*, 17 (2), 124–31.

Hadley, Bree. 2008. Mobilising the Monster: Modern Disabled Performers' Manipulation of the Freakshow. *M/C Journal*, 11 (3). Available: http://www.journal.mediaculture.org.au/index.php/mcjournal/article/viewArticle/47 (accessed 30 October 2009).

Hadley, Bree. 2007. *Mirage*. Australian Stage Online, Thursday 3 May 2007. Available: http://www.australianstage.com.au/reviews/brisbane/mirage--igneous-334.html (accessed 1 February 2012).

Hadley, Bree, Rajak, Jelena, Filmer, Andrew, and Caines, Rebecca, with Read, Alan. 2010. The 'Dirty Work' of the Lie. *Performance Research*, 15 (2), 123–9.

Hadley, Bree, Trace, Genevieve, and Winter, Sarah. 2010. Uncertainties that Matter: Risk, Response-ability, Ethics, and the Moment of Exchange in Live Art. *About Performance*, 10, 137–51.

Haraway, Donna J. 1991 *Simians, Cyborgs and Women*. New York: Routledge.

Hawthorn, Lucy. 2007. *Small Metal Objects*: Ordinary Guise. *RealTime Arts*, Special Edition: *Ten Days on the Island*, 23 March–1 April 2007. Available: http://www.realtimearts.net/feature/search/8491 (accessed 20 February 2009).

Heddon, Deirdre. 2008. *Autobiography and Performance*. Basingstoke: Palgrave Macmillan.

Henderson, Bruce, and Ostrander, Noam, eds. 2010. *Understanding Disability Studies and Performance Studies*. London and New York: Routledge.

Hickey Moody, Anna. 2009. *Unimaginable Bodies: Intellectual Disability, Performance and Becomings*. Rotterdam: Sense Publishers.

Holmwood, Leigh. 2009. Trafalgar Square plinth becomes surprise web hit for Sky Arts. *The Guardian*, 29 July 2009. Available: http://www.guardian.co.uk/media/2009/jul/29/trafalgar-square-plinth-antony-gormley (accessed 30 May 2010).

Houchin, John. 2008. Bodily Fear: Recent American Performance Controversies. In Censorship and Performance. *Theater*, 38 (3).

Houghton Mifflin Company. 2000. *The American Heritage Dictionary of the English Language*, 4th edn. Westport, CT: Houghton Mifflin/Harcourt.

Inclusion in the Arts & Media of People with Disabilities. 2010. New Study Reveals Lack of Characters with Disabilities on Television. IAMPWD.org. Available: http://www.iampwd.org/new-study-reveals-lack-characters-disabilities-television (accessed 10 April 2011).

Jain, Sarah. 1999. The Prosthetic Imagination: Enabling and Disabling the Prosthesis Trope. *Science Technology and Human Values*, 24, 31–54.

Jarram, Steph. 2010. Example of Disability – Dr House. *As Media*. Available: http://stephjarramlcasmedia.blogspot.com/2010/11/example-of-disability-dr-house.html (accessed 10 April 2010).

Johnston, Kirsty. 2012. *Stage Turns: Canadian Disability Theatre*. Montreal: McGill Queens University Press.

Jones, Alison. 2010a. Interview with Author, Liverpool.

Jones, Alison. 2010b. *Portrait of the Artist by Proxy*. YouTube, 2 February 2010. Videorecording. Available: http://www.youtube.com/watch?vL_zMee24DQI (accessed 1 February 2012).

Jones, Jonathan. 2009. The fourth plinth: It was just Big Brother all over again. *The Guardian*, 9 October 2009. Available: http://www.guardian.co.uk/artanddesign/2009/oct/09/fourth-plinth-gormley-trafalgar-square (accessed 30 May 2010).

Kennedy, Maeve. 2009. Fourth plinth project ends with cheers, tears and a Hillsborough tribute. *The Guardian*, 14 October 2009. Available: http://www.guardian.co.uk/artanddesign/2009/oct/14/trafalgar-square-fourth-plinth-ends (accessed 30 May 2010).

Kennedy, Dennis. 2009. *The Spectator and the Spectacle: Audiences in Modernity and Postmodernity*. Cambridge and New York: Cambridge University Press.

Keidan, Lois. 2007. Access All Areas. In I. Ivkovic and T. Medak, eds, *Extravagant Bodies*. Zagreb: Kontejner, 122–37.

Keidan, Lois. 2004. Live Art UK Vision Paper: *A Question of Live Art*. London: Live Art Development Agency. Available: http://www.liveartuk.org/downloads/Live_Art_UK_VISION_PAPER.pdf (accessed 31 October 2009).

Kochhar Lindgren, Kanta. 2006. *Hearing Difference: The Third Ear in Experimental, Deaf, and Multicultural Theater*. Washington DC: Gallaudet University Press.

Kociemba, David. 2010a. 'This isn't something I can fake': Reactions to *Glee's* Representations of Disability. *Transformative Works and Cultures*, 5. Available: http://journal.transformativeworks.org/index.php/twc/article/viewArticle/225/185 (accessed 1 April 2011).

Kociemba, David. 2010b. *Glee's* 'Dream On' vs. Reality. *Watcher Junior*, 19 May 2010. Available: http://blog.watcherjunior.tv/2010/05/glees-dream-on-vs-reality.html (accessed 1 April 2011).

Kociemba, David. 2010c. 'Proud Mary': Glee's Very Special Sham Disability Pride Anthem. *In Media Res*, 9 April 2010. Available: http://mediacommons.futureofthebook.org/imr/2010/04/09/proud-mary-glee-s-very-special-sham-disability-pride-anthem (accessed 1 April 2011).

Kosofsky Sedgwick, Eve. 1990. *Epistemology of the Closet*. Berkeley, CA: University of California Press.

Kuppers, Petra. 2011. *Disability Culture and Community Performance*. Basingstoke: Palgrave Macmillan.

Kuppers, Petra. 2009. 'Your darkness also/rich and beyond fear': Community Performance, Somatic Poetics and the Vessels of Self and Other', *MC Journal*, 12 (5). Available: http://journal.media-culture.org.au/index.php/mcjournal/article/viewArticle/203 (accessed 1 February 2012).

Kuppers, Petra. 2007. The Rhetoric of the Wheelchair. *TDR: The Drama Review*, 51 (4), 80–8.

Kuppers, Petra. 2004. *Disability and Contemporary Performance: Bodies on Edge*. New York and London: Routledge.

Lakmaier, Noemi. 2010. Interview with Author, London.

Lehmann, Hans Thies. 2006. *Postdramatic Theatre*. Trans. Karen Jürs Munby. London and New York: Routledge.

Lévinas, Emmanuel. 1998. *On Thinking-of-the-Other: Entre Nous*. Trans. M. B. Smith and B. Harshav. New York: Columbia University Press.

Lévinas, Emmanuel. 1996a. Is Ontology Fundamental?. In *Emmanuel Levinas: Basic Philosophical Writings*. Ed. A. Peperzak, S. Critchley and R. Bernasconi. Bloomington and Indianapolis, IN: Indiana University Press, 1–10.

Lévinas, Emmanuel. 1996b. Transcendence and Height. In *Emmanuel Levinas: Basic Philosophical Writings*. Ed. A. Peperzak, S. Critchley and R. Bernasconi. Bloomington and Indianapolis, IN: Indiana University Press, 11–31.

Lévinas, Emmanuel. 1996c. Meaning and Sense. In *Emmanuel Levinas: Basic Philosophical Writings*. Ed. A. Peperzak, S. Critchley and R. Bernasconi. Bloomington and Indianapolis, IN: Indiana University Press, 33–64.

Lévinas, Emmanuel. 1996d. Subsitution. In *Emmanuel Levinas: Basic Philosophical Writings*. Ed. A. Peperzak, S. Critchley and R. Bernasconi. Bloomington and Indianapolis, IN: Indiana University Press, 79–96.

Lévinas, Emmanuel. 1991a. *Totality and Infinity*. Trans. A. Lingis. Dordrecht: Kluwer.

Lévinas, Emmanuel. 1991b. *Otherwise Than Being or Beyond Essence*. Trans. A. Lingis. Dordrecht: Kluwer.

Lewis, Victoria. 2006. *Beyond Victims and Villains: Contemporary Plays by Disabled Playwrights*. New York: Theatre Communications Group.

Live Art Development Agency. 2012. *Access All Areas: Live Art and Disability*. London: Live Art Development Agency.

Live Art Development Agency, 2008. What Is Live Art? Available: http://www.thisisliveart.co.uk/about_us/what_is_live_art.html (accessed 31 October 2009).

Logan, Brian. 2007. Streets Ahead. *The Guardian*, 7 November 2007. Available: http://www.guardian.co.uk/stage/2007/nov/07/theatre4 (accessed 20 February 2009).

Low, Lenny Ann. 2007. Small Metal Objects: Passers-by Becoming Unwitting Extras in a Play Performed in a Public Space. *Sydney Morning Herald*, 5 January 2007. Available: http://www.smh.com.au/news/arts-reviews/small-metal-objects/2007/01/05/1167777264303.html (accessed 20 February 2009).

Mazer, Sharon. 2001. 'She's so fat…': Facing the Fat Lady at Coney Island's Sideshows by the Seashore. In J. Evans Braziel and K. LeBesco, eds, *Bodies out of Bounds: Fatness and Transgression*. Berkeley, CA: University of California Press, 257–76.

McConachie, Bruce. 2008. *Engaging Audience: A Cognitative Approach to Spectating in the Theatre*. London and New York: Palgrave Macmillan.

McHenry, Lalita. 2007. Is There a Gene Responsible for our Obsession with Perfection? Disability, Ethics and Responsibility. *Performance Paradigm*, 3. Available: http://www.performanceparadigm.net/wp-content/uploads/2007/06/05-mchenry.pdf

McNeilly, Jody. 2006. Reflected Presence in Dialogue. Research Paper. University of Sydney Department of Performance Studies. 18 November 2006. Available: http://archive.igneous.org.au/MIRAGE-Jody%20McNeilly.pdf (accessed 1 June 2010).

Milful, Tim. 2007. Review: Everything Has Value: Seeing *Small Metal Objects* in the Queen Street Mall. *MC Reviews*, 8 March 2007. Available: http://reviews.media-culture.org.au/article.php?sid1985 (accessed 20 February 2009).

Millett Gallant, Ann. 2010. *The Disabled Body in Contemporary Art*. Basingstoke: Palgrave Macmillan.

Mitchell, David T., and Snyder, Sharon L. 2006. *Cultural Locations of Disability*. Chicago, IL: University Of Chicago Press.

Mitchell, David T., and Snyder, Sharon L. 2001. Re-Engaging the Body: Disability Studies and the Resistance to Embodiment. *Public Culture*, 13 (3), 367–89.

Mitchell, David T., and Snyder, Sharon L. 2000. *Narrative Prosthesis: Disability and the Dependencies of Discourse*. Ann Arbor, MI: University of Michigan Press.

Moore, Tammy. 2010. Noemi Lakmaier: Disabled Artist Talks About Her Exciting Installation at the Belfast Festival. *Culture Northern Ireland*, 18 October 2010. Available: http://www.culturenorthernireland.org/article/3613/Noemi_Lakmaier (accessed 10 April 2010).

Myers, Kimberly Rena. 2004. Coming Out: Considering the Closet of Illness. *Journal of Medical Humanities*, 25 (4), 255–70.

Needham, Alex. 2009. Why the fourth plinth was a life-affirming portrait of Britain. *The Guardian*, 9 October 2009. Available: http://www.guardian.co.uk/artanddesign/2009/oct/09/fourth-plinth-one-and-other-gormley (accessed 30 May 2010).

Norfolk, Andrew. 2009. Dancer Rita Marcalo to have Epileptic Fit on Stage. *The Times*, 20 November 2009. Available: http://www.freerepublic.com/focus/f-news/2390798/posts (accessed 10 April 2011).

Oddey, Alison, and White, Christine, eds. 2009. *Modes of Spectating*. Bristol: Intellect Books.

Ouch Team. 2009. Interview – 13 Questions: Liz Crow. BBC – Ouch! (Disability), 25 November 2009, Available: http://www.bbc.co.uk/ouch/interviews/13_questions_liz_crow.shtml (accessed 30 May 2010).

Parker Starbuck, Jennifer. 2006. Becoming-Animate: On the Performed Limits of 'Human'. *Theatre Journal*, 58 (4), 649–68.

Paterson, Mary. 2011. Access All Areas. Open Dialogues, 7 March 2011. Available: http://open-dialogues.blogspot.co.uk/2011/03/reflections-on-access-all-areas.html (accessed 28 February 2012).

Performing Lines. n.date. *Small Metal Objects*: Back to Back Theatre. PerformingLines.org.au. Available: http://performinglines.org.au/productions/small-metal-objects/ (accessed 20 November 2011).

Phelan, Peggy. 1993. *Unmarked: The Politics of Performance*. London and New York: Routledge.

Phil. 2009. The Trouble with *Glee*. RockyTimeWarp.com, 30 November 2009. Available: http://www.rockytimewarp.com/2009/11/the-trouble-with-glee/ (accessed 1 April 2011).

Rayner, Alice. 1994. *To Act, To Do, To Perform: Drama and the Phenomenology of Action*. Ann Arbor, MI: University of Michigan Press.

Richardson, Owen. 2005. Small Metal Object. *The Age*, 9 October 2005. Available: http://www.theage.com.au/news/arts-reviews/small-metal-obje cts/2005/10/08/1128563036372.html (accessed 20 February 2009).

Ridout, Nicholas. 2009. *Theatre & Ethics*. Basingstoke: Palgrave Macmillan.

Ridout, Nicholas. 2007. *Stage Fright, Animals, and Other Theatrical Problems*. New York: Cambridge University Press.

Roy Williams, Emma. 2009. Epilepsy on Stage. *The Epilepsy Diaries*, 30 November 2009. Available: http://theepilepsydiaries.blogspot.com/2009/11/epilepsy-on-stage.html (accessed 10 April 2011).

Sandahl, Carrie. 2004. Black Man, Blind Man: Disability Identity Politics and Performance. *Theatre Journal*, 56, 597–602.

Sandell, Richard, Dodd, Jocelyn, and Garland Thomson, Rosemarie, eds. 2010. *Re-Presenting Disability: Activism and Agency in the Museum*. London and New York: Routledge.

Schaefer, Karine. 2003. The Spectator as Witness: Binlids as Case Study. *Studies in Theatre and Performance*, 23 (1), 5–20.

Schneider, Rebecca. 1997. *The Explicit Body in Performance*. London and New York: Routledge.

Shannon, Bill. 2009a. Disability: Personal, Political, Cultural. WhatIsWhat.com, Available: http://www.whatiswhat.com/page/disability-personal-political-cultural (accessed 31 October 2009).

Shannon, Bill. 2009b.Weight of Empathy. WhatIsWhat.com. Available: http://www.whatiswhat.com/content/weight-empathy (accessed 31 October 2009).

Shannon, Bill. 2009c. A Brief Explanation of my Phenomenological Art. WhatIsWhat.com. Available: http://www.whatiswhat.com/content/brief-explanation-my-phenomenological-art (accessed 31 October 2009).

Shannon, Bill. 2009d. Public Works. WhatIsWhat.com. Available: http://www.whatiswhat.com/page/shannon-public-works-window-bench-and-traffic (accessed 31 October 2009).

Shannon, Bill. 2009e. *Regarding the Fall*. WhatIsWhat.com. Available: http://www.whatiswhat.com/page/regarding-fall (accessed 31 October 2009).

Shannon, Bill. 2008. Bill Shannon Challenges Notions of Disability. YouTube, 12 May 2008. Videorecording. Available: http://www.youtube.com/watch?vsddowvYNCUo&featurerelated (accessed 31 October 2009).

Shildrick, Margrit. 2002. *Embodying the Monster*. London: Sage Publications.

Siebers, Tobin. 2010. *Disability Aesthetics*. Ann Arbor, MI: University of Michigan Press.

Siebers, Tobin. 2008. *Disability Theory*. Ann Arbor, MI: University of Michigan Press.

Siebers, Tobin. 2001. Disability in Theory: From Social Constructionism to the New Realism of the Body. *American Literary History*, 13 (4), 737–54.

Smith, S. E. 2010a. No *Glee* for Disabled People: The Fox smash hit show's ese of nondisabled actors in disabled roles is yet another example of TV handling disability atrociously. *The Guardian*, 19 August 2010. Available: http://www.guardian.co.uk/commentisfree/2010/aug/19/no-glee-for-disabled-people (accessed 1 April 2011).

Smith, S. E. 2010b. Representation: Actors With Disabilities Playing Character's with Disabilities. *Disabledfeminists.com*. Available: http://disabledfeminists.com/2010/09/22/representation-actors-with-disabilities-playing-characters-with-disabilities (accessed 1 April 2011).

Smith, S. E. 2009. The Transcontinental Disability Choir: *Glee*-ful Appropriation. *Bitch Magazine*, 12 November 2009. Available: http://bitchmagazine.org/post/glee-ful-appropriation (accessed 1 April 2011).

Soboslay, Zsuzsanna. 2008. Performance Alchemies. *RealTime Arts*, 77 (3), August. Available: http://www.realtimearts.net/article.php?id8348 (accessed 30 July 2010).

States, Bert O. 1985. *Great Reckonings in Little Rooms: On the Phenomenology of Theater*. Berkeley, CA: University of California Press.

Stephens, Elizabeth. 2006. Cultural Fixations of the Freak Body: Coney Island and the Postmodern Sideshow. *Continuum: Journal of Media and Cultural Studies*, 20 (4), 485–98.

Stokes, Paul. 2009. Epileptic actress attempts to induce fit on stage. *The Telegraph*, 19 November 2009. Available: http://www.telegraph.co.uk/culture/theatre/theatre-news/6606339/Epileptic-actress-attempts-to-induce-fit-on-stage.html (accessed 10 April 2011).

Sutherland, Allan. 2009a. Epilepsy as Live Art Isn't Controversial. *Theatre Blog, The Guardian*, 20 November 2009. Available: http://www.guardian.co.uk/stage/theatreblog/2009/nov/20/epilepsy-live-art-rita-marcalo (accessed 10 April 2011).

Sutherland, Allan. 2009b. Review: Liz Crow at Centre Stage on Antony Gormley's Fourth Plinth. Disability Arts Online, 9 August 2009. Available: http://www.disabilityartsonline.org/Liz-Crow-one-and-other (accessed 30 May 2010).

Templeton, Andrew. 2008. Small Metal Objects: Beautiful Logic. *RealTime Arts*, Special Feature: *Small Metal Objects*, 9 February 2008. Available: http://www.realtimearts.net/feature/RealTime_@_PuSH/8919 (accessed 20 February 2009).

Thain, Alana. 2008. The In-tensions of Extensions: Compagnie Marie Chouinard's *bODY rEMIX/ gOLDBERG vARIATIONS*. *Differences*, 19 (1), 71–95.

Thom, Paul. 1993. *For an Audience: A Philosophy of the Performing Arts*. Philadelphia, PA: Temple University Press.

Thomas, Lorraine. 2001. Disability is not so beautiful: A Semiotic Analysis of Advertisements for Rehabilitation Goods. *Disability Studies Quarterly*, 21 (2).

Tracey, Emma. 2009. Interviews – 13 Questions: Dance Artist Rita Marcalo, BBC Ouch! (Disability), 9 December 2009. Available: http://www.bbc.co.uk/

ouch/interviews/13_questions_dance_artist_rita_markalo.shtml (accessed 10 April 2011).

Valentine, Kristin Bervig. 2002. Yaqui Easter Celebrations and the Ethics of Intense Spectatorship. *Text and Performance Quarterly*, 22 (4), 280–96.

Verrent, Jo. 2009. Review: Jo Verrent sees Rita Marcalo's *Involuntary Dances*. Disability Arts Online, 12 December 2009. Available: http://www.disability artsonline.org/?location_id1110 (accessed 10 April 2011).

Warren, Bernie. 1988. *Disability and Social Performance: Using Drama to Achieve Successful 'Acts of Being'*. Cambridge, MA: Brookline Books.

Williamson, Aaron. 2008. *Aaron Williamson – Performance/Video/Collaboration*. London: Live Art Development Agency.

Index

204   *Index*

bibliotheca SelfCheck System

Customer name: De St. Croix, Cassie
Customer ID: 2006446

Items that you have borrowed

Title: Disability arts and culture : methods and
approaches
ID: 108177
Due: 16 November 2022

Title: Disability, public space performance and
spectatorship : unconscious performers
ID: 104071
Due: 16 November 2022

Title: Divided portraits : identity and disability
ID: R57122
Due: 16 November 2022

Title: Into art : positive experiences of disabled
artists
ID: 51376
Due: 16 November 2022

Total items: 4
Account balance: £0.00
26 October 2022
Borrowed items: 13
Overdue: 0
Hold requests: 4
Ready for collection: 4

Thank you for using the bibliotheca SelfCheck
System.

106071